Practical Cloud-Native Java Development with MicroProfile

Develop and deploy scalable, resilient, and reactive
cloud-native applications using MicroProfile 4.1

Emily Jiang
Andrew McCright
John Alcorn
David Chan
Alasdair Nottingham

Jory,

Great to see you @OSsummit 2022!

Tanner,

Jory thinks you might like this book!

Hope you enjoy this book!

Emily Jiang

BIRMINGHAM—MUMBAI

Practical Cloud-Native Java Development with MicroProfile

Copyright © 2021 Packt Publishing

Group Product Manager: Richa Tripathi
Publishing Product Manager: Shweta Bairoliya
Senior Editor: Storm Mann
Content Development Editor: Vaishali Ramkumar
Technical Editor: Karan Solanki
Copy Editor: Safis Editing
Project Coordinator: Manisha Singh
Proofreader: Safis Editing
Indexer: Manju Arasan
Production Designer: Sinhayna Bais

First published: August 2021

Production reference: 2130921

Published by Packt Publishing Ltd.
Livery Place
35 Livery Street
Birmingham
B3 2PB, UK.

ISBN 978-1-80107-880-1

www.packt.com

To my husband, Francis Yang, for his love, endless support, and managing our house-building project while I was writing this book. To my sweet daughter, Emma Yang, for her support and looking after her younger brother. To my adorable son, Adam Yang, for his understanding and unconditional love.

– Emily Jiang

To my wife, Jamie, for always supporting me and believing in me. And to my three kids, who sacrificed time with their dad for more than a few nights and weekends.

– Andrew McCright

To my wife, Rebecca, for her support throughout the writing of this book, and across the decades. And to all those who contributed over the years to the creation of the Stock Trader cloud-native application.

– John Alcorn

To my lovely partner in crime, Stephanie Van, for always being there for me. Also, to our dog, Milo. You're the bestest doggo ever.

– David Chan

To all the people who have contributed to making Java, Jakarta EE, and MicroProfile a success.

– Alasdair Nottingham

Foreword

Whenever there are significant shifts in computing architectures, we find the need to adapt and to evolve application architectures and the toolboxes leveraged by developers. These toolboxes need to be sensitive to the shifts and enable their exploitation, not just toleration.

Cloud computing and microservices offer an opportunity to build applications differently than in the past. For example, scaling is more economical and practical with the presence of pay-as-you-go cloud resources such as compute and storage. But given the nature of the applications being constructed and evolved, scalability is expected and it is supposed to efficiently leverage those resources. The developer's role in leveraging cloud-provider native services, managing reliability and robustness as well as keeping track of all the moving parts that go with a microservices-based approach requires new thinking that starts with your programming language and how you use it. Those moving parts are then placed into an agile DevOps world where the velocity of each iteration is expected to improve. *Practical Cloud-Native Java development with MicroProfile* provides a broad and deep look at the relevant topics you need to consider as you and your organization ramp up cloud adoption and tackle application portfolio modernization.

Since the early days of Java, there have been frameworks that have been created and matured to enable large-scale consumption of the technology at scale for a variety of application architectures. The earliest J2EE specifications, the JEE era and Jakarta work, provide substance and insight as we now address the new normal of cloud computing. MicroProfile is accelerating the maturation of techniques and offering a path forward from the prior thinking that helped make Java a staple in most large organizations. The authors of this book bring with them years and years of experience from both the middleware definition and implementation side of the business and from the application side, having worked with countless clients to demonstrate the art of the possible and bring new business systems to life. I know they have saved me several times when clear precise technical answers were needed quickly.

In my own work with customers back in the early 2000s, I often would say that the next great legacy would be that of Java code. In recent years, it has become obvious that this is the case. There are a lot of core mission-critical applications built on Java and JEE, each representing the standards and patterns representative of the era in which they were created. Many have evolved to a state of being complex to change and to a state of being considered monolithic. With the expectations of increased velocity combined with the notion of what is now more practical because of cloud architectures and because of orchestration technologies such as Kubernetes, the challenge is set, that is for sure.

While that might all sound familiar and reasonable, it might lead you to ask questions such as what is the north star that you want to modernize toward? Or, you might ask how one goes about simplifying developers' tasks while not hiding the realities of this new world. MicroProfile can be at the center of the programming model part of that north star. MicroProfile, its features, and the practical guidance you will find in the chapters that lie ahead allow you to consistently tackle these modernization challenges in a safe and simple way. Things such as health checks and liveness/readiness settings (MicroProfile Health) are examples that come to mind for me. They are part of this whole notion of observability and monitoring, which is essential in dynamic cloud-based environments. MicroProfile Health and MicroProfile Metrics are the basis of this. MicroProfile provides structure and support that enables your microservices with minimal effort on the part of the programmer, yet yields valuable insights for the SREs that play a vital role in agile development. That is from a technical perspective.

Given the openness of the approach to defining and evolving MicroProfile, there is also less risk of vendor lock-in, not to mention a great environment for incubating innovation both in specification and implementation. This is what we need. This way, you can get on with the reason we do this application stuff in the first place, the business value offered by the features you're working on creating or evolving.

If you are like me and struggle to consume abstract architectural pictures and conceptual guidance that isn't backed by real code and told in the voice of someone who has done it, you will enjoy reading this book. In this book, you will find the concepts that are necessary for the cloud architectures we aspire to all supported by concrete examples. That is the recipe. Please enjoy this book and all it has to offer.

Eric Herness

IBM Fellow and Vice-President

Cloud Engagement Hub CTO

Contributors

About the authors

Emily Jiang is a Java Champion and a cloud-native architect with practical experience of building cloud-native applications. She is a MicroProfile guru, leading several MicroProfile specifications, as well as the implementations in Open Liberty. She is also a well-known international conference speaker. You can connect with her via Twitter (@emilyfhjiang).

I would like to thank the whole MicroProfile community for the great work. A special callout to Kevin Sutter and John Clingan for their outstanding leadership! Thanks to my colleagues at IBM, particularly Ian Robinson, Melissa Modjeski, Nikki Woodward, Thorsten Gau, Mandy Chessell, and Theony Mousa for their wholehearted support and trusting me to write this book. Thanks to the Packt team (Shweta, Vaishali, Storm, Prajakta, and others) for leading us through this enjoyable journey. Many thanks to Ivar Grimstad for providing many excellent review comments. Finally, thanks to my dear family for their unreserved support and love.

Andrew McCright is IBM's web services architect with 20 years of experience building Enterprise Java runtimes. He leads the MicroProfile Rest Client and GraphQL projects and contributes to Open Liberty, Jakarta REST, CXF, RESTEasy, and more. He is also a blogger.

Many thanks to Packt (Storm, Vaishali, Shweta, and many others!) for believing in us to put this book together and helping us along the way. Thanks to my colleagues at IBM and the MicroProfile and Jakarta organizations who have helped me so much in my career – and for enabling me to write this book. Thanks also to my family for their love and support to make this possible. And finally, thanks to my Lord and Savior, Jesus Christ.

John Alcorn is an application modernization architect in the Cloud Engagement Hub, specializing in helping customers modernize their traditional Java EE applications in the cloud. He developed and maintains the Stock Trader application, which shows how to build a composite application out of MicroProfile-based microservices in Java. You can connect with John via Twitter (@jwalcorn).

I would like to thank the members of the WebSphere Bring-Up lab in Rochester for their support throughout my career, including Ryan Claussen, Karri Carlson-Neumann, Kyle Schlosser, Greg Hintermeister, Deb Banerjee, Raunak Sresthra, Truman Brown, and especially our long-time leader, Eric Herness.

David Chan is a software developer at IBM who works on the observability and serviceability components of the Open Liberty project. He is involved with the MicroProfile project with a specialization in the MicroProfile Metrics component.

I want to thank Don Bourne, Felix Wong, Prashanth Gunapalasingam, and Ellen Lau. I couldn't ask for any better role models and teammates than you guys. Big thanks to the team at Packt for helping guide our way throughout.

Alasdair Nottingham is a software developer and lead architect for Open Liberty and WebSphere. He has been involved with the MicroProfile and Jakarta EE projects to a varying extent since their inception.

Many thanks to Packt, my coauthors, and the book reviewers for making this book possible. Thank you to Alex Mulholland, Erin Schnabel, Melissa Modjeski, and Ian Robinson for their support throughout my career. Thank you to my wife for her support as I missed multiple opportunities to hike, kayak, and swim with her while writing this book. I also want to thank my brother, David Nottingham, for encouraging my interest in computers and pushing me to make the move from the UK to North America.

About the reviewers

Ivar Grimstad is the Jakarta EE developer advocate at the Eclipse Foundation. He is a Java Champion and JUG Leader based in Sweden. Besides advocating for the Jakarta EE technologies, Ivar contributes to the Jakarta EE specifications, as well as being the PMC lead for **Eclipse Enterprise for Java (EE4J)**. He is also one of the specification leads for Jakarta MVC and represents the Eclipse Foundation in the JCP Executive Committee.

Ivar is also involved in MicroProfile, Apache NetBeans, and a wide range of other open source projects and communities. He is a frequent speaker at international developer conferences.

Michael P. Redlich is an author, speaker, and accomplished IT professional with experience that includes over 30 years at ExxonMobil Research & Engineering, over 20 years facilitating the Garden State Java User Group, over five years as a Java editor for InfoQ, and 25 years of speaking at conferences such as Oracle CodeOne, Emerging Technologies for the Enterprise, Trenton Computer Festival, and various other Java User Groups. His latest passions include MicroProfile, Jakarta EE, Micronaut, Helidon, and MongoDB.

Table of Contents

Section 2: MicroProfile 4.1 Deep Dive

4

Developing Cloud-Native Applications

5

Enhancing Cloud-Native Applications

6

Observing and Monitoring Cloud-Native Applications

7

MicroProfile Ecosystem with Open Liberty, Docker, and Kubernetes

Section 3: End-to-End Project Using MicroProfile

8

Building and Testing Your Cloud-Native Application

9

Deployment and Day 2 Operations

Section 4: MicroProfile Standalone Specifications and the Future

10

Reactive Cloud-Native Applications

11

MicroProfile GraphQL

12

MicroProfile LRA and the Future of MicroProfile

Preface

MicroProfile provides a set of APIs to facilitate the building of cloud-native applications with best practices. Once you have learned MicroProfile, you can develop a standard cloud-native application, which can be deployed to many runtimes without worrying about migration.

This book provides a hands-on approach to implementation and associated methodologies that will have you up and running and productive in no time. It comes with an end-to-end application to demonstrate how to build a cloud-native application using MicroProfile 4.1 and then deploy it to the cloud.

By the end of this book, you will be able to understand MicroProfile and use the APIs in your cloud-native application development with confidence.

Who this book is for

This book is for Java application developers and architects looking to build efficient applications using an open standard framework that performs well in the cloud. DevOps engineers who want to understand how cloud-native applications work will also find this book useful. A basic understanding of Java, Docker, Kubernetes, and cloud is needed to get the most out of this book.

What this book covers

Chapter 1, Cloud-Native Applications, defines the concept of cloud-native applications and briefly discusses best practices.

Chapter 2, How Does MicroProfile Fit Into Cloud-Native Application Development?, provides an overview of MicroProfile and then describes the specifications of MicroProfile in terms of fulfilling the requirements of cloud-native applications.

Chapter 3, Introducing the IBM Stock Trader Cloud-Native Application, presents the Stock Trader application with high-level architecture and describes its functionality and design.

Chapter 4, Developing Cloud-Native Applications, explains the details of JAX-RS, JSON-B, JSON-P, CDI, and the MicroProfile Rest Client, and then demonstrates how to use them to build cloud-native applications using some code examples.

Chapter 5, Enhancing Cloud-Native Applications, explains how to configure your cloud-native application using MicroProfile Config, ensuring that the application behaves under all kinds of conditions using MicroProfile Fault Tolerance. Finally, you will understand how to secure the applications using MicroProfile JWT.

Chapter 6, Observing and Monitoring Cloud-Native Applications, covers Day 2 operations in terms of how to observe the health status and operation status of cloud-native applications and then how to identify faults using MicroProfile Open Tracing.

Chapter 7, MicroProfile Ecosystem with Open Liberty, Docker, and Kubernetes, explains how to deploy cloud-native applications to the cloud and how it interacts with cloud infrastructures such as Docker, Kubernetes, and Istio.

Chapter 8, Building and Testing Your Cloud-Native Application, covers how to build the real-world, cloud-native application, Stock Trader, from scratch and gradually utilize MicroProfile specifications to fulfill the best practices of cloud-native applications.

Chapter 9, Deployment and Day 2 Operations, discusses how to deploy the Stock Trader application via Operator and talks about Day 2 operations, such as post-deployment maintenance.

Chapter 10, Reactive Cloud-Native Applications, explains the difference between imperative and reactive applications and demonstrates how to use reactive messaging to build reactive applications.

Chapter 11, MicroProfile GraphQL, expands on why you need to use MicroProfile GraphQL for queries, followed by a demonstration of how to use GraphQL to build queries.

Chapter 12, MicroProfile LRA and the Future of MicroProfile, explains what cloud-native application transactions are and demonstrates how to use MicroProfile LRA to perform cloud-native transactions, followed by the future roadmap of MicroProfile.

To get the most out of this book

You need to have Java 8 or 11 installed on your computer. To run through the sample code, you need to have the latest version of Maven installed.

Software/hardware covered in the book	Operating system requirements
Java 8 or above	Windows, macOS, or Linux
Maven	

If you are using the digital version of this book, we advise you to type the code yourself or access the code from the book's GitHub repository (a link is available in the next section). Doing so will help you avoid any potential errors related to the copying and pasting of code.

Download the example code files

You can download the example code files for this book from GitHub at `https://github.com/PacktPublishing/Practical-Cloud-Native-Java-Development-with-MicroProfile`. If there's an update to the code, it will be updated in the GitHub repository.

We also have other code bundles from our rich catalog of books and videos available at `https://github.com/PacktPublishing/`. Check them out!

Download the color images

We also provide a PDF file that has color images of the screenshots and diagrams used in this book. You can download it here: `https://static.packt-cdn.com/downloads/9781801078801_ColorImages.pdf`.

Conventions used

There are a number of text conventions used throughout this book.

`Code in text`: Indicates code words in text, database table names, folder names, filenames, file extensions, pathnames, dummy URLs, user input, and Twitter handles. Here is an example: "Mount the downloaded `WebStorm-10*.dmg` disk image file as another disk in your system."

A block of code is set as follows:

```
@Provider
public class ColorParamConverterProvider
  implements ParamConverterProvider {

  @Override
  public <T> ParamConverter<T> getConverter(Class<T> rawType,
    Type genericType, Annotation[] annotations) {
    if (rawType.equals(Color.class)) {
      return (ParamConverter<T>) new ColorParamConverter();
    }
    return null;
  }
}
```

When we wish to draw your attention to a particular part of a code block, the relevant lines or items are set in bold:

```
global:
  auth: basic
  healthCheck: true
  ingress: false
  istio: false
  istioNamespace: mesh
  route: true
  traceSpec: "com.ibm.hybrid.cloud.sample.stocktrader.broker.
    BrokerService=fine:*=info"
  jsonLogging: true
  disableLogFiles: false
  monitoring: true
  specifyCerts: false
```

Any command-line input or output is written as follows:

```
kubectl create configmap app-port --from-literal port=9081
```

Bold: Indicates a new term, an important word, or words that you see on screen. For instance, words in menus or dialog boxes appear in **bold**. Here is an example: "We've learned that there are some useful tools such as **GraphiQL** that can simplify testing."

> **Tips or important notes**
> Appear like this.

Get in touch

Feedback from our readers is always welcome.

General feedback: If you have questions about any aspect of this book, email us at customercare@packtpub.com and mention the book title in the subject of your message.

Errata: Although we have taken every care to ensure the accuracy of our content, mistakes do happen. If you have found a mistake in this book, we would be grateful if you would report this to us. Please visit www.packtpub.com/support/errata and fill in the form.

Piracy: If you come across any illegal copies of our works in any form on the internet, we would be grateful if you would provide us with the location address or website name. Please contact us at copyright@packt.com with a link to the material.

If you are interested in becoming an author: If there is a topic that you have expertise in and you are interested in either writing or contributing to a book, please visit authors.packtpub.com.

Share your thoughts

Once you've read *Practical Cloud-Native Java Development with MicroProfile*, we'd love to hear your thoughts! Scan the QR code below to go straight to the Amazon review page for this book and share your feedback.

https://packt.link/r/1-801-07880-7

Your review is important to us and the tech community and will help us make sure we're delivering excellent quality content.

Section 1: Cloud-Native Applications

In this section, you will learn what it means for an application to be *cloud-native*. You will also learn about the basics of MicroProfile and how it provides the tools you need to build your own cloud-native Java applications. In this section, you will also learn about the real-world sample application that will be used throughout the rest of the book.

This section comprises the following chapters:

- *Chapter 1, Cloud-Native Applications*
- *Chapter 2, How Does MicroProfile Fit Into Cloud-Native Application Development?*
- *Chapter 3, Introducing the IBM Stock Trader Cloud-Native Application*

1

Cloud-Native Applications

When talking about **cloud-native applications**, it is important to have a shared understanding of what cloud-native means. There is often an assumption that cloud-native and microservices are the same thing, but actually, microservices are just *one* architectural pattern that can be used when building cloud-native applications. That leads us to the questions: what is a cloud-native application, and what are the best practices for building them? This will be the focus of this chapter.

In particular, we will cover these main topics:

- What is a cloud-native application?
- Introducing distributed computing
- Exploring cloud-native application architectures
- Cloud-native development best practices

This chapter will provide some grounding for understanding the rest of the book as well as helping you to be successful when building cloud-native applications.

What is a cloud-native application?

Back in 2010, Paul Freemantle wrote an early blog post about cloud-native (`http://pzf.fremantle.org/2010/05/cloud-native.html`) and used the analogy of trying to drive a horse-drawn cart on a 6-lane highway. No matter how much better a highway is as a road, there is a limit to how much a cart can transport and how quickly. You need vehicles that are designed for driving on a highway. The same is true of applications.

An application designed to run in a traditional data center is not going to run well on the cloud compared to one that was designed specifically to take advantage of the cloud. In other words, a cloud-native application is one that has been specifically designed to take advantage of the capabilities provided by the cloud. The **Stock Trader** application from *Chapter 8*, *Building and Testing Cloud-Native Applications*, is an example of such an application. A real-world example of microservices is Netflix.

Perhaps at its core, the promise of the cloud is being able to get compute resources on-demand, in minutes or seconds rather than days or weeks, and being charged based on incremental usage rather than upfront for potential usage – although, for many, the attraction is just no longer having to manage and maintain multiple data centers. The commoditization of compute resources that the cloud provides leads to a very different way of thinking about, planning for, and designing applications, and these differences significantly affect the application. One of the key changes in application design is the degree to which applications are distributed.

Introducing distributed computing

Most cloud-native architectures involve splitting an application into several discrete services that communicate over a network link rather than an in-process method invocation. This makes cloud-native applications implicitly distributed applications, and while **distributed computing** is nothing new, it does increase the need to understand the benefits and pitfalls of distributed computing. When building distributed applications, it is important to consider and understand the eight fallacies of distributed computing. These are as follows:

- The network is reliable.
- Latency is zero.
- Bandwidth is infinite.
- The network is secure.

- Topology doesn't change.
- There is one administrator.
- Transport cost is zero.
- The network is homogeneous.

In essence, what these fallacies mean is that a network call is slower, less secure, less reliable, and harder to fix than invoking a Java method call or a C procedure. When creating cloud-native applications, care needs to be taken to ensure these fallacies are correctly accounted for, otherwise, the application will be slow, unreliable, insecure, and impossible to debug.

An application consisting of multiple services interacting across the network can produce many benefits, such as the ability to individually scale and update services, but care must be taken to design services to minimize the number of network interactions required to deliver the ultimate business solution.

As a result, several cloud-native architectures can be used to build cloud-native applications that present different tradeoffs between the benefits and challenges of distributed computing.

Exploring cloud-native application architectures

Since 2019, there has been increasing discussion in the industry about the pros and cons of microservices as a **cloud-native application architecture**. This has been driven by many microservice-related failures and as a result, people are now discussing whether some applications would be better off using different architectures. There has even been the start of a renaissance around the idea of building monoliths, after several years of those kinds of applications being seen as an anti-pattern.

While it is attractive to think of cloud-native as just being a technology choice, it is important to understand how the development processes, organization structure, and culture affect the evolution of cloud-native applications, the system architecture, and any ultimate success. Conway's Law states the following:

Any organization that designs a system will produce a design whose structure is a copy of the organization's communication structure.

A simple way of thinking of this is if your development organization is successful at building monoliths, it is unlikely to be successful at building microservices without some kind of reorganization. That doesn't mean every team wanting to do cloud-native should go out and reorganize; it means that you should understand your strengths and weaknesses when deciding what architecture to adopt. You should also be open to reorganizing if necessary.

This section discusses a number of the more popular cloud-native application architectures out there and the pros and cons of using them. Let's start with microservices.

Microservices

Although Netflix didn't invent the idea of **microservices**, their use of the architecture did popularize it. A single microservice is designed to do one thing. It doesn't, despite the name, mean that service is small or lightweight – a single microservice could be *millions* of lines of code, but the code in the microservice has a high level of cohesion. A microservice would never handle ATM withdrawals and also sell movie tickets. Identifying the best way to design a cloud-native application into a series of well-designed microservices is not a simple task; different people might take different views of whether a deposit into and withdrawal from a bank account would warrant a single microservice or two.

Microservices usually integrate with each other via REST interfaces or messaging systems, although gRPC and GraphQL are growing in popularity. A web-facing microservice is likely to use a REST or GraphQL interface, but an internal one is more likely to use a messaging system such as Apache Kafka. Messaging systems are generally very resilient to network issues, since once the messaging system has accepted the message, it will store the message until it can be successfully processed.

The key promise of the microservice-based architecture is that each microservice can be independently deployed, updated, and scaled, allowing teams that own disparate microservices to work in parallel, making updates without the need to coordinate. This is perhaps the biggest challenge with microservice architectures. It is relatively common for well-meaning developers who set out to build microservices to end up building a distributed monolith instead. This often occurs because of poorly defined and poorly documented APIs between services and insufficient acceptance testing, resulting in a lack of trust in updating a single microservice without impacting the others. This is called a *distributed monolith* because you end up with all the disadvantages of a monolith and microservices and miss out on the benefits.

In an ideal world, a development organization building microservices will align the microservices with an individual development team. This may be difficult if there are more microservices than development teams. As the number of microservices a team manages increases, more time will be spent managing the services rather than evolving them.

Monoliths

Monoliths are strongly associated with pre-cloud application architectures and are considered an anti-pattern for cloud-native applications. For that reason, it might seem strange that this appears in a discussion of cloud-native architecture. However, there are some reasons for including them.

The first is really just the reality that monoliths are the simplest kind of application to build. While the individual services cannot be independently scaled, as long as the monolith has been designed to scale, this may not be an issue.

The second is that there are a lot of monoliths out there and many enterprises are moving them to the cloud. **MicroProfile** provides additional APIs to retrofit many cloud-native behaviors into an existing app.

The trick with a monolith is ensuring that despite the colocation of services in a single deployment artifact, the monolith can start quickly enough to enable dynamic scaling and restart if there is an application failure.

Typically, a small development organization will benefit from monoliths since there is only a single application to build, deploy, and manage.

Macroservices

Macroservices sit somewhere between a monolith and a microservice architecture and are also referred to as *modular monoliths*. With macroservices, the services are combined into a small number of monoliths that interoperate in the same way that a series of microservices would.

This provides many of the benefits of microservices but significantly simplifies the operations environment since there are fewer things to manage. If a macro-service has been written well, then individual services in that macro-service can be broken out if they would benefit from an independent life cycle. A well-known example of a macro-service is **Stack Overflow**. Stack Overflow (`https://www.infoq.com/news/2015/06/scaling-stack-overflow/`) is famously a monolith except for the tagging capability, which is handled in another application due to the different performance needs. This split moves it from being a pure monolith into the realm of macroservices (although Stack Overflow uses the term *monolith-plus*).

This architecture can work especially well when a development organization is organized into a smaller number of teams than the number of services.

Function as a Service

Function as a Service (FaaS), often referred to as *serverless*, is an architecture where a service is created as a function that is run when an event occurs. The function is intended to be fast starting and fast executing and can be triggered by things such as HTTP requests or messages being received. FaaS promises that you can deploy the function to a cloud, and it is started and executed by the event trigger, rather than having to have the function running *just in case*. Typically, public cloud providers that support FaaS only charge for the time the function is running. This is very attractive if the event is relatively uncommon since there is no financial cost in having a system running for when an uncommon event occurs.

The challenge with this architecture is that your function needs to be able to start quickly and usually has to finish executing quickly too; as a result, it isn't suitable for long-running processes. It also doesn't remove the server; the server is still there. Instead, it just shifts the cost from the developer to the cloud provider. If the cloud provider is a public cloud, then that is their problem, since they are charging for the function runtime, but if you are deploying to a private cloud, this becomes your problem, thereby removing some of the benefits.

Event sourcing

Often, we think of services as providing a REST endpoint, and services make calls to them. In fact, factor VII of the Twelve-Factor App (discussed in the next section) *explicitly* states this. The problem with this approach is that a REST call is implicitly synchronous and prone to issues if the service provider is running slow or failing.

When providing an external API to a mobile app or a web browser, a REST API is often the best option. However, for services within an enterprise, there are many benefits to using a messaging system such as Kafka and using **asynchronous events** instead. A messaging system that can guarantee that the message will be delivered allows the client and service to be decoupled such that an issue with the service provider doesn't prevent the request from occurring; it just means it'll be processed later. A one-to-many event system makes it easy for a single service to trigger multiple different actions with just a simple message send. Different actions can be taken by different services receiving a copy of the message and if new behavior is required, an additional service can receive the same message without having to change the sending service. A simple illustration of this might be that an event that orders an item can be processed by the payment service, the dispatch service, a reorder service, and a recommendation service that provides recommendations based on past purchases.

One of the trends with cloud-native applications is that data is moved from a centralized data store closer to the individual services. Each service operates on data it holds, so if something happens to slow down the data store for one service, it doesn't have a knock-on effect on others. This means that new mechanisms are required to ensure data consistency. Using events to handle data updates helps with this, since a single event can be distributed to every service that needs to process the update independently. The updates can take effect even if the service is down when the update is triggered. Another advantage of this approach is that if the data store fails, it can be reconstructed by replaying all the events.

Having chosen the architecture (or architectures) for building your cloud-native application, the next step is to start building it, and to do that, it is a good idea to understand some of the industry best practices around cloud-native application development.

Cloud-native development best practices

There are many best practices that, if followed, will improve the chances that your cloud-native application will be a success. Following these best practices doesn't guarantee success, just as ignoring them doesn't guarantee failure, but they do encode key practices that have been shown to enhance the chances of success. The most famous set of best practices is the **Twelve-Factor App**.

Twelve-Factor App

The Twelve-Factor App (`https://12factor.net`) is a set of 12 best practices that, if followed, can significantly improve the chance of success when building cloud-native applications. Some of the factors would be considered obvious by many software developers even outside of cloud-native, but taken together, they form a popular methodology for building cloud-native applications. The 12 factors are as follows:

- Code base
- Dependencies
- Config
- Backing services
- Build, release, run
- Process
- Port binding
- Concurrency

- Disposability
- Dev/prod parity
- Logs
- Admin processes

I – Code base

The first factor states that a cloud-native application consists of a single **code base** that is tracked in a version control system, such as Git, and that code base will be deployed multiple times. A deployment might be to a test, staging, or production environment. That doesn't mean that the code in the environments will be identical; a test environment will obviously contain code changes that are proposed but haven't been proven as safe for production, but that is still one code base.

II – Dependencies

It has been common development practice for Java applications to use **dependencies** stored in Maven repositories such as Maven Central for some time. Tools such as Maven and Gradle require you to express your dependencies in order to build against them. While this practice absolutely requires this, it goes beyond just build-time dependencies to runtime ones as well. A 12-factor application packages its dependencies into the application to ensure that a single development artifact can be reliably deployed in any suitable environment. This means that having an administrator provide the libraries in a well-known place on the filesystem is not acceptable since there is always a chance the administrator-deployed library and the application-required one are not compatible.

When considering this practice, it is important to make a clear decision about what the cloud-native application is, since at some point there will be a split between what the application provides and what the deployment environment provides. This factor triggered a trend in enterprise Java away from WAR files to executable JAR files, since many viewed the application server as an implicit dependency. However, that just shifted the implicit dependency down a level; it didn't remove it. Now the implicit dependency is Java. To a certain extent, containerization addresses this issue and at the same time, it removes the need to rearchitect around an executable JAR file.

III – Config

Since a 12-factor application may have many deployments and each deployment may connect to different systems with different credentials, it is critical that **configuration** be externalized into the environment. It is also common to read in the media about security issues caused by a developer accidentally checking credentials into a version control system, which would not happen if the configuration was stored externally to the code base.

Although this factor states that configuration is stored in environment variables, there are many who are uneasy about the idea of storing security-sensitive configuration in environment variables. The key thing here is to externalize configuration in a way that can be simply provided in production.

IV – Backing services

Backing services are treated as attached resources. It should be possible to change from one database to another with a simple change in configuration.

V – Build, release, run

All applications go through some kind of **build, release, run** process, but a 12-factor application has strict separation between those phases. The build phase involves turning the application source into the application artifact. The release phase combines the application artifact with the configuration so it can be deployed. The run phase is when it is actually executing. This strict separation means that a configuration change is never made in the run phase since there is no way to roll it back to the release stage. Instead, if a configuration change is required, a new release is made and run. The same is true if a code change is required. There is no changing the code that is running without going through a build and a run. This makes sure that you always know what is running and can easily reproduce issues or roll back to a prior version.

VI – Process

A 12-factor application consists of one or more **stateless processes**. This does not mean that each request is mapped to a single process; it is perfectly reasonable in Java to have a single JVM processing multiple requests at the same time. This means that the application should not rely on any one process being available from one request to another. If a single client is making 20 requests, the assumption must be that each request is handled by a separate process with no state being retained between processes. It is a common pattern to store the server-side state associated with a user. This state should always be persisted to an external datastore, so if a follow-on request is sent to a different process, there is no impact on the client.

VII – Port binding

Applications export services via **port binding**. What this means is that an HTTP application should not rely on being installed into a web container, but instead it should declare a dependency on the HTTP server and cause it to open a port during startup. This has led many to take the view that a 12-factor Java application must be built as an uber-jar, but this is just one realization of the idea of building a single deployment artifact that binds to ports. An alternative and significantly more useful interpretation is to use containers; containers are very much built around the idea of port binding. It should be noted that this practice does not always apply; for example, a microservice driven by a Kafka message would not bind to a port. Also, many FaaS platforms do not provide an API for port binding.

VIII – Concurrency

Concurrency in Java is typically achieved by increasing the resources allocated to a process so more threads can be created. With 12-factor, you increase the number of instances rather than the compute capacity. There is a limit to how easy it is to add compute capacity to a single machine, but adding a new virtual machine of equivalent size is relatively easy. This practice is related to factor VI, so they complement and reinforce each other. Although this could be read to suggest a single process per request model, a Java-based application is more than capable of running multiple threads more efficiently than having a 1:1 ratio between process and request.

IX – Disposability

Every application should be treated as **disposable**. This means making sure the process starts quickly, shuts down promptly, and copes with termination. Taking this approach makes the application scale out well and quickly, as well as being resilient to unexpected failure, since a process can be quickly and easily restarted from the last release.

X – Dev/prod parity

Lots of application problems manifest themselves because of differences between **development and staging environments**. In the past, this happened because installing and starting all the downstream software was difficult, but the advent of containers has significantly simplified this experience, making it possible to run many of these systems in earlier environments. The advantage of this is that you no longer experience problems because your development database interprets SQL differently from the dev environment.

XI – Logs

Applications should write **logs**, and these should be written to the process output as opposed to being written to the filesystem. When deployed, the execution environment will take the process output and forward it to a final destination for viewing and long-term storage. This is very useful in Kubernetes, where logs stored inside the container do not persist if the container is destroyed, and they are easier to obtain using the Kubernetes `log` function, which follows the process output and not the log files.

XII: Admin processes

Admin processes should be run as one-off processes separate from the application and they should not run in line with application startup. The code for these application processes should be managed with the main application such that the release used for normal flow can be used to execute the admin task. This makes sure the application and the admin code do not diverge.

Other best practices

The concept of the 12-factor application has been around for a while; it is important to remember with any methodology that what works for some people may not work for others, and sometimes the methodology needs to evolve as our understanding of how to be successful does. As a result, several other best practices are often added to the 12 factors discussed previously. The most common relates to the importance of describing the service API and how to test it to ensure that changes to one service do not require the coordinated deployment of client services.

APIs and contract testing

While the 12-factor methodology details a lot of useful practices for the creation and execution of cloud-native applications, it does little to talk about how application services interact and how to ensure that changing one doesn't cause another to need to change. Well-designed and clearly documented **APIs** are critical to ensuring that changes to a service do not affect the clients.

It isn't enough to just have documentation for the API; it is also important to ensure that changes to the service provider do not negatively affect the client. Since any bug fix could result in a change, it is often possible for the provider to believe a change is safe and accidentally break a client. This is where **contract testing** can come in. The advantage of contract testing is that each system (the client and the server) can be tested to ensure that changes to either do not violate the contract.

Security

One of the most noticeable gaps in the 12-factor methodology is the lack of best practices around security. From a certain perspective, this is because there is an existing set of best practices for securing applications and these apply as much to cloud-native applications as they do to traditional applications. For example, the third practice on config addresses, at least partly, how to protect credentials (or other secrets) by externalizing them outside of the application, However, this factor doesn't talk about how to securely inject secrets into the environment and how they are stored and secured. Something that depends on the deployment environment. This is discussed in more detail in *Chapter 7, MicroProfile Ecosystem with Open Liberty, Docker, and Kubernetes.*

Breaking things down into microservices adds additional complexity that doesn't apply in a monolith. With a monolith, you can trust the various components of the application because they are co-deployed often in the same process space. However, when a monolith is broken down into microservices and network connections are used, other mechanisms need to be used to maintain trust. The use of **JSON Web Tokens** (**JWTs**) is one such mechanism of managing and establishing trust between microservices. This is discussed in more detail in *Chapter 5, Enhancing Cloud-Native Applications.*

GraphQL

There is a default assumption involved in much of cloud-native thought that the APIs exposed are REST-based ones. However, this can lead to increased network calls and excessive data being sent across the network. **GraphQL** is a relatively new innovation that allows a service client to request the exact information it needs from a data store over an HTTP connection. A traditional REST API has to provide all the data about the resource, but often only a subset is required. Network bandwidth and client-side data processing is often wasted when using RESTful APIs since data is provided that the client does not use. GraphQL solves this by allowing the client to send a query to the service requesting exactly the data they need and no more. This reduces the data being transported and fetched from the backing data store. MicroProfile provides a Java-based API for writing a GraphQL backend, which makes it easy to write a service that provides such a query-based API for clients.

Summary

In this chapter, we have learned what a cloud-native application is and learned about some architectures for building them. We have also learned about some best practices for building cloud-native applications and why they exist, so we can determine whether and when to apply them. This provides a good grounding for applying what you'll learn in the rest of the book to be able to be successful in building and deploying cloud-native applications.

In the next chapter, we will explore what MicroProfile is and how it can be used to build cloud-native applications.

2

How Does MicroProfile Fit into Cloud-Native Application Development?

This chapter provides you with an overview of **MicroProfile** and describes the specifications of MicroProfile in terms of fulfilling the requirements of cloud-native applications. In this chapter, we first look at the history of MicroProfile concerning why it was created and for what purpose, and then we will explore the content of MicroProfile. This will give you a high-level understanding of each MicroProfile specification so that you will understand how MicroProfile fits into cloud-native application development and why you should adopt MicroProfile technologies. Finally, we will look at the MicroProfile code generator, **MicroProfile Starter**, focusing on how to create cloud-native applications. This is useful because it will help you get started with MicroProfile from scratch.

We will cover the following topics in this chapter:

- MicroProfile overview
- MicroProfile specifications
- MicroProfile Starter

MicroProfile overview

Let's start by reflecting on the history of MicroProfile, why it was set up, and how it progressed and established its working group. In this section, we look at two different sub-topics: the *history of MicroProfile* and the *characteristics of MicroProfile*. We'll begin by looking at the history. It is important to understand the release cycle and what is included in various MicroProfile releases so that we can choose which version to use, and that we have a sense of how fast MicroProfile releases new versions.

History of MicroProfile

Seeing the slowly advancing pace of Java EE, a few major industry players, including IBM, Red Hat, Payara, Tomitribe, and others, got together in 2016 to discuss how to make server-side Java frameworks move faster and to address the new challenges associated with the new microservice space. As a result of this collaboration, MicroProfile was born in the fall of 2016. It was designed to help Java developers develop cloud-native applications without needing to learn new languages.

MicroProfile 1.0 was announced in September 2016 at JavaOne. This first release of MicroProfile 1.0 consisted of CDI, JSON-P, and JAX-RS. In December 2016, MicroProfile joined the Eclipse Foundation under the Apache License v2.0 (Alv2.0). MicroProfile 1.1 was released in August 2017 and included the first new MicroProfile specification, MicroProfile Config 1.0. From 2017 to 2019, MicroProfile did three releases per year: in February, June, and October.

In 2020, following the release of MicroProfile 3.3, MicroProfile was requested by Eclipse Foundation to set up its working group before any further major or minor releases could be performed. It took nearly 1 year for the community to decide whether to set up its own working group or merge with the Jakarta EE working group. Eventually, IBM, Red Hat, and Tomitribe decided to pursue a separate working group. With the working group requirement of a minimum of 5 corporate members, it took the community some time to acquire 2 more corporate members. In October, **Atlanta Java User Group** (**AJUG**) and Jelastic joined forces with IBM, Red Hat, and Tomitribe to form the MicroProfile working group. Finally, in October 2020, the working group charter was approved. Soon afterward, Payara, Oracle, Fujitsu, Garden State JUG, and iJUG joined the MicroProfile working group.

After the MicroProfile working group was established in October 2020, the MicroProfile community immediately prepared the MicroProfile 4.0 release using the newly established release process. On 23 December, MicroProfile 4.0 was released. The latest MicroProfile version 4.1 got released recently in July 2021. Here is the timeline for MicroProfile releases:

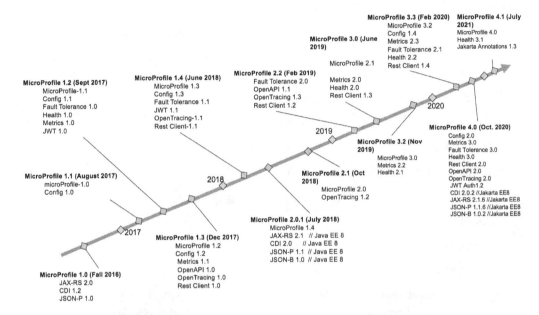

Figure 2.1 – MicroProfile release timeline

As you can see from *Figure 2.1*, MicroProfile has a fast release cadence. As well as this, MicroProfile has other identifying characteristics. In the next section, we will look at them.

Characteristics of MicroProfile

MicroProfile grew very quickly thanks to its unique characteristics of openness and diversity. These are detailed as follows:

- Openness and transparency: MicroProfile is open to the public in terms of meetings, projects, contributions, and suchlike. There is no hierarchy, and everyone has the same right to voice their opinions. No one has a veto right.

- Diversity: The community is diverse. Its contributors are made up of many major players, including IBM, Red Hat, Tomitribe, Payara, Java User Groups, and other individuals and groups. Everyone is welcome to join MicroProfile and voice their opinion. The way to join the conversation is via the MicroProfile Google group, accessible via **Join the Discussion** on `microprofile.io`.

- Many runtime implementations: MicroProfile evolves APIs, specifications, and **Technology Compatibility Kits** (**TCKs**). It only creates APIs, but it does not include implementations. However, there is no lack of implementations. There are around a dozen implementations, as follows:

  a) Open Liberty (`https://openliberty.io/`)

  b) WebSphere Liberty (`https://www.ibm.com/cloud/websphere-liberty`)

  c) Quarkus (`https://quarkus.io/`)

  d) Wildfly (`https://www.wildfly.org/`)

  e) Payara (`https://www.payara.fish/`)

  f) TomEE (`https://tomee.apache.org/`)

  g) Helidon (`https://helidon.io`)

  h) Launcher (`https://github.com/fujitsu/launcher`)

  i) KumuluzEE (`https://ee.kumuluz.com/`)

  j) Piranha Cloud (`https://piranha.cloud/`)

  k) Apache Geronimo (`https://geronimo.apache.org/`)

- Lightweight, iterative processes: MicroProfile establishes a pattern that moves fast and adopts an iterative process. It adapts to changes, allows breaking changes between releases, and adopts a semantic versioning policy, which means a major version release containing breaking changes. However, MicroProfile tries to minimize the number of breaking changes. When there are breaking changes, the changes must be clearly documented in the release notes of the corresponding specifications.

Due to the aforementioned characteristics of MicroProfile, its adoption rate increased rapidly. As a result, more and more companies started investing in MicroProfile technologies. MicroProfile is now seen as the standard for developing cloud-native applications. We will take a closer look at each individual MicroProfile specification in the next section.

MicroProfile specifications

At this point, you might be wondering what MicroProfile consists of. As you may know, MicroProfile evolves **Application Programming Interfaces** (**APIs**) in terms of developing cloud-native applications. MicroProfile has several specifications that offer various capabilities for cloud-native applications. As a cloud-native application developer, it's important to understand these.

The MicroProfile 4.0 release includes four specifications from Jakarta EE 8 and eight MicroProfile specifications, as follows:

Jakarta EE specifications:

- Jakarta Contexts and Dependency Injection (CDI) 2.0
- Jakarta RESTful Web Services (JAX-RS) 2.1
- Jakarta JSON Binding 1.0
- Jakarta JSON Processing 1.1

MicroProfile specifications:

- MicroProfile Config 2.0
- MicroProfile Fault Tolerance 3.0
- MicroProfile Health 3.0
- MicroProfile JWT Propagation 1.2
- MicroProfile Metrics 3.0
- MicroProfile OpenAPI 2.0
- MicroProfile OpenTracing 2.0
- MicroProfile Rest Client 2.0

MicroProfile specifications are grouped under different release categories. MicroProfile has the concept of **platform release** and **standalone release**. In this section, we will cover both concepts in detail.

Platform release

The platform release consists of 12 specifications, 4 of them being from Jakarta EE. These specifications can be divided into three subgroups (three layers) based on their usage:

- **Building cloud-native applications**: CDI, JAX-RS, Rest Client, JSON-B, and JSON-P
- **Enhancing cloud-native applications**: Open API, Fault Tolerance, JWT Propagation, and Config
- **Observing and monitoring cloud-native applications**: Open Tracing, Health, and Metrics

Let's explore each of these groups in turn.

Technologies for developing cloud-native applications

Cloud-native applications can be developed using **CDI, JAX-RS, JSON-B,** or **JSON-P.** MicroProfile Rest Client is used for connecting cloud-native applications. Coming up next is a quick overview of these technologies. *Chapter 4, Developing Cloud-Native Applications,* will explain them in more detail.

CDI – Contexts and Dependency Injection

CDI (`https://github.com/eclipse-ee4j/cdi`) is a Jakarta EE API specification that provides a core framework for managing dependencies. It enables loosely coupled cloud-native application development. CDI supports dependency injection and manages the life cycle of the dependencies. The life cycle of a bean is specified via the scope annotations, such as `@ApplicationScoped`, `@RequestScoped`, and `@Dependent`. The `@ApplicationScoped` annotation means only one instance exists per cloud-native application. The dependency injection is specified via the `@Inject` annotation, which is defined in the Jakarta injection specification.

JAX-RS – Jakarta RESTful Web Services

JAX-RS (`https://github.com/eclipse-ee4j/jaxrs-api/`) is a Jakarta EE API specification that provides mechanisms for creating RESTful services. In *Chapter 1, Cloud-Native Application*, the sixth factor, *Processes*, in **Twelve-Factor App**, can be fulfilled by JAX-RS. JAX-RS provides many annotations to transform a **Plain Old Java Object** (**POJO**) into a web resource. These annotations include `@Path`, `@GET`, `@PUT`, `@POST`, `DELETE`, `@Produces`, and `@Consumes`. Let's look at these instances individually:

- `@Path` specifies the relative path for a resource or a method.

- `@GET`, `@PUT`, `@POST`, and `@DELETE` specify the HTTP request type.

- `@Produces` specifies the response media type, such as `MediaType.APPLICATION_JSON`.

- `@Consumes` specifies the accepted media type.

- The following is an example of a JAX-RS service. It declares a `GET` operation with the endpoint, such as `http://localhost:9080/system/properties`. When this URL is invoked, the system properties will be returned. Since `@Produces` specifies the `MediaType.APPLICATION_JSON` format, the payload format will be in a format called **JavaScript Object Notation** (**JSON**):

```
@ApplicationScoped // (1)
@Path("/properties") // (2)
public class PropertyController {
```

```
    @GET // (3)
    @Produces(MediaType.APPLICATION_JSON) // (4)
    public Properties getProperties() {
        return System.getProperties();
    }
}
```

Let's take a look at the four commented lines in this code snippet:

1. The `@ApplicationScoped` annotation, defined in the CDI, states that the life cycle of the `PropertyController` resource is singular, with only one instance existing per application.

2. The `@Path` annotation specifies the relative path to the `PropertyController` resource to be `/properties`.

3. The `@GET` annotation indicates the JAX-RS operation type.

4. The `@Produces(MediaType.APPLICATION_JSON)` annotation mandates the payload to be in JSON format.

By now, you should have a basic understanding of JAX-RS. In the next section, we will take a look at how to connect RESTful services using MicroProfile Rest Client.

MicroProfile Rest Client

MicroProfile Rest Client (`https://github.com/eclipse/microprofile-rest-client`) provides a type-safe approach to invoke RESTful services over HTTP. You can use `@RegisterRestClient` to declare a type-safe interface, as shown in the following code snippet.

The following example defines the type-safe interface for the JAX-RS operation, `PropertyController.getProperties()`, as shown in the previous section:

```
@RegisterRestClient(baseUri="http://localhost:9081/system")
  // (1)
public interface PropertiesClient {
    @GET // (2)
    @Produces(MediaType.APPLICATION_JSON) // (3)
    @Path("/properties") // (4)
    public Properties getProperities();
}
```

Let's take a look at the four commented lines in this code snippet:

1. The `@RegisterRestClient` annotation registers the `PropertiesClient` interface as a RESTful client.

2. The `@GET` annotation indicates that the `getProperties()` method is a GET operation.

3. The `@Produces(MediaType.APPLICATION_JSON)` annotation specifies the payload format as a JSON format.

4. The `@Path` annotation declares the relative path to the `getProperties()` operation.

The type-safe clients support both CDI and programmatic lookup. The following code snippet demonstrates how to use CDI to inject the `PropertiesClient` RESTful client and then invoke its `getProperties()` method:

```
@Path("/client")
@ApplicationScoped
public class ClientController {
@Inject @RestClient
private PropertiesClient; // (1)
    @GET
    @Path("/props")
    @Produces(MediaType.APPLICATION_JSON)
    public Properties displayProps() throws
       IllegalStateException, RestClientDefinitionException,
        URISyntaxException {
        return propertiesClient.getProperities(); // (2)
    }
}
```

Let's take a look at the two commented lines in this code snippet:

1. The `@Inject` (defined by **Jakarta Injection**) and `@RestClient` (a CDI qualifier defined by **MicroProfile Rest Client**) annotations inject an instance of `PropertiesClient` into the `propertiesClient` variable.

2. Call the backend operation, `getProperties()`, which is `PropertyController.getProperties()`.

Alternatively, you can use the `RestClientBuilder` programmatic API to get hold of the client, which will be discussed in *Chapter 4, Developing Cloud-Native Applications.*

In the preceding example, the response from the JAX-RS service is in JSON format, the most popular response format. We will look at JSON in the next section in terms of how to convert to, and from, an object to a JSON object.

JSON-B and JSON-P

JSON is the prominent format for transmitting data in cloud-native applications. JSON supports two data structures: **objects** and **arrays**. The objects are sets of key-value pairs, enclosed by curly brackets, while arrays collect these objects into a set.

Both **JSON-B** (`https://github.com/eclipse-ee4j/jsonb-api`) and **JSON-P** (`https://github.com/eclipse-ee4j/jsonp`) are Jakarta EE API specifications that convert POJOs to and from JSON data. The first version of JSON-P was released a few years before JSON-B. JSON-P provides both streaming and data models for JSON processing.

JSON-B provides a mechanism for converting Java objects to/from JSON messages. It provides several methods to serialize/desterilize a Java object to/from JSON. JSON-B provides a higher-level API than JSON-P. JSON-B works well with JAX-RS and JAX-RS 2.1 mandates the use of JSON-B to automatically convert the returned object to JSON data in the HTTP response.

Technologies for enhancing cloud-native applications

After building cloud-native applications, the job is not done yet, unfortunately. You will need to think about how to improve the application. The next task is to improve its reliability and maintainability. Do you want to freely change its config value without recompiling your applications, for example, the port number? Do you want your application to be resilient, functioning all the time no matter what? Do you want your application to be secure, which means unauthorized requests are not permitted? Do you need help to work out what your applications are doing when you have got tens or hundreds of applications?

If the answer to any of the aforementioned questions is *yes*, you will need to add some essential **Quality of Services(QoS)** , which includes the following:

- Configuration
- Resilience
- Security
- Documentation

MicroProfile Config provides a way to configure applications without the need for redeployment. **MicroProfile Fault Tolerance** makes the application more resilient. **MicroProfile JWT Authentication** secures applications in a portable and simple way, while **MicroProfile Open API** is used to document applications. Next, we will provide a quick overview of these technologies, and we will go deeper into each of them in *Chapter 5, Enhancing Cloud-Native Applications*.

MicroProfile Config

MicroProfile Config (`https://github.com/eclipse/microprofile-config`) defines an easy and flexible system to retrieve application configurations. The configurations are defined in config sources, which can be supplied by applications. There are two ways to retrieve configuration: **CDI** or **programmatic lookup**. Let's look at each of these in turn:

- **Injecting configuration via CDI**: Upon looking up a property named `"customer.name"`, the following code snippet can be used to retrieve its value:

```
@Inject @ConfigProperty(name="customer.name") String
customerName;
```

- **Programmatic lookup**: A property named `customer.name` can also be looked up programmatically via the following APIs:

```
Config = ConfigProvider.getConfig();
String customerName = config.getValue("customer.name",
  String.class);
```

The property defined in the `microprofile-config.properites` file on the classpath, environment variable, and system properties is available to the cloud-native applications automatically. This means that MicroProfile Config can also access the values of fields from Kubernetes `ConfigMaps` or `Secrets` that are mapped to the Pod as environment variables. The following code snippet demonstrates the `customer.name` property defined in `microprofile-config.properties`, in the format of a Java property file:

```
customer.name=Bob
```

MicroProfile Config enables the externalization of the configuration. The configuration stored in the environment can be accessed by the cloud-native applications via the Config APIs. This specification fulfills the third factor, **Configuration**, in **Twelve-Factor App**, as mentioned in *Chapter 1, Cloud-Native Application*. You have learned how to configure your application. Next, we will briefly discuss how to make your application resilient using MicroProfile Fault Tolerance.

MicroProfile Fault Tolerance

MicroProfile Fault Tolerance (`https://github.com/eclipse/microprofile-fault-tolerance/`) defines a set of annotations for making cloud-native applications resilient. These annotations are as follows:

- `@Retry`: Recovers from a brief network glitch. This allows you to define how many times the retry can be performed, what exceptions can trigger the retry, the time duration for the retries, and so on.

- `@Timeout`: Defines the maximum allowed response time. This is used for time-critical operations. It defines the maximum time duration for the corresponding operation to respond.

- `@CircuitBreaker`: Fails fast and avoids the repeatable indefinite wait or timeout. You can specify the rolling window for a circuit to be checked, the failure ratio for the circuit to open, the exceptions that the circuit breaker considers or ignores, and so on.

- `@Bulkhead`: Isolates failures and avoids bringing the whole system down. There are two types of bulkhead. When this annotation is used together with the `@Asynchronous` annotation, this means **thread isolation**, which means the method with this annotation will be executed on a child thread. Otherwise, it means **semaphore isolation**, which means the method will be executed on the parent thread.

- `@Fallback`: Provides an alternative solution for a failed execution. You should always use this annotation to ensure a resilient cloud-native application to respond to all kinds of situations. This annotation provides an alternative operation if the original method returns an exception.

- The aforementioned annotations can be used together, which improves the resilience of your cloud-native applications. Once your application is configurable and resilient, the next step is to think about how to prevent sensitive information from being obtained by irrelevant parties. This is where MicroProfile JWT Propagation comes into play.

MicroProfile JWT Propagation

MicroProfile JWT (short for JSON Web Token) Propagation (`https://github.com/eclipse/microprofile-jwt-auth/`) provides a portable and interoperable way to secure cloud-native microservices. It is used in conjunction with Jakarta EE Security, which provides APIs, such as `@RolesAllowed`, to secure JAX-RS endpoints.

MicroProfile JWT Propagation establishes a way to pass in the user info to the backend so that the backend can determine whether the invocation is allowed. MicroProfile JWT Propagation is built on top of a JWT with a couple of additional claims: **upn** and **groups**. It defines an API, `JsonWebToken`, which extends the `java.security.Principal` interface. This API makes a set of claims available via getter accessors.

JAX-RS applications can access `JsonWebToken` from the `SecurityContext` annotation:

```
@GET
@Path("/getGroups")
public Set<String> getGroups(@Context SecurityContext sec) {
    Set<String> groups = null;
    Principal user = sec.getUserPrincipal();
    if (user instanceof JsonWebToken) {
        JsonWebToken jwt = (JsonWebToken) user;
        groups= = jwt.getGroups();
    }
    return groups;
}
```

Alternatively, it can also be injected:

```
@Inject private JsonWebToken jwt;
@Inject @Claim(standard= Claims.raw_token) private String
    rawToken;
@Inject @Claim("iat") private Long dupIssuedAt;
@Inject @Claim("sub") private ClaimValue<Optional<String>>
    optSubject;
```

MicroProfile JWT Authentication also ensures single sign-on and the runtime will automatically reject the requests with insufficient **access rights** or a lack of the appropriate claims. Once your application is configurable, resilient, and secure, you then need to think about how to document your application. You can document your application using MicroProfile OpenAPI.

MicroProfile OpenAPI

MicroProfile OpenAPI (`https://github.com/eclipse/microprofile-open-api/`) provides a set of annotations and models that automatically produce OpenAPI v3 documents for JAX-RS applications. A fully processed OpenAPI document is available at `http://myHost:myPort/openapi`, as a `GET` operation. Some MicroProfile Open API implementations such as Open Liberty (`https://openliberty.io/`) also provide the Swagger UI integration and exposes the endpoint, `http://myHost:myPort/openapi/ui`, which allows the endpoints to be tested out.

Note

MicroProfile OpenAPI produces a set of Java interfaces and annotations that allow Java developers to produce OpenAPI v3 documents from their JAX-RS. MicroProfile OpenAPI was heavily influenced by OpenAPI v3, but they are not the same.

As a cloud-native developer, your job is nearly done. You could deploy your application to the cloud. If everything goes well, you will have an easy job. However, if something goes wrong, you might have a difficult time figuring out where the problem lies. In order to help with service, you will need to learn about the technologies for observing and monitoring your applications. Read along to find out what you can do to help with serviceability.

Technologies for observing and monitoring cloud-native applications

Upon completing the development of cloud-native applications, the next stage is **day 2 operation**, where monitoring, maintenance, and troubleshooting come into play. **MicroProfile Health**, **MicroProfile Metrics**, and **MicroProfile Open Tracing** provide support in these areas. Next is a quick overview of these technologies to give you a basic understanding of how these technologies work together to help with day 2 operation. *Chapter 6, Observing and Monitoring Cloud-Native Applications*, will cover this in more detail.

MicroProfile Health

MicroProfile Health (`https://github.com/eclipse/microprofile-health/`) provides readiness and liveness checks with the `@Readiness` and `@Liveness` annotations, accordingly. The `@Readiness` annotation is applied to a `HealthCheck` implementation to define a readiness check procedure, while `@Liveness` is applied to a liveness check procedure. The response of the `HealthCheck` procedure can be either *UP* or *DOWN*.

The response of the readiness check determines whether the cloud-native application is ready to serve requests. If the response is *UP*, the cloud infrastructure, such as **Kubernetes**, will route requests to the Pod it lives in. If the response is *DOWN*, Kubernetes will not route requests to the Pod. The response of the liveness check means whether the cloud-native application is still alive. With a response of *DOWN*, Kubernetes will destroy the Pod that the cloud-native application lives in and start a new one.

MicroProfile Health defines the `http://myHost:myPort/health/ready` and `http://myHost:myPort/health/live` endpoints to be exposed by its implementations to represent the status of readiness and liveness of the entire runtime accordingly, which can be used for Kubernetes readiness and liveness checks.

MicroProfile Metrics

MicroProfile Metrics (`https://github.com/eclipse/microprofile-metrics/`) defines a mechanism for cloud-native applications to expose metrics for monitoring. It defines three scopes of metrics: **base**, **vendor**, and **application**. MicroProfile Metrics defines a number of APIs for application developers to provide additional application metrics. These metrics can be accessed via the endpoints of `http://myHost:myPort/metrics/base`, `http://myHost:myPort/metrics/vendor`, and `http://myHost:myPort/metrics/application`. The endpoint of `http://myHost:myPort/metrics` lists the aggregation of all three scopes of the metrics. The data exposed via REST over HTTP can be in JSON format or **OpenMetrics** text format, which can be consumed by the monitoring tools such as **Prometheus** so that the metrics can be represented as a graph in a dashboard.

MicroProfile OpenTracing

MicroProfile OpenTracing (`https://github.com/eclipse/microprofile-opentracing/`) provides implicit support for JAX-RS applications to participate in distributed tracing without adding any distributed tracing code to their cloud-native applications. It provides a mechanism to automatically inject `SpanContext` information into any outgoing JAX-RS request and then start a span for any outgoing JAX-RS request and finish the `Span` when the request completes. MicroProfile OpenTracing adopts **OpenTracing** (`https://opentracing.io/`) and its implementation must make `io.opentracing.Tracer` available to each application.

MicroProfile OpenTracing exposes the trace spans that tracing tools such as **Jaeger** or **Zipkin** can use to gather the data and graph them in a dashboard.

You have learned the essential specifications from MicroProfile. However, there are some extra specifications following standalone releases. Let's look at these to see whether you could use some of them in your applications.

Standalone releases

From 2018, a few more MicroProfile specifications were released: **MicroProfile Reactive Streams Operators**, **MicroProfile Messaging**, **MicroProfile Context Propagation**, and **MicroProfile GraphQL**.

The MicroProfile community would like to get more feedback before merging these specifications into the umbrella release. As a consequence, they remain as standalone specifications. *Chapter 10, Reactive Cloud-Native Applications*, and *Chapter 11, MicroProfile GraphQL*, will discuss these specifications in more detail. For now, let's have an overview of each:

- **MicroProfile Reactive Streams Operators** (`https://github.com/eclipse/microprofile-reactive-streams-operators/`) defines an API for manipulating reactive streams by providing operators such as `map`, `filter`, and `flatMap`. It also provides APIs to be used by MicroProfile Messaging.

- **MicroProfile Messaging** (`https://github.com/eclipse/microprofile-messaging/`) defines a messaging mechanism for declaring CDI beans producing, consuming, and processing messages via the annotations of `@Incoming` for consuming messages and `@Outgoing` for publishing messages.

- **MicroProfile Context Propagation** (`https://github.com/eclipse/microprofile-context-propagation/`) introduces APIs for propagating contexts across units of work that are thread-agnostic. It provides a mechanism for pushing the contexts from the parent thread to the child thread, which allows the asynchronous APIs such as `CompletionStage`, `CompletableFuture`, and `Function`, to work better in cloud-native applications with some associated contexts. MicroProfile Context Propagation enables asynchronous programming to be context-aware because the new threads can inherit some contexts from parent threads, such as `Security Context`, `CDI Context`, `Application Context`, `Transaction Context`, and other applications defined in `ThreadContext`.

- **MicroProfile GraphQL** (`https://github.com/eclipse/microprofile-graphql/`) provides a set of APIs for developing GraphQL-based applications, such as `@Query` and `@Mutuation`, for building GraphQL queries and mutations, accordingly.

So far, we have learned about all the MicroProfile specifications in short order. If you don't understand some of them, don't worry as we will cover them in more depth in the following chapters.

You might now be wondering how to create a cloud-native application using MicroProfile, and whether there are any tools to help with creating a cloud-native application. We will cover this in the next section.

MicroProfile Starter

MicroProfile Starter (`https://start.microprofile.io/`) is a code generator for developing cloud-native applications using MicroProfile. This tool can be accessed via the web, command line, or IDE plugins. In this section, we will learn about the MicroProfile Starter tool for creating cloud-native applications.

Accessing MicroProfile Starter via the web

The following screenshot shows the **User Interface** of MicroProfile Starter, which can be used to create cloud-native applications and then download the ZIP:

Figure 2.2 – MicroProfile Starter UI

In the preceding UI, we can specify the following:

- **groupId**: The generated application's Maven group ID.

- **artifactId**: The generated application's Maven artifact ID.

- **MicroProfile Version**: The version of the MicroProfile release.

- **MicroProfile Runtime**: The selected runtime that supports the chosen MicroProfile release version. In *Figure 2.2*, MicroProfile version 3.3 is selected, and then three runtimes that implement MicroProfile version 3.3 are displayed: **Open Liberty**, **Wildfly**, and **Payara Micro**.

- **Java SE Version**: Once we have chosen our favorite runtime, we can then choose the Java SE version. If a runtime supports multiple Java SE, we can then select which Java SE version you want. For example, Open Liberty supports both Java SE 8 and Java SE 11. Once we have selected Open Liberty, we can then choose either Java SE 8 or Java SE 11.

- **Examples for specifications**: The MicroProfile specifications that the generated applications are going to use. Clicking on the checkbox will select the corresponding MicroProfile specifications and the code sample will include the chosen MicroProfile specifications. If TypeSafe Rest Client or JWT Auth is selected, two cloud-native applications will be generated to demonstrate the client-server architecture. If you want to create a MicroProfile application from scratch, you don't need to choose any of the checkboxes. In this case, you will have the structure set up and you can write your business code straightaway.

Accessing MicroProfile Starter via the command line

MicroProfile Starter has command-line support, which is useful if you want to automatically generate cloud-native applications on the command line or as part of the automation process.

You can find all information via the following command, where the output displays all of the supported features with the corresponding commands:

```
curl 'https://start.microprofile.io/api'
```

In the output from the aforementioned command, you can find further commands to use for creating a specific cloud-native application for a chosen runtime, MicroProfile version, and so on.

Accessing MicroProfile Starter via an IDE plugin

MicroProfile Starter can also be accessed via IDE plugins, namely, the **Visual Studio Code MicroProfile extension pack** or **Intellij IDEA MicroProfile plugin**, which we will look at now.

Visual Studio Code plugin

The **Visual Studio Code Extension Pack for MicroProfile** (https://marketplace. visualstudio.com/items?itemName=MicroProfile-Community.vscode-microprofile-pack) can be downloaded and installed onto Visual Studio Code (https://code.visualstudio.com).

This extension pack also includes **Language Server Support for MicroProfile**, **Open Liberty Tools**, **Quarkus**, and **Payara Tools**.

IntelliJ IDEA plugin

IntelliJ IDEA (`https://www.jetbrains.com/idea/`) offers a MicroProfile Starter plugin (`https://plugins.jetbrains.com/plugin/13386-microprofile-starter`) for you to access MicroProfile Starter directly from the Intellij IDE. You can simply install the plugin and start using MicroProfile Starter. When using the plugin, you can input the same fields as shown in *Figure 2.2*, and then an application will be created.

Summary

In this chapter, we have learned all of the MicroProfile specifications and discussed how they can help with creating cloud-native applications. We then added various QoS, such as configuration, resilience, security, and monitoring. With this, you will have a basic idea of how to design your cloud-native application with best practices to make it secure, configurable, resilient, intelligent, and monitorable. In the chapters to follow, we will learn these technologies in more depth.

Furthermore, after going through the MicroProfile specifications, we then introduced MicroProfile Starter, a tool to develop cloud-native applications. This tool can be accessed via the web, command line, Visual Studio plugin, or IntelliJ IDEA plugin. You will be able to use these tools to create your cloud-native applications from scratch.

In the next chapter, we will introduce a real-world, cloud-native application that utilizes MicroProfile technologies to solve some common problems, and we will also learn how MicroProfile helps with the challenges posed by real-world use cases.

3
Introducing the IBM Stock Trader Cloud-Native Application

Throughout this book, we'll be using an example application known as **IBM Stock Trader** to demonstrate various concepts and techniques. This open source example is intended to show people how to develop, deploy, and use a typical cloud-native application that is composed of various microservices and leverages various external services such as databases, messaging systems, and internet services. All microservices are containerized and deployed (via an operator) to a Kubernetes cluster such as the **OpenShift Container Platform**.

As the name implies, the IBM Stock Trader example exists in the financial domain, simulating a brokerage application that tracks the stocks each customer has purchased in their portfolio. While it doesn't actually buy or sell anything, it does look up current actual prices of specified stocks and computes an overall portfolio value that maps to a customer loyalty level. It also simulates an account balance from which it debits commissions paid per trade and tracks the **return on investment** (**ROI**) for each portfolio. As well as this, it has optional pieces that do things such as send out notifications when new loyalty levels are reached and analyze submitted feedback to see if free (no commission) trades should be granted, demonstrating how it interacts with real-world systems such as Slack, Twitter, or **International Business Machine Corporation's** (**IBM's**) Watson.

As we discuss each MicroProfile 4.x technology in upcoming chapters, we'll be referring back to how this example demonstrates the usage of each. We'll include code snippets from various microservices that comprise the example, explaining the benefits the application derives from using each MicroProfile technology.

In this chapter, we're going to cover the following main topics:

- Overview of the IBM Stock Trader application
- Mandatory microservices and external services
- Optional microservices and external services

By the end of this chapter, you will be familiar with the application, how to use it, how the various parts fit together to make a composite application, and which parts you can ignore if you're in a hurry.

Overview of the IBM Stock Trader application

Created and enhanced over the past 3-4 years, this polyglot example demonstrates how to create containerized microservices, targeting a variety of application runtimes. For the most part, these microservices are deliberately kept simple so that readers don't get bogged down in the deep technical intricacies that would likely exist in a real brokerage application. That said, it is very much intended to be significantly more instructive than the various *Hello World*-level examples often shown in beginners' documentation for cloud-native programming.

The example consists of about a dozen microservices that interact with about a dozen external dependencies (most of which are optional). There is also a Helm chart and an OpenShift operator (which wraps the Helm chart) used for deployment of the example, which will be covered in *Chapter 9, Deployment and Day 2 Operations*.

In this section, we will provide a high-level overview of the application, the microservices that comprise it, and what they do. Let's start by looking at **user interfaces** (**UIs**).

UIs

Before diving into all of the backend microservices running in the cloud, let's look at what is provided as a client for you to use in your web browser. There is actually a choice of **graphical UI** (**GUI**) clients for this example. There's a simple Java servlet /JSP-based UI called **Trader** that deliberately uses very simplistic **HyperText Markup Language** (**HTML**) to render results so that the servlet code is easily understandable. Let's take a look at this simplistic client in the following screenshot:

○ Create a new portfolio
◉ Retrieve selected portfolio
○ Update selected portfolio (add stock)
○ Delete selected portfolio

	Owner	Total	Loyalty Level
○	Thursday	$479.48	BASIC
○	Raunak	$1,177,712.46	PLATINUM
○	Karri	$10,431.96	BRONZE
○	Alex	$12,049.00	BRONZE
◉	John	$76,720.39	SILVER
○	Eric	$120,835.00	GOLD
○	Charlie	$3,004,905.16	PLATINUM

Submit   Log Out

Figure 3.1 – Simple Java servlet-based UI: Trader

As you can see, this client provides a list of the portfolios and allows you to view the details of one, modify one, create a new one, or delete one. You have to log in successfully to use the client and have the option to submit feedback, which can lead to free (no-commission) trades. It will show your current loyalty level, your account balance, and your ROI.

There is also a fancier user interface called **Tradr** that is written in Node.js using the **Vue.js UI framework** and that provides a more modern experience; this requires JavaScript to be enabled in your browser. Let's take a look at that one too—you can see it in the following screenshot:

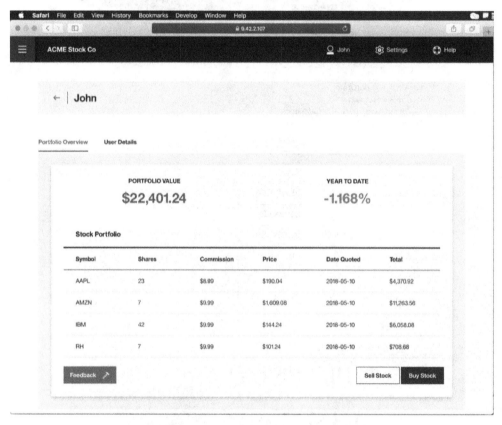

Figure 3.2 – Fancy Node.js-based UI: Tradr

Both clients have the same functionality. The fancier one is a bit more complicated to understand when reading its code, but it presents a much more professional-looking, responsive experience. Trader looks as though it was written at the end of the twentieth century, while Tradr looks as though it was written in the modern day.

There is also a command-line client called `loopctl` that runs a specified number of iterations (on parallel threads) of actions upon portfolios, which can be used for performance and throughput testing, as illustrated here:

```
sh-4.4$ ./loopctl.sh 1 1
1:  GET /broker
```

```
[{"owner": "Raunak", "total": 1,160,209.07, "loyalty":
"PLATINUM", "balance": -89.82, "commissions": 139.82, "free":
0, "nextCommission": 5.99, "sentiment": "Unknown", "stocks":
{}}, {"owner": "Karri", "total": 10,413.06, "loyalty":
"BRONZE", "balance": 31.02, "commissions": 18.98, "free": 0,
"nextCommission": 8.99, "sentiment": "Unknown", "stocks":
{}}, {"owner": "Alex", "total": 12,049.00, "loyalty":
"BRONZE", "balance": 41.01, "commissions": 8.99, "free": 0,
"nextCommission": 8.99, "sentiment": "Unknown", "stocks":
{}}, {"owner": "John", "total": 79,544.03, "loyalty":
"SILVER", "balance": 16.04, "commissions": 33.96, "free": 0,
"nextCommission": 7.99, "sentiment": "Unknown", "stocks":
{}}, {"owner": "Eric", "total": 120,835.00, "loyalty":
"GOLD", "balance": 43.01, "commissions": 6.99, "free": 0,
"nextCommission": 6.99, "sentiment": "Unknown", "stocks":
{}}, {"owner": "Charlie", "total": 3,004,905.16, "loyalty":
"PLATINUM", "balance": 34.02, "commissions": 15.98, "free": 0,
"nextCommission": 5.99, "sentiment": "Unknown", "stocks": {}}]
```

```
2:   POST /broker/Looper1
```

```
{"owner": "Looper1", "total": 0.00, "loyalty": "Basic",
"balance": 50.00, "commissions": 0.00, "free": 0,
"nextCommission": 9.99, "sentiment": "Unknown", "stocks": {}}
```

```
3:   PUT /broker/Looper1?symbol=IBM&shares=1
```

```
{"owner": "Looper1", "total": 127.61, "loyalty": "Basic",
"balance": 40.01, "commissions": 9.99, "free": 0,
"nextCommission": 9.99, "sentiment": "Unknown", "stocks":
{"IBM": {"symbol": "IBM", "shares": 1, "price": 127.61, "date":
"2021-03-12", "total": 127.61, "commission": 9.99}}}
```

```
4:   PUT /broker/Looper1?symbol=AAPL&shares=2
```

```
{"owner": "Looper1", "total": 369.67, "loyalty": "Basic",
"balance": 30.02, "commissions": 19.98, "free": 0,
"nextCommission": 9.99, "sentiment": "Unknown", "stocks":
{"AAPL": {"symbol": "AAPL", "shares": 2, "price": 121.03,
"date": "2021-03-12", "total": 242.06, "commission": 9.99}
{"IBM": {"symbol": "IBM", "shares": 1, "price": 127.61, "date":
"2021-03-12", "total": 127.61, "commission": 9.99}}}
```

In the interest of brevity, only the first 4 of the 12 steps in each iteration are shown in the preceding output. In short, it creates a new portfolio, buys and sells stock in it, and deletes it, and does these dozen steps as many times as you request, on as many parallel threads as you want, and reports timings.

No matter which of the three clients you use, they all make **REpresentational State Transfer** (**REST**) calls to the same **Broker** microservice, which in turn reaches out to the other microservices as needed, as we'll see in the next section.

Architectural diagram

Let's take a look at a diagram showing how all of the pieces fit together. It may look a little overwhelming at first but, per the advice from *The Hitchhiker's Guide to the Galaxy*, "*don't panic!*". Most of the microservices and dependencies you see in the following diagram are optional:

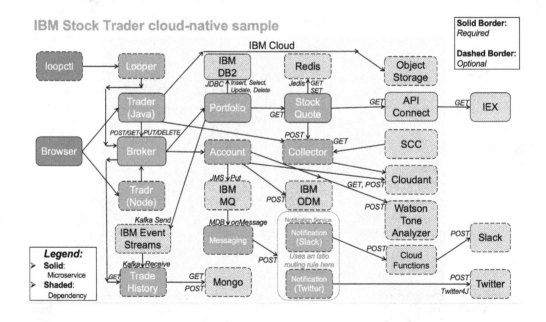

Figure 3.3 – Architectural diagram

There is a GitHub repository at `https://github.com/IBMStockTrader` for each of the solid color boxes shown in *Figure 3.3*. As per standard GitHub naming conventions, each microservice name is converted to all lowercase, and a dash is used between words in a multi-word name; for example, the **Stock Quote** microservice is available at `https://github.com/IBMStockTrader/stock-quote`.

There is also a Docker Hub repository at `https://hub.docker.com/u/ ibmstocktrader` for each of these microservices. You can of course build each from their source code in GitHub (which we'll discuss in *Chapter 8, Building and Testing your Cloud-Native Application*) and push the images to whichever image repository you want, such as the one built into your OpenShift cluster. But to make it easier to deploy the example, there are pre-built images provided as well. If you use the operator to deploy the example, it will default to pulling the images from Docker Hub, but you can replace the default image and tag fields for each microservice to pull from any image repository.

In the following sections, we'll look at each microservice in the application, as well as its dependencies.

Mandatory microservices and external services

As mentioned earlier, the core part of the example is just that which is needed to do the basics of creating portfolios and buying/selling stock. Those parts of the example have a solid border around each box, as shown in *Figure 3.3*.

The following subsections will describe each of the microservices and their dependencies that are required in order to exercise the primary functionality of the **IBM Stock Trader** application—that is, the ability to create portfolios and buy and sell stocks within them.

Trader

Trader is the standard UI client for the example. As seen earlier in *Figure 3.1*, it presents a list of existing portfolios, allowing you to create new ones, update existing ones (by buying or selling stocks), and delete portfolios. It communicates, via REST service calls, with the Broker microservice, passing a **JavaScript Object Notation (JSON) Web Token (JWT)** for **single-sign-on (SSO)** purposes.

It is implemented via a set of simple Java servlets and JSPs that, as with most of the Stock Trader microservices, runs atop the open source Open Liberty application server, running in the **Universal Base Image (UBI)**, which is a **Red Hat Enterprise Linux (RHEL)** 8.4 container with the Open J9 Java 11 **virtual machine (VM)**.

There are choices for how this client performs authentication. The default and easiest way is to log in against a hardcoded list of credentials defined in a `basicRegistry` stanza within the `server.xml` file of the Trader microservice, such as `stock/trader` as the **identifier (ID)**/password.

LDAP

Another option you can choose with the Trader microservice is to log in against your company's **Lightweight Directory Access Protocol (LDAP)** server. This way, your employees can log in against their corporate user registry, such as with their serial number or email address. Note that if you are deploying the example to an OpenShift cluster in the public cloud and your user registry server runs in an on-premises data center behind a firewall, then you'll need to set up a **virtual private network (VPN)** connection back to that LDAP server.

OIDC

The final option for authentication with the Trader microservice is to log in using an **OpenID Connect (OIDC)** server. This option is often used if you want to require authentication via a third-party provider out on the internet, such as logging in via your Facebook, Twitter, or GitHub credentials. For testing purposes, you can also deploy your own OIDC server locally into your OpenShift cluster, such as by using the operator (in OperatorHub) for **Red Hat SSO (RH-SSO)**, which is based on the open source **Keycloak** project.

Broker

Architects often recommend using a **model-view-controller (MVC)** architecture with a multi-tiered application. With the Stock Trader example, the JSON is the *model*, Trader (or the optional Tradr or Looper) is the *view*, and the **Broker** microservice serves as the *controller*.

It is a stateless microservice that, as with most of the microservices in this example, exposes a REST interface via the **Jakarta RESTful Web Services (JAX-RS)**. It coordinates calls to various other microservices such as **Portfolio** and the optional **Account** and **Trade History**. It does not directly depend on any external services.

Portfolio

This microservice takes care of all of the stock-related operations for a given portfolio. It reaches out to the **Stock Quote** microservice to get the current price of the desired stock.

Conceptually, it is a stateful microservice; however, it does not maintain any state in memory. Instead, it connects to a relational database to persist and access its data. That database can be running locally in your OpenShift cluster or out in the cloud, or in an on-premises data center (which, if so, would require a VPN connection to reach). The microservice uses **Java Database Connectivity (JDBC)** to interact with the database, and optionally uses **Kafka** to post a message to a topic.

JDBC database

Portfolio uses two tables in a relational database, named `Portfolio` and `Stock`. There is a row in the `Portfolio` table corresponding to each row you see in the table in the client. There is also a row in the `Stock` table for each stock purchased. The `Stock` table has a foreign key back to the `Portfolio` table, and a `cascade delete` rule on the relationship that will remove all of the stocks for a given portfolio if that portfolio is deleted.

Since this example was created by IBMers and is often used to demonstrate how to connect up a cloud-native application to various IBM products, usually IBM's **Db2** (part of the IBM *Cloud Pak for Data*) is used as the relational database. However, it has been tested with other **JDBC** providers, such as the open source **Apache Derby**. Note that no code needed to change in the microservice to switch providers; only the `server.xml` file and the `Dockerfile` (to copy the JDBC **Java ARchive (JAR)** file into the container) needed updates to choose a different relational database vendor.

Here's a graphical view of the resources that Portfolio uses in a **Db2-as-a-Service** database hosted in the IBM cloud:

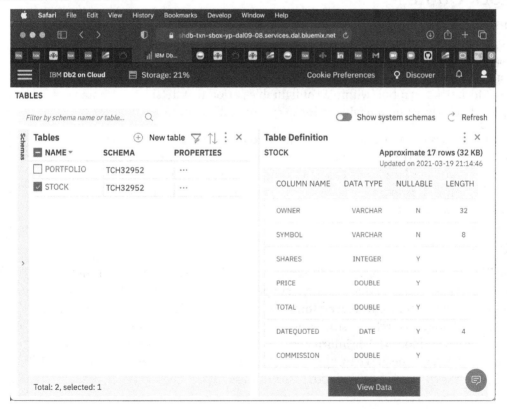

Figure 3.4 – Details of the IBM Db2 on cloud database used by Portfolio

In the preceding screenshot, you can see the details of the table holding each of the stocks that have been purchased; the **OWNER** column is a foreign key back to the portfolio containing the stocks.

Kafka

Portfolio also has an optional dependency on **Kafka**. If configured, Portfolio will publish a message to a Kafka topic whenever a stock is traded. The optional Trade History microservice will subscribe to this topic, using MicroProfile Reactive Messaging (which we'll discuss further in *Chapter 10, Reactive Cloud-Native Applications*), and act upon the message.

Usually, the **IBM Event Streams** product (from the IBM *Cloud Pak for Integration*) is chosen as the Kafka provider. However, other providers could be used, such as **AMQ Streams** from Red Hat, if desired.

Stock Quote

This is the simplest microservice in the example. It merely calls a REST **application programming interface** (**API**) in the cloud that returns the current price of the specified stock (quotes are 15 minutes delayed from this free service; more real-time quotes cost money). There is also an optional caching service that can be used so that calls for the same stock ticker symbol (within a configurable period that defaults to 1 hour) can be returned quickly, without having to make another call out onto the internet.

Note that this is the only microservice that is configured to run on Red Hat's **Quarkus** application framework. All of the other Java-based microservices run on Open Liberty. Quarkus is another Java MicroProfile implementation. The Java code is the same either way; the only difference is in how it is built and configured and which starting-point Docker container it runs in.

API Connect

The REST API that Stock Quote calls is implemented in **API Connect** (part of the *IBM Cloud Pak for Integration*). You can simply accept the defaults and it will use a pre-provisioned instance with everything already set up. This API fronts a free service out in **IEX Cloud** that returns stock prices with a 15-minute delay (getting more real-time prices costs money). For information on how to set up this API in your own instance of API Connect, see https://medium.com/cloud-engagement-hub/introducing-api-connect-a0218c906ce4.

> **Note**
> This API used to use a different free stock price service from Quandl, but that service went offline; the nice thing was that nothing in the Stock Trader example had to change—it was simply an update to the implementation of the API from API Connect, which still presented the same operation signature.

Redis

Stock Quote uses **Redis** as its optional caching service. If not present, then each call will result in a trip out to the internet to get the stock price. By caching each stock's price in Redis, it means you can scale the Stock Quote microservice up to as many pods as you want and be sure that no matter which one you get routed to each time, you will get a consistent answer. It also means that in true *serverless* fashion (where stuff not recently used gets stopped to save money and restarted **just in time** (**JIT**) when new requests arrive), you can scale all the way down to zero pods when not needed and be sure that when you get scaled back up to handle new requests, you can still benefit from the previously cached data.

Optional microservices and external services

There are also several optional parts of the example that you would only set up if you wanted certain extra bells and whistles available (such as having it send a tweet when you level up from **SILVER** to **GOLD**). Those parts have a dashed border in the architectural diagram.

Most people setting up the example skip many (or sometimes all) of the following pieces in the interest of simplicity. But each of these demonstrates how to do some additional things in a cloud-native manner, so they serve as good examples of how to utilize additional **Java Enterprise Edition** (**EE**)/**Jakarta EE** and **MicroProfile** technologies.

In this section, we will take a look at each of these optional microservices and their dependencies. The first of these is the alternate UI we saw earlier.

Tradr

The more attractive UI is called **Tradr**. Its source code (the only non-Java microservice in the example) is a bit more complicated to read, but it provides a much more modern, responsive interface, as is generally expected these days of professional websites. It calls the exact same REST services from the Broker microservice—it just renders the results in a more appealing way.

Note that, whereas Trader offers a choice of authentication approaches, with the default being a very simple approach requiring no extra setup, the Tradr client requires the use of OIDC. This means you have to do extra setup, to either stand up your own OIDC server in your OpenShift cluster or to adjust the configuration of an external OIDC server (which often requires registering a callback **Uniform Resource Locator** (**URL**) pointing back to the OpenShift route for Tradr).

Account

This optional microservice takes care of things associated with a portfolio that are above and beyond the list of which stocks it holds. This includes the loyalty level, the account balance, commissions paid, the owner's sentiment, and any free trades they have earned. Those fields will just show Unknown (for strings) or -1 (for numbers) if this microservice is not configured.

Although the Portfolio microservice chose to use an old-fashioned **Structured Query Language** (**SQL**)-based database, this one demonstrates the use of a more modern NoSQL database to store each JSON document: IBM **Cloudant** (from the IBM *Cloud Pak for Data*).

Cloudant

Note that whereas the Portfolio microservice had to do an object-to-relational mapping (such as turning the one-to-many containment relationship between Portfolio and Stock into a foreign key with a cascade delete rule), that isn't necessary for the Account microservice. The exact same JSON that gets returned by each of the REST operations on this JAX-RS-based microservice is what is stored in the Cloudant database, as we can see here:

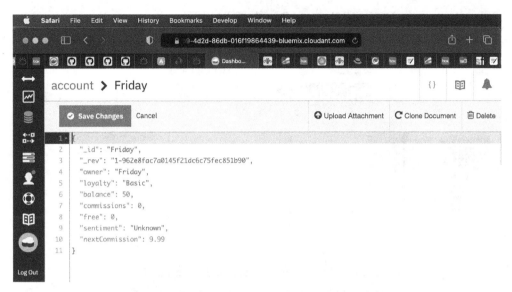

Figure 3.5 – An example Account document stored in IBM Cloudant

In the preceding screenshot, we can see the data that Account manages, including the loyalty level and the account balance. Note that the _id and _rev fields are ones added by Cloudant itself to manage how you find a specific document (_id) and revisions on a document (_rev).

ODM

Rather than hardcode the business rule for determining the loyalty level in Java, this microservice externalizes that rule to a business rules engine. This allows us to adjust thresholds, such as how high the portfolio's total value must reach to achieve **GOLD** status, on the fly via a dashboard, without having to change and redeploy the microservice.

The example uses the IBM **Operational Decision Manager** (**ODM**), from the IBM *Cloud Pak for Automation*, as its business rules engine. There is a ruleset ZIP file in the Account Git repository (https://github.com/IBMStockTrader/account/blob/master/stock-trader-loyalty-decision-service.zip) that you can import into the Decision Center UI and deploy to a Decision server. If ODM isn't configured, the loyalty level will just remain at its starting value forever.

Let's take a look at the **Decision Center** UI in the following screenshot:

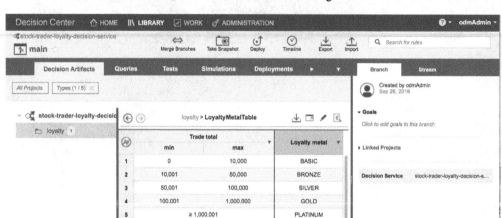

Figure 3.6 – The IBM ODM Decision Center UI, showing our decision table

Here, we can see the decision table, showing the various thresholds. For example, once your portfolio's total value crosses **US dollars** (**USD**) $50,000, its loyalty level goes from **BRONZE** to **SILVER**.

Jakarta Messaging

When the loyalty level changes (meaning you have ODM configured and have bought enough stock—for example, the default threshold, as you can see in *Figure 3.6*, is $100,000 to reach **GOLD**), the Account microservice will post a message to a **Jakarta Messaging** queue. There are downstream microservices that will react to that message.

Usually, the IBM **MQ** product, from the *IBM Cloud Pak for Integration*, is used as the Jakarta Messaging provider. You can also choose other providers—for example, the example has been tested with Open Liberty's built-in **Java Message Service** (**JMS**) provider as well. As with JDBC providers, no Java code needs to change in order to pick a different provider; the change is just an update to the `server.xml` file and a line in the `Dockerfile` to copy the Jakarta Messaging `.rar` file into the container.

Watson Tone Analyzer

Normally, whenever you buy or sell a stock, a commission is debited from your account balance. However, it is possible to earn a free (zero commission) trade by using the **Submit Feedback** button. Whatever text you type will be sent to the IBM *Watson Tone Analyzer* (hosted in the IBM Cloud), and a `sentiment` will be determined and returned. You get one free trade for submitting most kinds of feedback, but there's a rule that will give you three free trades in order to soothe you if it determines your sentiment is **Angry**.

If you don't configure the Watson Tone Analyzer, you'll get back **Unknown** and no free trades.

Trade History

This microservice keeps a record of every trade you made, when you made it, and what the stock cost when you made it. Without this microservice, the example only knows aggregate information. For example, if you bought 10 shares of IBM stock a month ago for $100, and 5 shares a week ago for $110, and 2 more shares today for $120, the Portfolio microservice would just know you now have 17 shares and what they are worth today ($2,040 in this example). The Trade History microservice remembers all of the details, so it would know you spent $1,790 and thus have an ROI of 14%. If this microservice isn't configured, the Trader and Tradr clients will just say **Unknown** for the ROI.

As mentioned in the discussion of the Portfolio microservice, this microservice subscribes to and consumes the messages that Portfolio publishes to the Kafka topic, such as would be managed by *IBM Event Streams*. It does so via **MicroProfile Reactive Messaging**.

Mongo

This microservice uses a **Mongo** database to persist the details of each trade. Its readiness probe checks to make sure Mongo is running at the specified endpoint via the specified credentials—if Mongo is unavailable, then the pods for this deployment will never reach a `Ready` state and thus nothing will ever consume the messages from the topic.

Messaging

This microservice consumes the JSON messages from the JMS queue about the change in loyalty level that the Account microservice sent. This microservice has the only Jakarta **Enterprise Bean** in the example, using a **Message Driven Bean** (MDB) to receive the messages. It then alerts you via the **Notification** microservice about the newly reached level. As with the Account microservice, this one also needs a Jakarta Messaging provider such as IBM MQ, as we can see in the following screenshot:

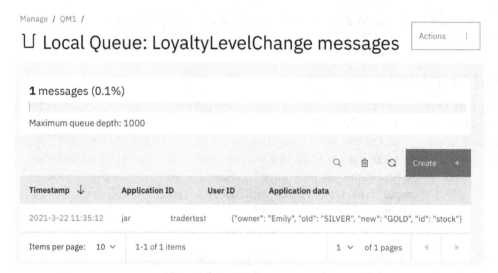

Figure 3.7 – The IBM MQ UI, showing a message sent by the Account microservice

Here, we see a simple JSON message on the MQ queue that gets processed by the Messaging microservice to provide a notification—in this case, about **Emily** having upgraded her loyalty level from **SILVER** to **GOLD**.

Notifications

There are two different flavors of the Notification microservice—one sends a tweet and the other posts to a Slack channel. Both have the same REST interface, so you just pick which you want to use when you deploy the example.

Notification-Twitter

The **Notification-Twitter** flavor uses the open source library from `twitter4j.org` to interact with Twitter's REST API to send a tweet.

Whereas most of the microservices in this example run on Open Liberty, this one runs on the **traditional WebSphere Application Server** (**tWAS**) in a Docker container.

For more information on how this was set up, see `https://medium.com/cloud-engagement-hub/experiences-using-the-twas-docker-container-557a9b044370`.

To configure the example to send tweets via your account, you need to get the **Open Authorization (OAuth)** credentials for your Twitter account. You'll need the consumer key and consumer secret, as well as the access token and access token secret. Here's an example tweet from Notification-Twitter:

Figure 3.8 – An example tweet sent by Notification-Twitter

In *Figure 3.8* you see the tweet from the `@IBMStockTrader` account that was sent when the loyalty level upgraded from **BRONZE** to **GOLD**.

Notification-Slack

This flavor of the Notification microservice posts a message to a Slack channel. As with the Twitter flavor, it does so whenever a JMS message about a loyalty-level change is processed. The microservice calls a *serverless* function that sends the actual post to Slack, as we see here:

Figure 3.9 – An example Slack message sent by Notification-Slack

As you can see, the message is much like what was sent to Twitter, but in this case, it was sent to a Slack channel instead.

The *serverless* function is implemented via the **Apache OpenWhisk** framework. You can either deploy OpenWhisk to your OpenShift cluster or use IBM's **Function-as-a-Service (FaaS)** known as *IBM Cloud Functions*. For details on how the action sequence was created that posts a message to the Slack channel, see `https://medium.com/cloud-engagement-hub/serverless-computing-and-apache-openwhisk-164676af8972`.

> **Note**
>
> There is also an Amazon Web Services (AWS) Lambda serverless function that Notification-Slack can invoke to cause the message to get posted to the Slack channel. It expects the same API definition as the OpenWhisk function, so no changes were needed to the Notification-Slack microservice - you just configure it with a different URL and credentials via the operator. Whether you choose IBM Cloud Functions or AWS Lambda, this shows that Kubernetes and serverless frameworks can work together harmoniously.

Collector

This microservice receives evidence from other microservices, persists it to IBM Cloudant, and makes it available for periodic scraping by a security/compliance tool such as the **Security and Compliance Center (SCC)** in the IBM cloud. Trader can be configured to send evidence about login attempts, and Stock Quote can be configured to send evidence about cache hits (in Redis). It receives evidence via REST (a POST request) and exposes evidence via REST (a GET request).

Unlike the other microservices, this one does not use **MicroProfile JWT (mpJWT)** for SSO; instead, it just uses basic auth (a simple user ID and password) since SCC would not know how to produce and sign such a JWT when it scrapes the /collector endpoint. This is similar to how **MicroProfile Metrics (mpMetrics)** does not use mpJWT, since a monitoring tool such as Prometheus would likewise not be able to create and attach such a JWT when it scrapes the /metrics endpoint.

Looper

The final optional microservice in this example is called **Looper**. This is a servlet used for performance and stress testing. Via a query parameter (which defaults to 1 if not specified) on its route URL, you can tell it to run a specified number of iterations of a dozen operations, which show off all of the **create, retrieve, update, and delete (CRUD)** operations available on the Broker microservice.

For example, the operator for this example (which will be described in detail in *Chapter 9, Deployment and Day 2 Operations*) has a checkbox to set up a **Horizontal Pod Autoscaler (HPA)** that will scale up each microservice to additional pods if they reach certain **central processing unit (CPU)** thresholds (and will scale back down when the CPU usage drops back off). By using Looper to put the example under load, you can see the HPA in action, and you can see that the resource usage graphs in the OpenShift console show the activity.

loopctl

One issue with requesting a large number of iterations of the Looper servlet is that you see no output until all of them are complete. In fact, most browsers, by default, will time out if the request takes an unreasonable amount of time to return.

To address this, there is a command-line client to the Looper servlet known as `loopctl`, which calls the `Looper` servlet in a loop.

You can tell it to run a specified number of iterations on a specified number of parallel threads. You saw the output of this command-line client earlier. To run it yourself, requesting 25 iterations on 4 parallel threads, the easiest approach is to go to the **Terminal** tab for the Looper pod in the OpenShift console and run `./loopctl.sh 25 4`, which would run 100 total iterations (temporarily creating portfolios named `Looper1`, `Looper2`, `Looper3`, and `Looper4`) and would output the average number of milliseconds per iteration.

Summary

You should now have a feel for the cloud-native example that will be used throughout this book. Though it may appear a bit daunting at first, the mandatory parts are quite easy to set up (especially if you use the pre-built images in Docker Hub), so you can be up and running with the basics of the example in a matter of minutes. Then, you can add whichever of the optional bonus capabilities you'd like at your own pace.

In the upcoming chapters, various MicroProfile technologies will be discussed in detail. Each will show snippets from particular microservices in this example. As you have seen, different microservices are meant to demonstrate different features of Jakarta EE and MicroProfile and provide a real running tutorial of how to integrate with various external services.

In *Chapter 8, Building and Testing your Cloud-Native Application* we'll examine how these microservices were developed so that you can learn how to develop such microservices yourself. In *Chapter 9, Step-by-Step Stock Trader Development*, we'll cover the deployment of the example in detail, as well as *day 2* operations you can perform.

In the next chapter, we will begin looking at each of the MicroProfile technologies themselves and see how they help Java developers create cloud-native applications that can run in, and deeply integrate with, an orchestrated, containerized environment in a public or private cloud.

Section 2: MicroProfile 4.1 Deep Dive

In this section, you will learn all about MicroProfile. This includes developing and consuming RESTful microservices and then enhancing them with APIs intended to add configuration options, fault tolerance, and more. You will also learn how to use MicroProfile technologies to observe your applications as well as debug them. Lastly, you will learn about cloud deployment options for your applications.

This section comprises the following chapters:

- *Chapter 4, Developing Cloud-Native Applications*
- *Chapter 5, Enhancing Cloud-Native Applications*
- *Chapter 6, Observing and Monitoring Cloud-Native Applications*
- *Chapter 7, MicroProfile Ecosystem with Open Liberty, Docker, and Kubernetes*

4

Developing Cloud-Native Applications

MicroProfile 4.1 builds on some **Jakarta EE** (formerly **Java Enterprise Edition**) **application programming interfaces (APIs)**—specifically, **Jakarta RESTful Web Services (JAX-RS)**, **Jakarta Contexts and Dependency Injection (CDI)**, **JavaScript Object Notation Processing (JSON-P)**, and **JSON Binding (JSON-B)**. Using only these technologies, it is possible to develop a perfectly capable cloud-native application. The MicroProfile community added a type-safe mechanism for invoking RESTful services known as the **MicroProfile Rest Client**. These technologies are essential for building Java-based microservices that can interoperate in the cloud. Learning to use these technologies will enable you to build robust and secure Java microservices.

In this chapter, we will explore all of the following topics:

- Developing a RESTful service with JAX-RS
- Managing the payload with JSON-P and JSON-B
- Consuming RESTful services with the MicroProfile Rest Client
- Managing life cycle and **dependency injection (DI)** with CDI

This chapter covers a wide spectrum of technologies and the functionality within each technology. When you have finished this chapter, you should have a broad and deep understanding of how to build reliable, robust RESTful applications that can communicate with each other using JSON.

Technical requirements

In order to build and run the samples mentioned in this chapter, you will need a Mac or PC (Windows or Linux) with the following software:

- **Java Development Kit** (**JDK**) version 8 or higher (`http://ibm.biz/GetSemeru`)

- Apache Maven (`https://maven.apache.org/`)

- A Git client (`https://git-scm.com/`)

- All of the source code used in this chapter is available on GitHub at `https://github.com/PacktPublishing/Practical-Cloud-Native-Java-Development-with-MicroProfile/tree/main/Chapter04`.

Once you have cloned the GitHub repository, you can start the Open Liberty server that these code samples will execute in by entering the `Chapter04` directory and running the following command from the command line:

```
mvn clean package liberty:run
```

You can then stop the server in the same command window by pressing *Ctrl* + *C*.

Now we've got the prerequisites taken care of, let's start by building a basic RESTful service.

Developing a RESTful service with JAX-RS

In this section, we will develop a few RESTful services using JAX-RS. We'll start with a simple example, and then we'll add more complex and powerful techniques such as exception handling, advanced conversion of **HyperText Transfer Protocol** (**HTTP**) data into Java objects (and vice versa), cross-cutting concerns, asynchronous methods, and DI.

JAX-RS is built around the idea of a **request-response** pipeline. On the server side, an HTTP request enters the pipeline, then the JAX-RS server invokes any pre-matching **filters** on the request. It then attempts to match the request with a JAX-RS **resource method**.

When the JAX-RS container receives an incoming request, it will perform the following process:

1. Invoke any registered pre-matching filters.
2. Attempt to match the request to a `resource` method. If no match can be made, the container will respond with an appropriate `not found` HTTP response.
3. Invoke any registered post-matching filters.
4. Perform conversion of HTTP data (such as the HTTP entity payload or parameters, headers, and so on) into Java objects consumable by the resource method if necessary.
5. Invoke the `resource` method.
6. Perform exception handling, if necessary.
7. Invoke any registered response filters.
8. Perform conversion of Java object(s) to HTTP response data, if necessary.
9. Return the HTTP response to the client.

This pipeline flow is illustrated in the following diagram:

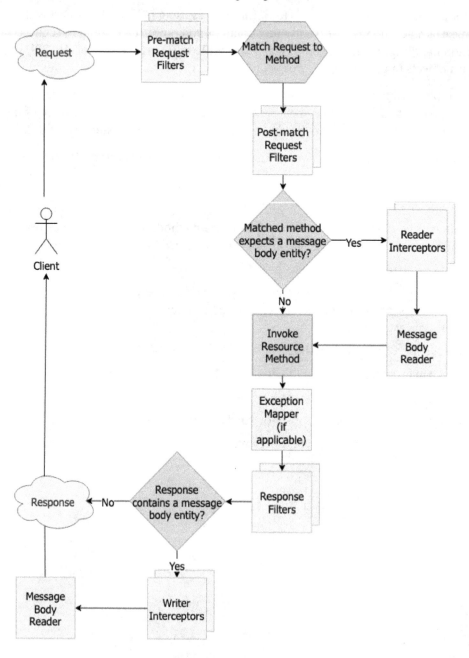

Figure 4.1 – JAX-RS server pipeline flow

In JAX-RS, there are three types of components, outlined as follows:

- **Resources**: The resources are what ultimately make the RESTful service what it is as they contain the business logic.

- **Providers**: Providers augment the application by performing tasks such as customizing the conversion of HTTP data into a Java object or vice versa, handling exceptions thrown from the resources, and intercepting the pipeline flow to perform supplementary tasks such as authorization or authentication, and more. Filters, `MessageBodyReader`, `MessageBodyWriter`, `ParamConverter`, `ExceptionMapper`, `ReaderInterceptor`, and `WriterInterceptor` are all providers.

- **Application subclasses**: An `Application` subclass is used to provide configuration for the JAX-RS application.

Now we understand the basic flow, let's create a simple JAX-RS application.

Hello World!

A JAX-RS application must contain at least one resource class. Providers are optional. An `Application` subclass is only necessary if you don't have a `web.xml` file that specifies an application path. So, a very simple application might look like this:

```
@ApplicationPath("/rest")
public class HelloWorldApp extends Application {}
@Path("/hello")
public class HelloWorldResource {

    @GET
    public String helloWorld() {
        return "Hello World!";
    }
}
```

If we build this code into a web application called `myApp.war` and deploy it into a JAX-RS container such as Open Liberty, we could quickly test it using an HTTP client by browsing to `http://localhost:9080/myApp/rest/hello` and we would see the text **Hello World!**.

This works because the @GET annotation on the helloWorld() method tells the JAX-RS container that this method should be invoked when a client issues a GET request to the /hello path of the /rest application path under the **context root** path. The context root path is usually the same name as the **Web application ARchive (WAR)** file but without the .war extension. By default, most HTTP clients (browsers, curl, and so on) use GET unless specified otherwise. This brings up a good point about tooling. When developing RESTful applications, it is extremely valuable to have a client tool that can issue different types of HTTP requests. Command-line tools such as curl are very useful, and there are several browser extension-based tools that would also work.

A more real-world example

Now we have built a simple JAX-RS application, let's build a more complex application—a thesaurus service where clients can search and update synonyms. We'll start with an **exception mapper**, as follows:

```
@Provider
public class NoSuchWordExceptionMapper implements
  ExceptionMapper<NoSuchWordException> {

    @Override
    public Response toResponse(NoSuchWordException ex) {
        return Response.status(404)
                    .entity(ex.getMessage()).build();
    }
}
```

Most applications will have **business exceptions**—exceptions specific to the application domain. For a thesaurus service, that might include a NoSuchWordException exception, which could be used to indicate that a searched word does not exist. It is clear in the application that somebody specified a word that does not exist, but it is not clear to an HTTP client. The NoSuchWordExceptionMapper provider class makes that possible. It enables the resource class methods to throw a NoSuchWordException exception, and the JAX-RS container will map the exception to an HTTP response (in this case, a 404 Not Found error).

Next is the resource class (the full source code is available at `https://github.com/PacktPublishing/Practical-Cloud-Native-Java-Development-with-MicroProfile/blob/main/Chapter04/src/main/java/com/packt/microprofile/book/ch4/thesaurus/ThesaurusResource.java`), as illustrated in the following code snippet:

```
@Path("/thesaurus/{word}")
@Consumes(MediaType.TEXT_PLAIN)
@Produces(MediaType.TEXT_PLAIN)
public class ThesaurusResource { // ...
```

There are a few new annotations on the resource class: `@Produces` and `@Consumes`. These annotations can be placed on resource classes or methods—as with most annotations of this type in JAX-RS, annotations on the method take priority over annotations on the class. These annotations help control the matching of requests and the entity providers (`MessageBodyReaders` and `MessageBodyWriters`) to be used in deserializing the HTTP entity from the request or serializing the HTTP entity in the response.

HTTP requests and responses may contain a header that indicates the **media type** (also known as the **Multi-purpose Internet Mail Extensions (MIME) type**) of the HTTP entity—`Content-Type`. HTTP requests may also contain a header that specifies the media type(s) that it expects to receive in the response—`Accept`. In the absence of these headers, all media types are allowed (denoted by, `*/*`).

In the previous example, the resource class specifies `MediaType.TEXT_PLAIN` or `text/plain`. Other media types include `text/html`, `application/json`, `application/xml`, `image/jpeg`, and much more. Specifying `text/plain` would prevent the resource methods from being invoked if a request contained a header such as `Content-Type: application/pdf` or `Accept: image/png`—instead of invoking the resource method, the JAX-RS container would return a `415 Unsupported Media Type` error.

> **Best practice**
>
> Always use `@Produces` and `@Consumes` to limit media types. This will place limits on the types of requests your service will respond to. It will ensure that your application (if properly tested) can handle requests of the specified media types.

This example also introduces new method-level HTTP verb annotations: `@POST`, `@PUT`, `@DELETE`, and `@PATCH`. As with `@GET`, these annotations specify which method should be invoked based on the HTTP request's **verb** (also known as method—**HTTP method** is probably the more commonly used term, but we will use *verb* in this book to disambiguate from Java methods). The JAX-RS API set includes these five verb annotations as well as `@HEAD` and `@OPTIONS`, which are less commonly used.

> **Special note**
>
> If the resource class contains a method annotated with `@GET` but not `@HEAD`, the JAX-RS container would invoke the `@GET` method for matching HTTP HEAD requests, but it would remove the entity. Likewise, if a resource class contains any HTTP verb annotation other than `@OPTIONS`, the JAX-RS container would return a response indicating all of the valid verbs that could be matched for that request. Using the preceding example, an `OPTIONS` request would result in a response with a header such as `Allow: DELETE, HEAD, GET, OPTIONS, PATCH, POST, PUT`.

This example also introduces the idea of HTTP parameters—specifically, `@PathParam("word") String word;`.

This annotation can be placed on fields or method parameters. The value of `@PathParm` is `word`, which corresponds to the template variable in the resource class's `@Path` value (`"/thesaurus/{word}"`). This means that for an HTTP request such as `http://localhost:9080/myApp/rest/thesaurus/funny`, the value injected into the `word` field would be `funny`.

There are other HTTP parameter types that can be used in JAX-RS, including `@QueryParam`, `@FormParam`, `@CookieParam`, `@HeaderParam`, and `@MatrixParam`, which all correspond to different parts of an HTTP request. JAX-RS also allows multiple HTTP parameter annotations to be aggregated on a single Java class and then referenced in the resource class or method as a `@BeanParam` parameter type. Here is an example of this:

```
public class ParamBean {
    private int id;

    @QueryParam("id")
    public void setId(int id) {
        this.id = id;
    }
    @HeaderParam("X-SomeHeader")
```

```
    public String someHeaderValue;

    @PathParam("path")
    public String pathParamValue;

    @Override
    public String toString() {
        return "ID: " + id + " X-SomeHeader: "
            + someHeaderValue + " path: " + pathParamValue;
    }
}
```

The `ParamBean` bean is just a **plain old Java object** (**POJO**) with fields or setters annotated with other `@*Param` annotations. Then, this POJO is injected into a resource, like this:

```
@GET
@Path("/beanparam/{path}")
public Response get(@BeanParam ParamBean params) {
    return Response.ok(params.toString()).build();
}
```

`@BeanParam` beans can be very useful for aggregating common sets of RESTful parameters to avoid writing repetitive code. Let's test this example from the command line using `curl`, as follows:

```
$ curl "http://localhost:9080/rest/beanparam/
  myPath?id=1234" -H "X-SomeHeader: MyHeaderValue"
ID: 1234 X-SomeHeader: MyHeaderValue path: myPath
```

One thing to be wary of is that not all parameters will be non-null, so you will need to check for null values, or you can use the `@DefaultValue` annotation. This applies to method parameters as well. An example is provided here:

```
@GET public String get(@QueryParam("startPage")
@DefaultValue("1") Integer startPage) { // ...
```

Notice that the value in the `@DefaultValue` annotation is always a string, but as long as it can be converted from a string to the parameter type (`Integer`, in this case), it will work. In the next section, we will learn how to convert data sent from a client into the Java objects in our application code.

Entity providers and ParamConverter

So far, our resource methods have mainly been dealing with strings or other primitives. The JAX-RS container is responsible for serializing and deserializing those objects, but what if we want to send and receive more complex objects? In those cases, we may need to implement some **entity providers** and/or `ParamConverter`.

Entity providers

Entity providers include `MessageBodyReader` and `MessageBodyWriter`, and they are responsible for deserializing HTTP entity data to a Java object and serializing a Java object to an HTTP entity, respectively.

Let's say that we have a `Person` object such as this:

```
public class Person {
    public enum Color {
        RED, BLUE, YELLOW, GREEN, ORANGE, PURPLE
    }
    private String firstName;
    private String lastName;
    private int age;
    private Color favoriteColor;
    //public getters/setters
}
```

And let's say that we have a `service` object such as this:

```
@Path("/person")
@Produces(MediaType.APPLICATION_JSON)
@Consumes(MediaType.APPLICATION_JSON)
public class PersonService {
    static List<Person> people = new ArrayList<>();

    @GET
```

```
@Path("/{id}")
public Person getPerson(@PathParam("id") int id) {
    try {
        return people.get(id);
    } catch (IndexOutOfBoundsException ex) {
        throw new WebApplicationException
            (Response.status(404).entity("ID " + id + "
                not found.").build());
    }
}


@POST
public int postPerson(Person person) {
    people.add(person);
    return people.lastIndexOf(person);
}
}
```

One thing to notice here is that the getPerson(...) method throws a new
WebApplicationException exception, passing it as a 404 response. This is another
way to map an exception to a response without needing an ExceptionMapper instance.

> **Best practice**
>
> Use ExceptionMappers when multiple resource methods may throw
> the same exception. Throw a WebApplicationException exception
> with a passed-in Response object only in cases where you don't have an
> appropriate business exception to throw or you only throw the exception from
> one resource method.

Another thing to notice is the use of APPLICATION_JSON as the media type that this
resource produces and consumes. The application/json media type is the most
common content type used in microservices. **JSON** is concise, human-readable, and easily
processed by most programming languages. Here is an example of JSON representing the
Person object from the previous sample code:

```
{
  "firstName": "John",
  "lastName": "Doe",
  "age": 33,
```

```
    "favoriteColor":"RED"
}
```

In order for a client to create a new `Person` object via the `POST` method, we need a `MessageBodyReader` instance. There are some built-in readers that would handle this nicely, but for now, we'll write and register our own, like this (the full source code is available at `https://github.com/PacktPublishing/Practical-Cloud-Native-Java-Development-with-MicroProfile/blob/main/Chapter04/src/main/java/com/packt/microprofile/book/ch4/entityandparamproviders/MyJsonReader.java`):

```java
@Provider
@Consumes(MediaType.APPLICATION_JSON)
public class MyJsonReader implements MessageBodyReader<Person>
{
    @Override
    public boolean isReadable(Class<?> type, Type
        genericType, Annotation[] annotations, MediaType
            mediaType) {
        return type.equals(Person.class) &&
            mediaType.isCompatible(MediaType
                .APPLICATION_JSON_TYPE);
    }


    @Override
    public Person readFrom(Class<Person> type,
        Type genericType, Annotation[] annotations,
            MediaType mediaType,
        MultivaluedMap<String, String> httpHeaders,
          InputStream entityStream)
                throws IOException, WebApplicationException {
        String s = new BufferedReader(new InputStreamReader
            (entityStream)).lines().collect
                (Collectors.joining(" ")).trim();
        if (!s.startsWith("{") || !s.endsWith("}")) {
            throw new WebApplicationException(Response
                .status(400).build());
        }
        Person p = new Person();
        // ... parse string into Peron object ...
```

```
        return p;
    }
}
```

Furthermore, in order to write a `Person` object as JSON in a response entity, we must register a JSON `MessageBodyWriter` instance, like this (the full source code is available at `https://github.com/PacktPublishing/Practical-Cloud-Native-Java-Development-with-MicroProfile/blob/main/Chapter04/src/main/java/com/packt/microprofile/book/ch4/entityandparamproviders/MyJsonWriter.java`):

```
@Provider
@Produces(MediaType.APPLICATION_JSON)
public class MyJsonWriter implements
  MessageBodyWriter<Person> {
    @Override
    public boolean isWriteable(Class<?> type, Type
        genericType, Annotation[] annotations, MediaType
          mediaType) {
        return type.equals(Person.class) && mediaType
          .isCompatible(MediaType.APPLICATION_JSON_TYPE);
    }

    @Override
    public void writeTo(Person p, Class<?> type, Type
        genericType, Annotation[] annotations, MediaType
          mediaType, MultivaluedMap<String, Object>
            httpHeaders, OutputStream entityStream)
        throws IOException, WebApplicationException {
            PrintStream ps = new PrintStream(entityStream);
            // print Person object to entity stream
    }
}
```

These providers could easily be combined into one `MyJsonEntityProvider` class that implements both interfaces. Both implementations use **input/output (I/O)** streams to represent the entity—`InputStream` to read an entity from a client request and `OutputStream` for writing the response entity. Both providers have a Boolean check to verify that this is the proper entity provider to invoke—in addition to the generic type specified (`Person`) and the `@Consumes/@Produces` values, returning `true` or `false` for the `isReadable` or `isWriteable` methods will tell the JAX-RS container whether this provider should be used to serialize/deserialize the data.

Another criterion for selecting among multiple providers would be the `@Priority` annotation—the JAX-RS container will select the provider with the highest priority (which is the lowest value—thus, `@Priority(1)` would be selected before `@Priority(2)`).

Ultimately, the value returned from the reader's `readFrom` method will be injected into the resource method's **entity parameter**. An entity parameter is any method parameter that is not annotated with `@Context` (more on this in the *Context injection* section) or `@*Param`. A resource method may contain zero or one entity parameters—any more will result in a deployment failure.

On the response side, the content written to the writer's `writeTo` entity stream will be written to the HTTP response sent back to the client.

If the amount of code complexity for writing and reading JSON seems a little daunting at this point, don't fret! We'll cover a simpler approach in the next section.

So, entity providers are responsible for serializing and deserializing HTTP entities to objects, but what about parameters such as query parameters, path parameters, and so on? These are deserialized with `ParamConverter`

ParamConverter

Building on our `PersonService` example, let's add a `PATCH` method allowing clients to change a person's favorite color, as follows:

```
@PATCH
@Path("/{id}")
public Person updateFavoriteColor(@PathParam("id") int
    id, @QueryParam("color") Color color) { // ...
```

We can invoke this method from the command line like this:

```
$ curl http://localhost:9080/rest/person/0?color=BLUE -X PATCH
{
```

```
"firstName": "John",
"lastName": "Doe",
"age": 33,
"favoriteColor":"BLUE"
}
```

We are able to update John's favorite color because the JAX-RS container was able to identify that `Color` is an enumerated type, and so it will invoke its `valueOf(String)` method to get the `Color` object that it injects when invoking the `updateFavoriteColor` method. But what happens when we specify the `color` in lowercase? Let's have a look at the following output to find out:

```
$ curl http://localhost:9080/rest/person/0?color=blue -X PATCH
-v
...
< HTTP/1.1 404 Not Found
...
<
```

Uh oh! The JAX-RS container could not match the request to a resource method (resulting in a `404 Not Found` response) because it could not convert `blue` to `Color.BLUE`. In order for our service to be more resilient or to handle more complex objects as parameters, we must use `ParamConverterProvider` and `ParamConverter` like this:

```
@Provider
public class ColorParamConverterProvider implements
    ParamConverterProvider {

    @Override
    public <T> ParamConverter<T> getConverter(Class<T>
        rawType, Type genericType, Annotation[] annotations) {
        if (rawType.equals(Color.class)) {
            return (ParamConverter<T>) new ColorParamConverter();
        }
        return null;
    }
}
```

ParamConverterProvider is responsible for returning an instance of a class that implements ParamConverter, such as this:

```
public class ColorParamConverter implements
  ParamConverter<Color> {

  @Override
  public Color fromString(String value) {
    return Color.valueOf(value.toUpperCase());
  }

  @Override
  public String toString(Color value) {
    return value.name();
  }
}
```

The first class, ColorParamConverterProvider, is the registered provider class. When a resource method has a parameter that needs to be converted from String to an object, the JAX-RS container will invoke the getContainer method of any registered ParamConverterProvider class until one returns a non-null ParamConverter instance.

The ColorParamConverter class simply capitalizes the string value to ensure that the enum's valueOf method will return the Color.BLUE color, regardless of whether the client request's query parameter was BLUE, Blue, blue, bLuE, and so on.

ParamConverter work for @QueryParam parameters as demonstrated, but also work for @CookieParam, @FormParam, @HeaderParam, @MatrixParam, and @PathParam parameters, and they can be used to convert a string to any object, and vice versa. The conversion from object to String is important on the client side. We'll discuss that in the *Consuming RESTful services with the MicroProfile Rest Client* section.

Intercepting requests and responses

There may be times when you need to check the input stream of a request before or after processing it in the MessageBodyReader entity provider. Likewise, there may be times where you want to perform additional processing to the output stream before or after processing it in the MessageBodyWriter entity provider. ReaderInterceptors and WriterInterceptors are intended for such tasks.

ReaderInterceptors and WriterInterceptors

In our `MessageBodyReader` entity provider, we make a lot of calls to trim strings, which can be expensive in terms of performance. One way we might be able to reduce such calls would be to remove whitespace from the entity stream in a `ReaderInterceptor` provider so that then the `MessageBodyReader` provider could always assume that the stream contains no whitespace characters. Here's an example of this:

```
@Provider
public class WhiteSpaceRemovingReaderInterceptor implements
   ReaderInterceptor {
    @Override
    public Object aroundReadFrom(ReaderInterceptorContext
        context) throws IOException, WebApplicationException {
        InputStream originalStream = context.getInputStream();
        String entity = // convert stream to string
        entity = entity.replaceAll("\\s","");
        context.setInputStream(new ByteArrayInputStream
            (entity.getBytes()));
        return context.proceed();
    }
}
```

When a client sends a multiline request entity with spaces, line feeds, or other white space, you can see that this will convert them with the system output, as follows:

```
PRE: {
 "firstName": "John",
 "lastName": "Doe",
 "age": 33,
 "favoriteColor":"RED"
}
POST: {"firstName":"John","lastName":"Doe","age":33,
   "favoriteColor":"RED"}
```

A common use case for `WriterInterceptors` is to reduce the response entity size by using GZIP compression—see a full example of this at `https://github.com/PacktPublishing/Practical-Cloud-Native-Java-Development-with-MicroProfile/blob/main/Chapter04/src/main/java/com/packt/microprofile/book/ch4/interceptorsandfilters/GzipWriterInterceptor.java`.

> **Special note about entity streams**
>
> While you can read the entity stream from multiple places (entity providers, reader or writer interceptors, filters—we'll cover these shortly), you can run into problems when you do. For example, your initial request entity stream may not support re-reading, so if you attempt to read it twice, you may end up with an `IOException` exception. In that case, you may need to reset the stream (if the stream supports resetting—each JAX-RS container may be a little different) or copy and replace the stream entirely as we did in our `ReaderInterceptor` example.

Filters

Where `ReaderInterceptors` and `WriterInterceptors` intercept the reading and writing of entity streams, **filters** intercept the overall request and response. Filters enable some powerful cross-cutting abilities in RESTful applications. So, what can we use filters for? We could probably fill the rest of this book with useful examples, from managing authentication, authorizing requests, redirecting requests, managing headers, aborting invalid requests before wasting server resources on them, audit logging requests/responses, detecting suspicious activity, providing application statistics, tracing requests/responses, throttling requests from specific clients, and more.

Let's start with an example that checks incoming requests for an API key and returns a useful response if none exists, if it is unrecognized, or if that API key has exceeded the maximum number of requests for the day (the full source code is available at `https://github.com/PacktPublishing/Practical-Cloud-Native-Java-Development-with-MicroProfile/blob/main/Chapter04/src/main/java/com/packt/microprofile/book/ch4/interceptorsandfilters/ApiKeyCheckFilter.java`). Have a look at the following code snippet:

```
@PreMatching
@Provider
public class ApiKeyCheckFilter implements
    ContainerRequestFilter {
    private final Map<String, Integer> apiInvocations = new
```

```
    ConcurrentHashMap<>();


    @Override
    public void filter(ContainerRequestContext
      requestContext) throws IOException {
        String apiKey = requestContext.getHeaderString
            (API_KEY_HEADER);
        if (apiKey == null) {
            requestContext.abortWith(Response.status(
              Status.UNAUTHORIZED).build());
            return;
        }
        // get count of recent invocations for this API key
        int currentInvocations = // ...
        if (currentInvocations == -1) {
            requestContext.abortWith(
                Response.status(Status.FORBIDDEN).build());
            return;
        }
        if (currentInvocations > MAX_REQUESTS_PER_INTERVAL) {
            requestContext.abortWith(
                Response.status(Status.TOO_MANY_REQUESTS)
                        .header(HttpHeaders.RETRY_AFTER, 5)
                        .build());
            return;
        }
    }
}
```

This example checks that the client sent an API key as an HTTP header, that the API key is valid (by its existence in the map), and that the user's key has not exceeded their quota of requests. If any of these conditions occur, the filter will abort the request and return a response with useful data for the client. If the filter method exits normally, then the request will proceed, and the JAX-RS container will attempt to match the request to a resource class and method.

Once the request has been matched to a resource method, the JAX-RS container will invoke post-match request filters. These filters are useful for performing **cross-cutting concerns** that are only applicable for valid requests. This could include audit logging (for tracking which RESTful APIs are used by which clients), custom authentication or authorization checks, more refined request validation, and so on. Post-match request filters implement the same interface (`ContainerRequestFilter`) as pre-match filters, but without the `@PreMatching` annotation. Post-match filters also enable more methods from the `RequestContext` object so that it knows which resource will be invoked. This is handy for situations where your filter may want to behave differently based on the resource class/method it will invoke.

Response filters are similar to request filters but are invoked after the resource method has been completed. Response filters can then further refine or transform the response. They could add or modify response headers or cookies. They could also replace the response entity entirely, though a `MessageBodyWriter` provider and/or `WriterInterceptor` provider might be more appropriate for that.

Dynamic providers

So far, all of the providers we have discussed will apply to all requests—or at least all matched requests—the only exception being entity providers, which will apply to all requests of the request's specified media type(s). But what if we want some providers to only be executed in certain circumstances, such as when a specific resource method is invoked or if the request contains specific content, or if the client's user is part of a special group? JAX-RS provides a few different mechanisms for more dynamic providers. First, we'll look at name binding.

Name binding allows users to place a custom annotation on one or more provider classes and one or more resource classes or methods. The JAX-RS container will then recognize that annotation and only invoke the provider if the target resource method or class is also annotated. For example, suppose we want to log certain requests; we might create an annotation like this:

```
@NameBinding
@Retention(RetentionPolicy.RUNTIME)
@Target({ElementType.METHOD, ElementType.TYPE})
public @interface Logged {}
```

The @NameBinding annotation is what tells the JAX-RS container to pay attention to this annotation. We can now create a filter that logs the request method, the **Uniform Resource Identifier (URI)**, and the request and response entity (the full source code is available at https://github.com/PacktPublishing/Practical-Cloud-Native-Java-Development-with-MicroProfile/blob/main/Chapter04/src/main/java/com/packt/microprofile/book/ch4/dynamicbinding/LoggingFilter.java). Have a look at the following code snippet:

```
@Logged
@Provider
public class LoggingFilter implements
  ContainerRequestFilter, ContainerResponseFilter {
    @Override
    public void filter(ContainerRequestContext
      requestContext) throws IOException {
        int requestID = idCounter.incrementAndGet();
        requestContext.setProperty("request.id", requestID);
        System.out.println(">>> " + requestID + " "
            + requestContext.getRequest().getMethod() + " "
            + requestContext.getUriInfo().getRequestUri()
            + " " + getAndReplaceEntity(requestContext));
    }

    @Override
    public void filter(ContainerRequestContext
        requestContext, ContainerResponseContext
            responseContext)
            throws IOException {
        int requestID = (int) requestContext.getProperty
            ("request.id");
        System.out.println("<<< " + requestID + " "
            + requestContext.getUriInfo().getRequestUri()
            + " " + responseContext.getEntity());
    }
    //...
}
```

This `filter` class is both a request and response filter. While it is very convenient to combine request and response filters (or perhaps even other provider types), it is important to note that the life-cycle behavior may change from one JAX-RS container to another. In general, it is considered a best practice not to store data in instance variables. If you want to store a piece of data from the request's filter method to be used in the response's filter method, a more portable approach would be to store that data in `requestContext` as a property, as we did for the request **identifier (ID)** in the preceding example.

Now, we would just add the `@Logged` annotation to the classes (all methods in the class) or methods that should be logged, so in the following example, only the `POST` method would be logged (the full source code is available at `https://github.com/PacktPublishing/Practical-Cloud-Native-Java-Development-with-MicroProfile/blob/main/Chapter04/src/main/java/com/packt/microprofile/book/ch4/dynamicbinding/DynamicResource.java`):

```
@Path("/dynamic")
public class DynamicResource {
    @GET
    public String getMessage() { // ...


    @POST
    @Logged
    public String postMessage(String message) { // ...
}
```

Another approach to dynamically apply providers is to use **dynamic features**. Dynamic features are providers themselves that determine, on each request, which providers to use. Dynamic features must implement one method, `configure`, which provides a `ResourceInfo` object that is used to determine specifics of the matched resource, and a `FeatureContext` object that is used to configure the providers and properties or view the application configuration for each request. The following example will add the `LoggingFilter` class to all resource methods that start with `get`:

```
@Provider
public class MyDynamicFeature implements DynamicFeature {

    @Override
```

```
    public void configure(ResourceInfo resourceInfo,
        FeatureContext context) {
        Method m = resourceInfo.getResourceMethod();
        if (m.getName().startsWith("get")) {
            context.register(LoggingFilter.class);
        }
    }
}
```

Since the `ResourceInfo` object will return the matched class and method, it is also possible to check the annotations of the matched resource. This makes it easy for dynamic features to register a provider for all requests of a specific HTTP verb (`if (resourceInfo.getResourceMethod().getAnnotation(GET.class) != null) { //...`) or methods with annotations that don't already have the `@NameBinding` annotation.

Name binding annotations and dynamic filters are powerful ways to control request and response processing.

Async

Enough with providers! Let's get back to the core of RESTful services—the resources. In many cases, the synchronous nature of the JAX-RS request/response flow is inefficient. For example, suppose your resources tend to pass a request to a data store that looks up or modifies data in a database. If your data store logic has a fixed set of threads performing the database operations, then when the service is under load, incoming requests may be queued. With the synchronous flow we've been working with so far, this means that the flow of execution would block inside the resource method waiting for the data-store logic to complete before completing the flow. This can be inefficient as one thread essentially waits for another to complete. That initial thread could be more efficient if it were to perform some other task while the data-store operations take place. Using **asynchronous** APIs in JAX-RS can obtain that increased efficiency.

AsyncResponse

Asynchronous methods in JAX-RS are created by adding an `AsyncResponse` parameter to the resource method, annotated with `@Suspended`. The `AsyncResponse` object may then be used to *resume* the request once the data has been fetched from the data store. Let's take a look at an example. Suppose we have a service that tracks people, like the one we used in the *Entity providers* section. We'll change the resource class around a little so that the data store access uses a separate `Executor` class to retrieve the data (the full source code is available at https://github.com/PacktPublishing/ Practical-Cloud-Native-Java-Development-with-MicroProfile/ blob/main/Chapter04/src/main/java/com/packt/microprofile/book/ ch4/async/AsyncPersonService.java). Have a look at the following code snippet:

```
@Path("/person")
public class AsyncPersonService {
    static ExecutorService executor =
        Executors.newFixedThreadPool(5);


    @GET
    @Path("sync/{id}")
    public Person getPersonSync(@PathParam("id") int id)
        throws InterruptedException, ExecutionException {
        Future<Person> someData = executor.submit(() ->
            getPerson(id));
        return someData.get();
    }


    private Person getPerson(int id) {//...
}
```

In this version of the code, the `getPersonSync` method will submit a request to the executor service to retrieve the `Person` object with the specified ID, then it will block until the executor service has completed the operation. In this case (for code simplicity), it is just pulling data out of a hash map, but if it were pulling data out of a remote database, the time spent blocking in the `someData.get()` call could be more substantial.

So, let's try to improve the efficiency so that we don't have to block. We can rewrite the `getPersonSync()` method to look like this:

```
@GET
```

```
@Path("async/{id}")
public void getPersonAsync(@PathParam("id") int id,
    @Suspended AsyncResponse ar) {
    executor.submit(() -> {
        ar.resume(getPerson(id));
    });
}
```

Now, the executor service is invoking the `getPerson(id)` method, but then passing the result to `ar.resume(...)`, which will pick up the request/response flow where it left off and return a response. The request thread that invoked the `getPersonAsync(...)` method immediately returns and can be used to service another request.

The `AsyncResponse` object can also be used to handle an exception. Let's say that we want to throw a `NoSuchPersonException` exception if the ID specified does not match any `Person` instance in the database. We might change the code to look like this:

```
executor.submit(() -> {
    Optional<Person> p = Optional.ofNullable(getPerson(id));
    if (p.isPresent())
        ar.resume(p.get());
    else ar.resume(new NoSuchPersonException());
});
```

When we resume a response with an exception, the JAX-RS container will attempt to map the exception to a suitable response, just as it does in the synchronous case.

Server-sent events

Another form of server-side async is **server-sent events (SSEs)**. SSEs are a part of the **HyperText Markup Language 5 (HTML 5)** specification and provide a way for a client to register and receive events asynchronously from a server.

JAX-RS has two ways of sending SSEs—streaming directly to each client and **broadcasting** to all clients. Let's take a look at how you might implement the first way, as follows (the full source code is available at `https://github.com/PacktPublishing/Practical-Cloud-Native-Java-Development-with-MicroProfile/blob/main/Chapter04/src/main/java/com/packt/microprofile/book/ch4/async/SseService.java`):

```
@Path("/sse")
@Produces(MediaType.SERVER_SENT_EVENTS)
```

```
public class SseService {
    @GET
    public void stream3Events(@Context SseEventSink
sink,                                      @Context Sse sse) {
        Executors.newSingleThreadExecutor().submit(() -> {
            try (SseEventSink sinkToClose = sink) {
                sink.send(sse.newEventBuilder()
                                .mediaType(TEXT_PLAIN_TYPE)
                                .data("foo")
                                .name("fooEvent")
                                .id("1")
                                .build());
                Thread.sleep(500);
                // repeat for 2/bar
                Thread.sleep(500);
                // repeat for 3/baz
            } catch (InterruptedException ex) {}
        });
    }
}
```

This is a contrived example, but it shows the method immediately returns after starting a new thread that sends a few text events to the client separated by a half-second delay.

This example shows us that in order for a JAX-RS resource to send SSEs, it must produce the SSE media type (MediaType.SERVER_SENT_EVENTS, or text/event-stream) and the method must receive Sse and SseEventSink parameters, both annotated with @Context. The Sse type is a utility class that can create events and broadcasters. The SseEventSink type represents the connection between the server and the client, so calling the send(...) method sends a new event to that specific client, and calling the close() method (which is done implicitly by the try-with-resources logic) will gracefully close the connection with the client.

The events we are sending have a text/plain media type—the media type is used to determine which MessageBodyWriter provider should be used to serialize that object passed to the data method. The name(...) and id(...) methods can provide additional context to each event sent. Only the data(...) method is required, though it is always a best practice to specify the media type.

If we were to invoke this service using `curl`, we would see something like this:

```
$ curl http://localhost:9080/rest/sse
event: fooEvent
id: 1
data: foo

event: barEvent
id: 2
data: bar

event: bazEvent
id: 3
data: baz
```

Another approach to sending events is to use a **broadcaster**. A broadcaster is basically a collection of `SseEventSinks`, and it will send events to all registered clients. Let's look at an example of code that we might add to our `SseService` class, as follows:

```
static SseBroadcaster broadcaster;
static ScheduledExecutorService executor =
    Executors.newSingleThreadScheduledExecutor();

private void startBroadcasting(Sse sse) {
    if (broadcaster == null) {
        broadcaster = sse.newBroadcaster(); //...
    }
}

@GET
@Path("/broadcast")
public void broadcast(@Context SseEventSink sink,
                      @Context Sse sse) {
    startBroadcasting(sse);
    broadcaster.register(sink);
    broadcaster.broadcast(sse.newEventBuilder()
        .mediaType(TEXT_PLAIN_TYPE)
        .data("new registrant")
```

```
            .build());
    }
```

As with the direct-stream approach, this approach also requires that the method produce a media type of `SERVER_SENT_EVENTS` and that the method has the `SseEventSink` and `Sse` parameter types.

First, we need to set `SseBroadcaster` as a static field. We do this because the default life cycle for JAX-RS resources is per request. We will discuss alternate life cycles in the *Managing life cycle and DI with CDI* section—that will simplify this code and improve performance too.

Once we have the broadcaster set, we then register the event sink with it. Once registered, the client associated with that event sink will receive all events sent from this broadcaster. In this example, we broadcast an event any time a new client is registered and every 5 seconds. Let's see what this looks like on the command line when using `curl` when we are the first client, and when a second client registers (from a separate command window), as follows:

```
$ curl http://localhost:9080/rest/sse/broadcast
      UnnamedEvent
data: new registrant

      UnnamedEvent
data: ping

      UnnamedEvent
data: ping
```

One thing to notice about this output is the `UnnamedEvent` text—this is because SSEs must have a name, so if no name is provided when it is built, the JAX-RS container creates a name for it. Other JAX-RS containers may use a different name if none is specified.

Context injection

We've already discussed injection when using the `@Context` annotation for SSE objects, but this annotation can be used for a lot more. **Context injection** can occur in both resources and providers. There are lots of useful things you can inject, as outlined here:

- `ResourceContext`: Used for initializing sub-resource locators
- `ResourceInfo`: Used for determining the matched resource class and method

- `HttpHeaders`: Used for reading HTTP headers in the client request
- `SecurityContext`: Used for determining the current user, their security role, and so on
- `UriInfo`: Used for reading the URI of the client request
- `Application`: Used for obtaining the application representing this RESTful service
- `Providers`: Used for accessing other JAX-RS providers
- `Sse` and `SseEventSink`: Discussed in the previous section

> **Best practice**
>
> In most cases, it is recommended that context injection occurs in fields rather than as parameters. The reason for this is that the Jakarta REST project is intending to deprecate the `@Context` annotation in favor of CDI's `@Inject` annotation, which does not target method parameters.

Javadoc (`https://jakarta.ee/specifications/restful-ws/2.1/apidocs/overview-summary.html`) is the best resource for understanding the capabilities of each of these injectable types. Here are a few basic examples:

```
@Context
SecurityContext secCtx;


@GET
public Response getSomeData() {
    if (secCtx.isUserInRole("special")) {
        return getSpecialResponse();
    }
    return getNormalResponse();
}
```

This example uses the role of the client's user principal to determine what entity response to return. The following example uses the `ResourceInfo` class to determine whether a `MessageBodyWriter` provider should be used or not:

```
@Provider
@Produces(MediaType.APPLICATION_JSON)
public class MySpecialJsonWriter implements
  MessageBodyWriter<Person> {
```

```
@Context
ResourceInfo resInfo;


@Override
public boolean isWriteable(Class<?> type, Type
  genericType, Annotation[] annotations, MediaType
  mediaType) {
    Class<?> resourceClass = resInfo.getResourceClass();
    return resourceClass.equals(SpecialResource.class)
       && type.equals(Person.class) && mediaType
        .isCompatible (APPLICATION_JSON_TYPE);
}
```

The injection of context objects into resources and providers enables us to develop powerful and flexible applications. Now, let's turn our attention to formatting the data our application will need to send and receive.

Managing the payload with JSON-P and JSON-B

While RESTful services in general and JAX-RS applications specifically can serve entities of any media type (plain text, **Extensible Markup Language (XML)**, **Portable Document Format (PDF)**, binary, and so on), JSON is the *standard du jour* for cloud-native applications. JSON is popular because it is both human-readable and easily parsed—libraries for JSON parsing and binding exist in virtually all modern languages.

In the *Entity providers* section, we got a taste of serializing and deserializing a Java object (`Person`) into JSON. In that section, we performed this by hand using string manipulation. While a manual approach can work, we're now going to discuss two APIs that enable simpler and more powerful control over JSON in Java.

JSON-P is a programmatic API for manipulating JSON, while JSON-B is a declarative (annotation-based) API for quickly and easily mapping an object to JSON or vice versa.

JSON-P

JSON-P has an object model API similar to the **Document Object Model** (DOM) for XML processing and a streaming API similar to the **Streaming API for XML** (StAX). Like their XML equivalents, the object model is better suited for making frequent changes or for using smaller documents as it is processed in memory. The streaming API is best suited for reading larger JSON documents or event-based processing. Both APIs can be used together, and the streaming API's parser will return objects such as `JsonObject`, `JsonArray`, and so on, which are part of the object model API.

Let's say we have some objects such as these:

```
public class Starship {
    private String name;
    private boolean hasHyperdrive;
    private List<Weapon> weapons;
    private int speedRating;
    //with public getters and setters
}


public class Weapon {
    private String name;
    private String type;
    private int damageRating;
    //with public getters and setters
}
```

And let's say we want to convert that into JSON content that looks like this:

```
{
  "name": "Coreillian Freighter",
  "hasHyperdrive": true,
  "speedRating": 22,
  "weapons": [
    {
      "name":"Quad Blaster Turret",
      "type":"Laser",
      "damageRating":24
    }
```

```
    ]
  }
```

We'll start out by converting an instance of `Starship` into a JSON string. We can do this by using the `Json` class to create object builders and array builders. These builders can create objects by adding properties or objects. So, to create the JSON for a starship, we would need an object builder for the starship and for each weapon, and then an array builder for all of the weapons. An example of this is available at `https://github.com/PacktPublishing/Practical-Cloud-Native-Java-Development-with-MicroProfile/blob/main/Chapter04/src/main/java/com/packt/microprofile/book/ch4/jsonp/JsonpConverter.java`.

Each object needs its own `JsonObjectBuilder` instance, and each array or collection needs its own `JsonArrayBuilder` instance. Then, you simply add items to them.

Deserializing a JSON string into an object works in the opposite way. First, you must extract `JsonObject` instance from `JsonReader`, like so:

```
JsonReader reader = Json.createReader(new StringReader(json));
JsonObject shipObject = reader.readObject();
```

Then, you must create a `Starship` instance and populate it from the properties in the `JsonObject`, like this:

```
Starship ship = new Starship();
ship.setName(shipObject.getString("name"));
ship.setHasHyperdrive(shipObject.getBoolean
   ("hasHyperdrive"));
//...
```

This approach uses the object model, which requires loading the entire JSON stream into memory before it can be converted into an object. For small JSON files, this is not an issue, and it allows the model to be stored in memory and re-accessed. It also allows the model to be changed over time before writing the JSON back to a stream.

The streaming approach requires far less memory and is capable of reading extremely large JSON streams without running out of memory. It accomplishes this by firing events as it reads the JSON and then discards that portion of the JSON. This is very efficient and performs better than the object model, but it requires more complex coding, and since the object model is not in memory, you cannot go back later to ask it: *Now, what was the value again?*

Using the same Java object and JSON stream as before, here is what the serialization code looks like (the full source code is available at https://github.com/PacktPublishing/Practical-Cloud-Native-Java-Development-with-MicroProfile/blob/main/Chapter04/src/main/java/com/packt/microprofile/book/ch4/jsonp/JsonpStreamingConverter.java):

```java
StringWriter sw = new StringWriter();
JsonGenerator generator = Json.createGenerator(sw);
generator.writeStartObject()
        .write("name", ship.getName())
        .write("hasHyperdrive", ship.isHasHyperdrive())
        .write("speedRating", ship.getSpeedRating())
        .writeStartArray("weapons");
for (Weapon w : ship.getWeapons()) {
    generator.writeStartObject()
            .write("name", w.getName())
            .write("type", w.getType())
            .write("damageRating", w.getDamageRating())
            .writeEnd();
}
generator.writeEnd()
        .writeEnd();
generator.close();
```

Similar to JsonObjectBuilder and JsonArrayBuilder, JsonGenerator can pass in map-like values to build the JSON object. Unlike the object model builder APIs, JsonGenerator cannot make changes—once the JSON is written, you cannot change the values. Both of the builders have remove methods, and the JsonArrayBuilder API has setter methods, allowing you to change previously configured values. The reason for having these two approaches is to allow you to make a decision between flexibility and efficiency.

For parsing JSON into an object, a stream-based approach is even more complex, as we can see here:

```java
Starship ship = new Starship();
JsonParser parser = Json.createParser(new StringReader(json));
while (parser.hasNext()) {
    Event event = parser.next();
```

```
if (event == Event.KEY_NAME) {
String keyName = parser.getString();
parser.next();
switch(keyName) {
case "name": ship.setName(parser.getString()); break;
//...
case "weapons": ship.setWeapons(parseWeapons(parser));
}
}
```

The parser works similar to a Java iterator, returning events to indicate things such as object start ({), object end (}), array start ([), array end (]), key names (for example, name and speedRating), and key values (for example, Coreillian Freighter and 24). It is important that each event is interpreted within its context. For example, an array might contain several objects, so it is necessary to keep track of which object is currently being parsed to avoid mixing up data. The parseWeapons method provides an example of this by separately parsing each item in the array, as illustrated in the following code snippet:

```
private List<Weapon> parseWeapons (JsonParser parser) {
    List<Weapon> weapons = new ArrayList<>();
    Event event = null;
    while ((event = parser.next()) != Event.END_ARRAY) {
        Weapon w = new Weapon();
        while (event != Event.END_OBJECT) {
            if (event == Event.KEY_NAME) {
                String keyName = parser.getString();
                parser.next();
                switch(keyName) {
                case "name": w.setName(parser.getString()); //...
                }
            }
            event = parser.next();
        }
        weapons.add(w);
```

```
        }
     return weapons;
  }
```

JSON-P provides a very powerful API set for reading and writing JSON programmatically. The code can tend to be a tad verbose, though. That's something that JSON-B can help with.

JSON-B

While JSON-P is very powerful and flexible, **JSON-B** is very simple and efficient at serializing and deserializing objects to JSON. JSON-B has some programmatic APIs but overall, it takes a declarative approach to writing/reading JSON. This means that the conversion of an object to JSON will be based on the object type's getter methods— and likewise, the conversion of JSON to object will be based on the object type's setter methods.

If we use the example objects of Starships and Weapons from JSON-P, the conversion of object to JSON and vice versa is very simple, as is illustrated here:

```
StringWriter sw = new StringWriter();
Jsonb jsonb = JsonbBuilder.create();
jsonb.toJson(ship, sw);
String json = sw.getBuffer().toString();
```

It is possible to convert directly to a string but using OutputStream or Writer is preferable, especially when dealing with large JSON objects. The primary objects here are Jsonb and the toJson(...) method. You can see the output here:

```
{"hasHyperdrive":true,"name":"Coreillian
Freighter","speedRating":22,"weapons":[{"damageRating":24,
"name":"Quad Blaster Turret","type":"Laser"}]}
```

This looks very similar to what we created using JSON-P, but it's all on one line and difficult to distinguish where one object ends and the next begins. For most JSON consumers that should not be a problem, but if we want to make it more human-readable, we can add some configuration by replacing the JsonbBuilder.create() method call with the following code:

```
Jsonb jsonb = JsonbBuilder.create(
     new JsonbConfig().withFormatting(true));
```

This will produce the following output:

```
{
    "hasHyperdrive": true,
    "name": "Coreillian Freighter",
    "speedRating": 22,
    "weapons": [
        {
            "damageRating": 24,
            "name": "Quad Blaster Turret",
            "type": "Laser"
        }
    ]
}
```

There are several other configuration options that you could use to handle the serialization of a Java object. For example, you could also add your own **deserializers** to provide some customization for certain objects. Deserializers work by allowing you to use a JsonParser from JSON-P to convert the object to JSON your own way.

Converting JSON back into an object is just as simple, as we can see here:

```
Starship shipFromJson = jsonb.fromJson(json,Starship.class);
```

And as with the toJson(...) method, you can use a string or a stream.

So, what happens if you have an object, but you want the JSON fields to have a different name than the Java property name? Or, maybe you don't want certain fields to be exposed as JSON at all? That's where annotations such as @JsonbProperty("someOtherName") and @JsonbTransient come in handy, and depending on where you place the annotation, it will have a different effect. If the annotation is on the getter, then it will only apply to serialization (conversion from Java to JSON). If the annotation is on the setter, then it will only apply deserialization. If the annotation is on the field itself, then it will apply to both. Let's consider the following code snippet:

```
public class Person {
    private String firstName;
    @JsonbTransient
    private String middleName;
```

```
    @JsonbProperty("familyName")
    private String lastName;
    private String favoriteColor;
    private int age;

    //...all other public unannotated getters/setters

    @JsonbProperty("favouriteColour")
    public String getFavoriteColor() {
        return favoriteColor;
    }

    @JsonbProperty("yearsOld")
    public void setAge(int age) {
        this.age = age;
    }
}
```

We would create an instance of `Person` and print it out to JSON, like so:

```
Person p = new Person();
p.setFirstName("John");
p.setMiddleName("Tiberius");
p.setLastName("Doe");
p.setFavoriteColor("Green");
p.setAge(25);
String jsonPerson = jsonb.toJson(p);
System.out.println(jsonPerson);
```

The output would look like this:

```
{
    "age": 25,
    "familyName": "Doe",
    "favouriteColour": "Green",
    "firstName": "John"
}
```

The `lastName` field has been converted to `familyName`, the `middleName` field has not been printed at all, and the `favoriteColor` field has been Britishized to `favouriteColour`. But if we tried to create a new `Person` instance from this JSON, we would get an incomplete `Person` instance. Let's take a look, as follows:

```
Person p2 = jsonb.fromJson(jsonPerson, Person.class);
System.out.println(p2.getFirstName());
System.out.println(p2.getMiddleName());
System.out.println(p2.getLastName());
System.out.println(p2.getFavoriteColor());
System.out.println(p2.getAge());
```

This would yield the following output:

```
John
null
Doe
null
0
```

The `middleName` field was missing from the JSON, so it is no surprise that it is null. Since the `@JsonbProperty("favouriteColour")` annotation is only on the getter, JSON-B will not convert the Britishized JSON field to the Americanized Java field. And since the `@JsonbProperty("yearsOld")` annotation is applied to the `setAge(...)` method, it will not be set since the JSON is still using the `age` field name.

The behavior differences depending on where an annotation is placed are important to note when using JSON-B.

Now, let's tie this back to JAX-RS. The JAX-RS specification says that a product that supports JSON-P must supply `MessageBodyReaders` and `MessageBodyWriters` for entity types of `JsonStructure`, `JsonObject`, `JsonArray`, `JsonString`, and `JsonNumber`. Furthermore, a product that supports JSON-B must supply `MessageBodyReaders` and `Writers` for any object type when the media type is `application/json`, `text/json`, `*/json`, or `*/*+json`. Any product that implements the entire MicroProfile set of specifications will have JAX-RS, JSON-P, and JSON-B. This means that for the most part, you can count on your JAX-RS container to handle the conversion of JSON to objects and back to JSON.

Now we've learned the easy way to work with JSON, let's learn how we can send requests and consume results using the client APIs.

Consuming RESTful services with the MicroProfile Rest Client

Thus far, we've covered how we can design elaborate RESTful services and how we can easily transform JSON into Java objects and vice versa. Next up, we need to consume those services using the client APIs. In a microservice architecture, RESTful clients are critical for invoking remote services.

JAX-RS Client APIs

One way to consume RESTful services is with the **JAX-RS Client APIs**. Similar to JSON-P (as opposed to JSON-B), these APIs tend to be more programmatic with more control over individual options, such as headers, path construction, and so on. Let's take a look at some code using the thesaurus example from earlier in this chapter, as follows:

```
String uri = "http://localhost:9080/rest/thesaurus";
Client client = ClientBuilder.newBuilder().build();
WebTarget target = client.target(uri).path(word);
Builder builder = target.request(MediaType.TEXT_PLAIN);
try (Response response = builder.get()) {
    int status = response.getStatus();
    assert status == 200;
} finally {
    client.close();
}
```

The client instance is built using `ClientBuilder`. In this example, it simply builds a `Client` instance, but you could use `ClientBuilder` to set configuration properties or register client-side providers. `Client` instances should be explicitly closed when you are done using them—they currently do not implement the `AutoCloseable` interface, but a future version of the JAX-RS specification will add that, allowing `Client` instances to be closed in a try-with-resources block.

`WebTarget` represents the destination of the client request. It has methods for appending path elements, resolving path template variables, adding query or matrix parameters, or specifying the expected response media type. In the previous example, we append the `word` variable to the `uri` variable with this line of code:

```
WebTarget target = client.target(uri).path(word);
```

Alternatively, we could change the `uri` variable to `http://localhost:9080/rest/thesaurus/{word}`, then we could use the following line of code:

```
WebTarget target = client.target(uri).resolveTemplate
    ("word", word);
```

Depending on the situation, either might be more usable.

An `Invocation.Builder` object is created by calling the `request(...)` method on the `WebTarget`—an optional media type parameter is used to determine what media type is expected for the response; it will set the `Accept` header. The `Invocation.Builder` object has methods such as `get(...)`, `post(...)`, `put(...)`, `delete(...)`, and other methods that represent the HTTP verb to use for the request. You can use the `method(...)` method to specify HTTP verbs that are not built into the API. It also has methods for setting cookies or headers.

The `Invocation.Builder` object also has `async()` and `rx()` methods that will return an asynchronous invoker and reactive invoker, respectively. These invokers enable users to retrieve the response asynchronously, which will generally improve performance.

The `Response` object represents the HTTP response from the remote server. From the `Response` object, you can check the status code of the response (`200`, `204`, `400`, `404`, `500`, and so on) and response headers, read the response entity, and more. Note that the `Response` object is `AutoCloseable`—it is always a good practice to close both `Response` and `Client` objects.

MicroProfile Rest Client

If the JAX-RS Client is similar to JSON-P, then the **MicroProfile Rest Client** API is similar to JSON-B. It uses annotations and a declarative approach to specify the HTTP endpoint and the entity object, header, and other data to be sent with the request. The MicroProfile Rest Client is type-safe, so the remote service is represented by a Java interface that is annotated similar to server-side JAX-RS resources—with `@Path`, `@GET`, `@PUT`, `@POST`, `@DELETE`, and so on, annotations. The MicroProfile Rest Client implementation provides an instance of the interface, which you can then invoke in order to invoke the remote service.

Let's take a look at an example, as follows (the full source code is available at `https://github.com/PacktPublishing/Practical-Cloud-Native-Java-Development-with-MicroProfile/blob/main/Chapter04/src/main/java/com/packt/microprofile/book/ch4/client/ThesaurusClient.java`):

```
@Path("/thesaurus/{word}")
@Consumes(MediaType.TEXT_PLAIN)
@Produces(MediaType.TEXT_PLAIN)
public interface ThesaurusClient {
    @GET
    String getSynonymsFor(@PathParam("word") String word)
        throws NoSuchWordException;

    @POST
    String setSynonymsFor(@PathParam("word") String word,
        String synonyms) throws WordAlreadyExistsException;
    // other methods matching ThesaurusResource ...
}
```

The methods here match the five resource methods in the `ThesaurusResource` class, with the exception that the `@PathParam` parameter is a method parameter. These methods all return a `String` object, but they could also return a `Response` object if it was important to view things in the response such as headers or status code, and so on. Usually, these things can be abstracted so that you can return the actual data type. This interface approach allows us to invoke the service by simply calling these methods. But first, we need to build an instance of this client. If we are in an environment that uses CDI (see the next section) and MicroProfile Config (see *Chapter 5, Enhancing Cloud-Native Applications*), then the framework can automatically build and inject the client instance. Otherwise (or if you just want to build the instance programmatically), you can use the `RestClientBuilder` API, like so:

```
ThesaurusClient thesaurus = RestClientBuilder.newBuilder()
    .baseUri(URI.create("http://localhost:9080/rest"))
            .build(ThesaurusClient.class);
```

This sets `baseUri`, the URI path up to the point where the `@Path` annotation is added. Similar to the JAX-RS `ClientBuilder` API, we could also use the `RestClientBuilder` API to specify properties for the client instance or register providers. Once we've built the client instance, we can invoke it like so:

```
thesaurus.getSynonymsFor(word);
```

Client-side providers

That's a nice way to invoke the service—a lot less code and it reads easier too! You might be thinking: *That method throws an exception—how does the implementation know when it should throw it?* Excellent question! The answer is `ResponseExceptionMapper`. It is basically the converse of JAX-RS `ExceptionMapper`—instead of mapping an exception to a response, they map a response to an exception. By default, MicroProfile Rest Client implementations will throw a `WebApplicationException` on any response with a status code of 400 or higher— those codes are client errors or server errors. To map more specific responses to exceptions, you would need to register one or more `ResponseExceptionMapper`, such as the following:

```java
public class NoSuchWordResponseMapper implements
    ResponseExceptionMapper<NoSuchWordException> {
    @Override
    public boolean handles(int status,MultivaluedMap<String,
        Object> headers) {
        return status == 404;
    }


    @Override
    public NoSuchWordException toThrowable(Response resp) {
        return new NoSuchWordException();
    }
}
```

This response exception mapper implements two methods. The first, `handles(...)`, is used to inform the client implementation of whether it should use this mapper for the current response. If it returns `true`, then the client implementation will invoke the `toThrowable(...)` method to obtain the exception it should throw. If the `handles(...)` method returns `false`, then the client implementation will check any other registered response exception mappers before assuming that the response was successful and simply returning a valid value to the client caller rather than throwing an exception.

> **Special note**
>
> The `toThrowable (...)` method should *return* the exception, not throw it. The client implementation will actually throw the exception; it just needs to know which exception to throw.

As with server-side providers, client-side providers need to be registered. There are two ways to register client providers. First, you can register them from the `RestClientBuilder` API before building the client, as illustrated in the following code snippet:

```
ThesaurusClient thesaurus = RestClientBuilder.newBuilder()
    .baseUri(URI.create("http://localhost:9080/rest"))
            .register(NoSuchWordResponseMapper.class)
            .build(ThesaurusClient.class);
```

A second way to register a client provider is to use one or more `@RegisterProvider` annotations on the client interface, like this:

```
@RegisterProvider(NoSuchWordResponseMapper.class)
public interface ThesaurusClient { //...
```

You can register as many of the same types of providers on the client side as you would on the server, including `MessageBodyReader` and `Writer`, `Reader`, and `WriterInterceptors`. You may not register `ExceptionMappers` or server-side filters (`ContainerRequestFilter` or `ContainerResponseFilter`). You may, however, register client-side filters (`ClientRequestFilter` or `ClientResponseFilter`)—they work in much the same way as server-side filters.

> **Tip**
>
> The `ClientRequestFilter` filter's `ClientRequestContext` has an `abortWith(Response)` method similar to the `ContainerRequestFilter` filter. This method can be useful in test code for mocking different server responses.

All of these client-side providers will work with either client, the JAX-RS Client and the MicroProfile Rest Client, except for `ResponseExceptionMapper`—these will only work with the MicroProfile Rest Client.

Async

Both JAX-RS Client and the MicroProfile Rest Client are capable of invoking services asynchronously. This is perhaps even more powerful on the client than on the server, as a client will often run in resource-constrained environments and may be called upon to perform multiple requests in order to achieve its goal.

The JAX-RS Client invokes services asynchronously by creating an `AsyncInvoker` instance that will produce `java.util.concurrent.Future` objects that reference the response objects or allow the user to specify an `InvocationCallback` that is notified when the response is available (or if there was an exception during the request/response). Here is an example of the `Future` approach:

```
AsyncInvoker invoker = builder.async();
Future<Response> future = invoker.get();
// do something else while waiting for the response...
try (Response response = future.get()) {
    // handle response...
} finally {
    client.close();
}
```

This code looks very similar to the synchronous code from earlier in this section and makes for a very simple way to perform asynchronous client requests. Next, let's see how we would use `InvocationCallbacks`, as follows (the full source code for this and the `Future` approach is available at https://github.com/PacktPublishing/Practical-Cloud-Native-Java-Development-with-MicroProfile/blob/main/Chapter04/src/main/java/com/packt/microprofile/book/ch4/client/JAXRSClient.java):

```
String uri = "http://localhost:9080/rest/thesaurus";
Client client = ClientBuilder.newBuilder().build();
for (String word : words) {
    WebTarget target = client.target(uri).path(word);
    Builder builder = target.request(MediaType.TEXT_PLAIN);
    AsyncInvoker invoker = builder.async();
    invoker.get(new InvocationCallback<String>() {
        @Override
```

```
        public void completed(String response) {
            sb.append(response + "\n");
        }
        @Override
        public void failed(Throwable th) {
            th.printStackTrace();
        }
    });
}
```

This example shows how you might look up multiple words. It sends multiple requests in parallel to the server, and the `completed` method of `InvocationCallback` is invoked when the response is available.

Asynchronous requests in the MicroProfile Rest Client are slightly different. The client interface methods must return `CompletionStage` that wraps the intended return type. So, we would modify our client interface to look like this (the full source code is available at `https://github.com/PacktPublishing/Practical-Cloud-Native-Java-Development-with-MicroProfile/blob/main/Chapter04/src/main/java/com/packt/microprofile/book/ch4/client/ThesaurusAsyncClient.java`):

```
@Path("/thesaurus/{word}")
@RegisterProvider(NoSuchWordResponseMapper.class)
@Consumes(MediaType.TEXT_PLAIN)
@Produces(MediaType.TEXT_PLAIN)
public interface ThesaurusAsyncClient {
    @GET
    CompletionStage<String> getSynonymsFor(@PathParam
        ("word") String word);


    @POST
    CompletionStage<String>setSynonymsFor
        (@PathParam("word") String word, String synonyms);
    //...similar methods for PUT, DELETE, and PATCH
}
```

Notice that none of these methods declare that they throw any exceptions. That is because any exception processing occurs after the processing of the returned `CompletionStage`. This is how we might invoke this client:

```
StringBuffer sb = new StringBuffer();
CountDownLatch latch = new CountDownLatch(wordsArr.length);
ThesaurusAsyncClient client = RestClientBuilder.newBuilder()
    .baseUri(URI.create("http://localhost:9080/rest"))
    .register(NoSuchWordResponseMapper.class)
    .build(ThesaurusAsyncClient.class);
Arrays.stream(wordsArr).parallel()
                        .map(client::getSynonymsFor)
                        .forEach(cs -> {
    cs.exceptionally(t -> {
        t.printStackTrace();
        return "unable to complete request";
    }).thenAccept(s -> {
        sb.append(s + "\n");
        latch.countDown();
    });
});
latch.await(5, TimeUnit.SECONDS);
```

Like the JAX-RS Client callback example, this example looks up the synonyms for multiple words simultaneously. By using `CompletionStage`, we can easily handle exceptions or perform additional processing inline.

Remember another form of asynchronous operations is SSEs. The JAX-RS Client APIs allow you to receive events in the form of `InboundSseEvent` objects. The MicroProfile Rest Client goes a step further and allows you to receive events using **Reactive Streams** `Publisher` objects. The events can be `InboundSseEvent` objects that allow you to read extra metadata on each event or as a specific Java type, so long as you have `MessageBodyReader` to convert the event into that type.

If we want to consume the SSE events from the service we wrote at the end of the *Building a RESTful Service with Jakarta REST* section, we might write a client interface that looks something like this:

```
@Path("/sse")
@Produces(MediaType.SERVER_SENT_EVENTS)
public interface SseClient {
    @GET
    Publisher<String> receiveSSEs();
```

The client interface is simple enough, right? So, this is how you might use it (the full source code is available at https://github.com/PacktPublishing/ Practical-Cloud-Native-Java-Development-with-MicroProfile/ blob/main/Chapter04/src/main/java/com/packt/microprofile/book/ ch4/async/MPSseConsumerResource.java):

```
client.receiveSSEs().subscribe(new Subscriber<String>() {
    @Override
    public void onSubscribe(Subscription s) {
        s.request(3);
    }
    @Override
    public void onNext(String s) {
        // handle event
    }
    @Override
    public void onError(Throwable t) {
        // exception while processing event
    }
    @Override
    public void onComplete() {
        // done receiving events
    }
});
```

Once the `Publisher` is returned from the client interface, a caller can subscribe to it and control the flow of the SSEs via the `request(int)` method of `Subscription`. The `onNext` callback method is invoked for each new event (so long as it has been requested). The `onError` callback is invoked when an error occurs (for example, not being able to find a `MessageBodyReader` that can deserialize the event). The `onComplete` callback is invoked when the connection with the server has been closed.

Propagating HTTP headers from server to client

Quite often, you may need to construct a RESTful service that needs to consume other RESTful services. This might be part of a gateway or delegation pattern, or it may be that your service needs to aggregate other services such as the following service, where a vacation service may need to make reservations for airlines, hotels, entertainment venues, and so on:

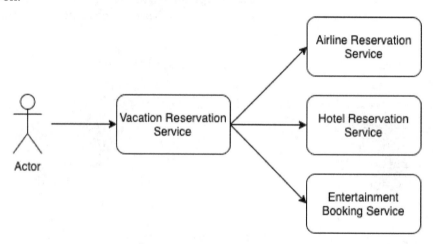

Figure 4.2 – Aggregating service

In these situations, it is often useful to propagate headers from the original request to the delegated requests. For example, suppose you want to reuse the authentication credentials sent on the original request when making the subsequent requests; the MicroProfile Rest Client has some built-in mechanisms that make this easy to do.

First, you must annotate your client interface with `@RegisterClientHeaders` and then specify a comma-separated list of headers that the container should automatically propagate in a MicroProfile Config property, like so:

```
org.eclipse.microprofile.rest.client.
propagateHeaders=Authorization,X-RequestID
```

Next, you can specify headers declaratively in the client interface, like this:

```
@RegisterRestClient
@ClientHeaderParam(name="AgentID", value="Bob's Travel Co.")
public interface AirlineReservationClient {
    @GET
    Reservation getReservation(String reservationID);

    @POST
    @ClientHeaderParam(name = "RequestID", value = "{newId}")
    String makeReservation(Reservation r);

    default String newId() {
        return UUID.randomUUID().toString();
    }
}
```

In this code, the `AgentID` header with the hardcoded value `Bob's Travel Co.` would be sent on every request from this client since the `@ClientHeaderParam` annotation is applied to the interface. When the `makeReservation` method is invoked, the MicroProfile Rest Client implementation will invoke the `newId` method to obtain the value of the `RequestID` header—the value of the header is the return value of a method because the annotation value is surrounded by curly braces.

Both of these approaches allow headers to be sent without needing to modify the signature of the client interface method.

Managing life cycle and DI with CDI

By default, JAX-RS resources are created for each request. While this might be useful in some cases, it would be far more efficient if they were singletons. That way, we wouldn't be creating new object instances (an expensive operation) for each request, and we wouldn't be generating excess garbage after the request is completed.

While we could create an `Application` subclass that returns the resources via the `getSingletons()` method, that would prevent the container from automatically discovering and registering resources and providers. Another reason to avoid that approach is that the `getSingletons()` method is deprecated in a future version of JAX-RS and will eventually be removed.

Instead, we can use **Context and Dependency Injection (CDI)**. CDI uses annotations to allow developers to declaratively manage object life cycles and perform injections of fields, constructors, and setter methods.

Scopes

CDI has several built-in **scopes** for declaring an object's life cycle. Some of the more common scopes are `@ApplicationScoped`, `@RequestScoped`, and `@Dependent`. As you can probably guess, an object annotated with `@ApplicationScoped` will *live* for the lifetime of the application, while an object annotated with `@RequestScoped` will only live for the lifetime of a single request.

The `@Dependent` annotation is a little special. Basically, objects annotated with it will inherit the scope of the object it is injected into. In the case of JAX-RS resource classes that are not really injected into anything, it inherits the scope of the JAX-RS container. For resource objects, that is **per request**, but for provider objects, that is **per application**.

This means that we can annotate our JAX-RS resource classes with `@ApplicationScoped` and then we can get rid of those pesky static fields and just use normal instance fields.

Injection

DI is another powerful piece of CDI. Using annotations, you can specify your dependencies and let the container handle all of the wiring. In the most basic cases where you want to inject a class or an instance of an interface where there is only one managed bean implementation of that interface, you can use `@Inject`, and CDI does the rest.

Let's take a look at an example. Suppose we have a class like this that we want to inject (the full source code for all CDI examples can be found at https://github.com/PacktPublishing/Practical-Cloud-Native-Java-Development-with-MicroProfile/tree/main/Chapter04/src/main/java/com/packt/microprofile/book/ch4/cdi):

```java
public interface MyDependency {
    int getInstanceId();
}


@RequestScoped
public class MyDependencyImpl implements MyDependency {
    static AtomicInteger COUNTER = new AtomicInteger();
    private final int instanceId = COUNTER.getAndIncrement();
    @Override
    public int getInstanceId() {
        return instanceId;
    }
}
```

We have a request-scoped bean that, when instantiated, will have a unique instance ID. Now, let's say that we want to inject it into a JAX-RS resource class that is managed by CDI, but we want the resource class to be application-scoped for better performance. It might look like this:

```java
@ApplicationScoped
@Path("/cdi")
public class MyCdiResource {
    @Inject
    MyDependency dependency;
    //...
}
```

This object, `MyCdiResource`, will only be instantiated once for the lifetime of the application, with no extra object creation or excess garbage. But the `MyDependency` object that is injected is **request-scoped**, meaning that for each request where it is accessed, CDI will create a new instance. We can see this when we invoke a `GET` method that returns the dependency instance ID, as the dependency's instance ID increments on each request, as illustrated here:

```
$ curl http://localhost:9080/rest/cdi
1
$ curl http://localhost:9080/rest/cdi
2
$ curl http://localhost:9080/rest/cdi
3
```

There may be times where you want to create your own bean that is injected. CDI provides a mechanism where you would use the `@Produces` annotation (same name but different package as the JAX-RS `@Produces` annotation for specifying media types). To use this, you would apply this annotation to a method on a CDI-managed bean; the object returned by that method will be injected appropriately. Let's see how this would look in a code example, as follows:

```
@ApplicationScoped
public class SomeOtherBean {
    @Produces
    public MyProducedDependency produceDependency() {
        return new MyProducedDependency(Math.random() * 10);
    }
}


@ApplicationScoped
@Path("/cdi")
public class MyCdiResource {
    //...
    @Inject
    MyProducedDependency producedDependency;
    //...
}
```

And in this case, since the `MyCdiResource` class is annotated with
`@ApplicationScoped`, the `MyProducedDependency` object is only built and
injected once for the lifetime of the application. If we were to change `MyCdiResource`
to be `@RequestScoped`, then the random number would change for each request. The
`producer` method is invoked when needed by the *consuming* bean.

So, what happens if you have more than one possible bean to inject? Your application
may fail to start with a `DeploymentException` exception, indicating ambiguous
dependencies. To resolve this, you can either use the `@Named` annotation or
qualifier annotations.

The `@Named` annotation may look something like this:

```
@ApplicationScoped
@Named("max")
public class MyOtherDependencyImpl implements MyDependency {
    //...
}

@ApplicationScoped
@Path("/cdi")
public class MyCdiResource {
    @Inject
    @Named("max")
    MyDependency dependency;
}
```

The `@Named` annotation with the same value, `max`, is applied to both the implementation
class *and* the injection point.

Qualifiers are a little more complex but add more flexibility. It first involves the creation of
a new annotation, like this:

```
@Documented
@Retention(RetentionPolicy.RUNTIME)
@Qualifier
public @interface Minimal { }
```

Then, we just add that annotation on both the class and injection target, like so:

```
@ApplicationScoped
@Minimal
public class MyThirdDependencyImpl implements MyDependency {
    //...
}


@ApplicationScoped
@Path("/cdi")
public class MyCdiResource {
    @Inject
    @Minimal
    MyDependency dependency;
}
```

Qualifiers can be used more extensively in other CDI artifacts such as interceptors and portable extensions. One such extension is built into the MicroProfile Rest Client implementation, which allows client instances to be built and injected into your CDI beans. It uses the @RestClient qualifier. For this to work, you would need to add the @RegisterRestClient annotation to the client interface. With this annotation, you can also specify the baseUri path. Alternatively, you could use MicroProfile Config to specify the baseUri path and other configuration options for the client instance. Here's what it might look like:

```
@Path("/thesaurus/{word}")
@RegisterProvider(NoSuchWordResponseMapper.class)
@RegisterRestClient(baseUri = "http://localhost:9080/rest")
public interface ThesaurusClient {
    @GET
    String getSynonymsFor(@PathParam("word") String word)
        throws NoSuchWordException;
    //...
}
```

Then, we could inject the client instance and use it like so:

```
@ApplicationScoped
@Path("/cdi")
```

```
public class MyCdiResource {
    @Inject
    @RestClient
    ThesaurusClient thesaurusClient;

    @GET
    @Path("/thesaurus/{word}")
    public String lookup(@PathParam("word") String word) {
        try {
            return thesaurusClient.getSynonymsFor(word);
        } catch (NoSuchWordException ex) {
            return "Sorry, that word is not found.";
        }
    }
}
```

While it might seem silly to create a RESTful service that then uses a client to access a different RESTful service in the same application, the principle is very common for microservice architecture. This service could be a gateway for the real thesaurus service, or perhaps the complete thesaurus is split across several **virtual machines** (**VMs**). The ability to provide or consume RESTful services where those services' life cycles and dependencies are managed declaratively can be very powerful indeed.

Summary

In this chapter, we've learned how to create and consume basic and complex RESTful services using industry-standard APIs such as JAX-RS, CDI, JSON-P, JSON-B, and the MicroProfile Rest Client. We've learned that some of these APIs provide very concise and type-safe approaches, while others provide additional flexibility at the cost of increased code complexity. Having completed this chapter, we can now create fully functioning micro-services utilizing REST and JSON. We can also improve the efficiency of these services by using asynchronous clients and appropriate life-cycle scopes.

In the next chapter, we will explore how we can improve the configurability and robustness of these services with other MicroProfile APIs.

5
Enhancing Cloud-Native Applications

In the previous chapter, *Chapter 4, Developing Cloud-Native Applications,* we learned how to build cloud-native applications. However, building cloud-native applications is just the start. The next step is to enhance the applications, by making them configurable, resilient, documentable, and secure. In this chapter, you will learn how to configure your cloud-native applications using MicroProfile Config, make your applications resilient using MicroProfile Fault Tolerance, document their APIs using MicroProfile OpenAPI, and finally, secure your applications using MicroProfile JWT. After this chapter, you should be able to use these technologies to improve the quality of your cloud-native applications. To fully comprehend this chapter, you will need some basic knowledge of Java, Maven, and Gradle.

We will cover the following topics:

- Configuring cloud-native applications using MicroProfile Config
- Making cloud-native applications resilient using MicroProfile Fault Tolerance
- Documenting cloud-native applications using MicroProfile OpenAPI
- Securing cloud-native applications using MicroProfile JWT

Configuring cloud-native applications using MicroProfile Config

MicroProfile Config (source code located at `https://github.com/eclipse/microprofile-config`) is the first specification created by the MicroProfile community. The concept of configuration has been around for a decade. You may recall in *Chapter 1, Cloud-Native Application*, we briefly discussed the **Twelve-Factor App**, in which the third factor *III. Config* (`https://12factor.net/config`) recommends that a twelve-factor app stores its configuration in an environment that is separate from the application code. This is because any configuration value update will not lead to the application code being rebuilt. But sometimes, it is not realistically possible to store all configs such as security credentials and much more in that environment. It is also common for some configuration to be stored in a database. Since the configuration could be in many different places, a mechanism for obtaining the configuration is required. Quite a few libraries provide this mechanism, such as Apache *DeltaSpike configuration* (`http://deltaspike.apache.org/documentation/configuration.html`), *Apache Tamaya* (`http://tamaya.incubator.apache.org/`), and many more.

MicroProfile Config was created as a standard so you would not need to worry about which library to pull into your applications.

In this section, we will learn how MicroProfile Config defines how configuration can be stored and retrieved by cloud-native applications.

Storing configuration

In MicroProfile Config, the configuration is stored in **ConfigSource**. A `ConfigSource` is a place where you can put configuration values. Environment variables, system properties, property files, databases, ZooKeeper, and much more can all be used as config sources. Each `ConfigSource` has an associated ordinal, which is used to indicate the importance of the `ConfigSource`. A `ConfigSource` with a higher ordinal means the configuration values it specifies will override the `ConfigSource` that specifies the same configuration with a lower ordinal.

For instance, the `customer_name property` is specified in a `ConfigSource` (ordinal = 200) with the value of `Bob`, and the same property is specified with the value of `Alice` in another `ConfigSource` (ordinal =120). Then when a cloud-native application looks up `customer_name`, the value `Bob` should be retrieved. The ordinal of a *ConfigSource* can be defined in the corresponding `ConfigSource` via the `config_ordinal` property, which indicates the ranking order of the enclosed config source. If not specified, the default config ordinal is 100.

There are two types of config sources: **default config source** and **custom config source**, which we discuss in the next subsections.

Default config sources

Default config sources are the ones mandated by MicroProfile Config and all MicroProfile Config implementations must provide them out of the box. MicroProfile Config mandates three default config sources to be supported out of the box:

- System properties with a default ordinal value of 400

- Environment variables with a default ordinal value of 300

- The property file META-INF/microprofile-config.properties found on the classpath with a default ordinal value of 100

The ordinal for the default config sources can be overridden by defining the property config_ordinal inside the config source. For instance, if you want to set the ordinal number for environment variables to 500, you can simply define an environment variable's config_ordinal with the value of 500.

Environment variable mapping rules

Some property names do not qualify as valid environment variables, because in some **Operating System (OS)**, environment variable names can only consist of uppercase letters, digits, and _ (underscore). MicroProfile Config defines a mapping rule when searching for a given config property (app.name) in an environment variable. The search will terminate once a match is found from the following list:

- The exact property name is found, such as app.name.

- If the property name contains some characters that are not letters or digits, convert these characters to _ and the transformed property name (app_name) will be found.

- If the property name contains some characters that are not letters or digits, convert the characters to _ and then convert all letters to uppercase and the transformed property name (APP_NAME) will be found.

Apart from the out-of-the-box config sources, you can create your own config sources using a file, a database, and much more. These config sources are called Custom Config Sources, which we discuss next.

Custom config source

Custom config source is a config source that you define in your application other than the default config source. To define a custom config source, you can follow these steps:

1. Implement the interface `ConfigSource` as follows:

```
public interface ConfigSource {
    String CONFIG_ORDINAL = "config_ordinal";
    int DEFAULT_ORDINAL = 100;
    default Map<String, String> getProperties() {
        Map<String, String> props = new HashMap<>();
        getPropertyNames().forEach((prop) ->
            props.put(prop, getValue(prop)));
        return props;
    }
    Set<String> getPropertyNames();
    default int getOrdinal() {
        String configOrdinal =
            getValue(CONFIG_ORDINAL);
        if (configOrdinal != null) {
            try {
                return Integer.parseInt(configOrdinal);
            } catch (NumberFormatException ignored) {
            }
        }
        return DEFAULT_ORDINAL;
    }
    String getValue(String propertyName);
    String getName();
}
```

The `getPropertyNames()`, `getValue(String propertyName)`, and `getName()` methods are the ones to be implemented.

2. Register the implementation of these functions using either of the following methods:

    a). Create a `META-INF/services/org.eclipse.microprofile.config.` `spi.ConfigSource` file with the fully qualified class name of the custom implementation.

    b). Add to `ConfigBuilder` programmatically via the following:

    ```
    ConfigBuider.withSources(ConfigSource... configSource)
    ```

Sometimes, you have sensitive configuration, and you need to store it somewhere safe. You might need to consider using **HashiCorp Vault** (`https://www.vaultproject.io/`), which manages secrets and stores sensitive data. If you store some secret properties in *Vault*, you can add *Vault* as a custom config source. Next, we'll look at another way of storing configuration using Kubernetes ConfigMaps and Secrets, which store configurations.

Kubernetes ConfigMaps and Secrets

Kubernetes ConfigMaps and **Secrets** are often used to store properties for cloud-native applications. You can use the following commands to declare properties as Kubernetes ConfigMaps or Secrets:

- Create a ConfigMap named `app-port`:

    ```
    kubectl create configmap app-port --from-literal
    port=9081
    ```

    The previous command creates a ConfigMap, `app-port`, in your cluster, and that ConfigMap contains a key called `port` with a value of `9081`. The `--from-literal` is used to store individual name-value pairs in this ConfigMap.

- Create a Secret, `app-credentials`:

    ```
    kubectl create secret generic app-credentials --from-
    literal username=Bob --from-literal password=TheBuilder
    ```

    This command is similar to creating a ConfigMap. The main difference between a Secret and ConfigMap is that a Secret only shows a Base64-encoded version of the text instead of cleartext.

After specifying a Kubernetes ConfigMap or Secret, you can map the ConfigMap or Secret to environment variables via the `deployment yaml` file:

```
env:
        - name: PORT
          valueFrom:
```

```
          configMapKeyRef:
            name: app-port
            key: port
            optional: true
     - name: APP_USERNAME
       valueFrom:
         secretKeyRef:
            name: app-credentials
            key: username
     - name: APP_PASSWORD
       valueFrom:
         secretKeyRef:
            name: app-credentials
            key: password
```

You can then use the following code to look up the properties:

```
@Inject @ConfigProperty(name="port", defaultValue="9080")
  int port;
@Inject @ConfigProperty(name="app.username") String user;
@Inject @ConfigProperty(name="app.password") String pwd;
```

Based on the defined mapping rules when looking up properties in the environment variables, port will be searched first, followed by PORT. Since the ConfigMap property app_port is optional, it is not required to be defined in the ConfigMap. If it is not found, the default value 9080 will be assigned to the variable port. As for the other property app.username, app.username is searched first, followed by app_username, and then APP_USERNAME.

So far, we have learned where to store property values, but sometimes, you might have to delete a property value. In this next section, we will learn how to erase a property.

Removing properties

In order to remove properties, you can simply remove the property entry from a config source. However, you might not be able to update a config source. In such circumstances, you can define a config source with a higher ordinal and define the property with a empty value. This effectively erases the config property. Therefore, any lookup for this property will resolve to an exception.

We have covered where to specify config properties. When we store the config property values, they are all expressed via strings. You might want to convert the strings to some other types, such as **int**, **float**, and so on. To achieve this, we will need some converters.

Converters

A **converter** converts a string to a target type. If a null value is passed to the converter, **NullPointerException** (**NPE**) will be thrown.

Just as there is more than one type of config source, there are a few types of converters:

- **Built-in converters**: They can convert strings to primitive and boxed types as well as class types.

- **Array converters**: They can convert a comma-separated string to an array.

- **Automatic converters**: An automatic convertor for a target type T is derived from a class where the class contains one of the following:

```
public static T of(String value)
public static T valueOf(String value)
public static T parse(CharSequence value )
public T(String value)
```

If more than one method is found, the method appearing at the top of the aforementioned list will be used for conversion.

- **Custom converters**: If the previous converters do not convert a string to the specified target type, you will have to define your own converter, which is called a custom converter. They can be defined by doing the following:

1) Implement the interface org.eclipse.microprofile.config.spi. Converter.

2) Register the converter by creating a META-INF/services/org.eclipse. microprofile.config.spi.Converter file with the fully qualified class name of the custom implementation or adding to ConfigBuilder programmatically via one of the following:

```
ConfigBuider.withConverters(converter)
ConfigBuilder.withConverter (Class<T> type,
    int priority, Converter<T> converter
```

There are several types of converters. There might be multiple converters for a given type. But the question arises, which converter will be used to transform the config string value to the given type? This is determined by converter priority.

Converter priority

Converter priority can be specified via the `@javax.annotation.Priority` annotation. If absent, the priority for a custom converter will default to 100. A converter with a higher priority overrides one with a lower priority.

We have covered how to specify the value of a config property with a string and then how to convert a string to a particular type. In the next section, we will learn how to look up config properties in cloud-native applications.

Config lookup

We have learned that config sources contain properties specified in strings and converters can convert strings to a target type. But the question arises, how do you retrieve a config property? This can be done either programmatically or via injection:

- **Retrieving config property via programmatic lookup**: In the following code, the property `customer.age` will be retrieved using the `getValue` method and converted to an integer using programmatic lookup:

```
Config = ConfigProvider.getConfig();
int age = config.getValue("customer.age", int.class);
```

- **Retrieving config property via CDI injection**: In the following, we use CDI injection to retrieve the property `customer.age`:

```
@Inject @ConfigProperty(name="customer.age") int age;
```

In your cloud-native applications, sometimes different values are specified during different project stages. For instance, you might use a different database in different project stages. When the project moves through different phases, the values associated with those stages will be injected into the corresponding config properties. This is called a **config profile**. We will cover this in more detail in the next section.

Understanding config profiles

Config profiles are an important concept that can be used to indicate project phases, such as development, testing, production, and so on. We'll first discuss how to define properties that use config profiles and then learn how to activate a particular profile.

Profile-aware properties

There are two ways to define profile-aware properties:

- Using the naming convention of *%<profile name>.<property name>*, for example, defining a property called %dev.customer.name in a config source.

- Defining the properties in a microprofile-config-<profile name>. properties file.

Activating a profile

An active profile is specified using the property mp.config.profile, which can be included in any config sources. If more than one config source specifies this property, the value from the config source with the highest ordinal is used.

Let's take a look at a few examples. Let's say we have the following config source, containing the following properties:

```
%dev.discount=0.1
%testing.discount=0.6
%live.discount=0.2
discount=0.15
```

If the value of mp.config.profile is set to dev, the value of the property discount will resolve to the value of %dev.discount, which is 0.1. Similarly, the value of the property discount will be 0.2 if the active profile is live. The value of the property discount will be 0.15 if no active profile is defined.

A config profile also works on the config source file microprofile-config. properties. Consider the following properties files provided by your application:

```
META-INF\microprofile-config.properties
META-INF\microrpofile-config-dev.properties
META-INF\microprofile-config-testing.properties
META-INF\microprofile-config-live.properties
```

If the value of mp.config.profile is set to dev, the config file META-INF\ microrpofile-config-dev.properties will be activated. Its content will be merged into META-INF\microrpofile-config.properties and override the property values for the same properties that exist in both files.

Sometimes the value of one property refers to another property. We call this a config reference. We will cover this topic in the next subsection.

Config references

A property value might reference a value from another property, which is called a **Config Reference**, also known as a property expression. The syntax for a property expression is *${another.property}*.

Consider the following example:

```
customer.name=${forename}-${surname}
forename = Bob
surname = Johnson
```

The value of `customer.name` will be `Bob-Johnson`. A property expression can be nested as well, in the format *${a${n}}*. In a nested expression, the inner expression will be resolved first.

As mentioned previously, a property can be specified in multiple config sources.

Sometimes you need to identify which config source supplies the value so that you can update the effective value if needed. In the next subsection, we will learn how to find out which config source is the winning config source.

Where is my property value from?

Sometimes you might be wondering which config source supplies the value for a particular property, since the same property might exist in multiple config sources. If you need to update the property value, you need to update the value from the winning config source. MicroProfile Config provides an API, `ConfigValue`, that enables you to find the winning config source. There are a couple of ways to obtain an object of `ConfigValue` for a specified property. You can use the following programmatic lookup to look up the config value for the property `host`:

```
ConfigValue configValueHost=ConfigProvider.getConfig()
.getConfigValue("host");
```

Alternatively, you can use CDI to obtain the config value for the `host` property, as shown here:

```
@Inject @ConfigProperty(name="host") ConfigValue
    configValueHost;
```

Then we can use the following method to retrieve some information about the winning config source and its value:

```
String configSourceForHost = configValueHost.getSourceName();
String valueOfHost = configValueHost.getValue();
```

Commonly, some properties are related, and they are often looked up together. It would be very useful if these properties were aggregated and mapped to a particular Java type.

Aggregate config properties

When looking up several related properties, it can be tedious to repeat the same configuration lookup statements. They might appear in different classes and some of the properties might be dynamic while others might be static, which might lead to an inconsistent state. In this situation, it is best practice to aggregate the related config properties in a CDI bean and annotate the CDI bean with the qualifier @ConfigProperties so that the property lookup is performed at the same time.

Let's take an example to see how @ConfigProperties works. The following is a custom ConfigSource:

```
config_ordinal=220
customer.forename=Bob
customer.surname=Builder
```

To look up the properties related to a particular customer, we can use @ConfigProperites, as shown next:

```
@ApplicationScoped
@ConfigProperties(prefix = "customer")
public class ConfigProps {
    private String forename;
    private String surname;
    public String getForename() {
        return forename;
    }
    public String getSurname() {
        return surname;
    }
}
```

When looking up the properties, you need to use the annotation
`@ConfigProperites(prefix="customer")`. The prefix can be omitted if the
prefix value is the same as the CDI bean prefix. If you specify a different prefix value, the
specified prefix value will override the value defined on the CDI bean and the specified
prefix will be used for looking up the properties.

Up till now, the config object has been provided by a Config specification implementation,
which loads the available config sources and converters. For some advanced use cases where
you need to control which config sources and converters are used, you might want to build
the config object yourself. MicroProfile Config also offers flexibility for such a use case.

Building a Config instance yourself

To build a Config instance, you will need to provide config sources and converters.
MicroProfile Config provides a builder for the config object to be built using the
following steps:

1. First, we need to create a builder as shown in the following code snippet by creating
   an instance of `ConfigProviderResolver` and then call the `getBuilder()`
   method to create an instance of a builder:

```
ConfigProviderResolver resolver =
    ConfigProviderResolver.instance();
ConfigBuilder builder = resolver.getBuilder();
```

2. We then add config sources and converters to the builder and then call the
   `build()` method to build a `config` object as follows:

```
Config = builder.addDefaultSources().withSources(aSource)
    .withConverters(aConverter).build();
```

3. Next, we need to register the `config` object so that we can always supply the same
   `config` object to the same `classloader` object, as shown here:

```
//register the config with the specified classloader
resolver.registerConfig(config, classloader);
```

4. Finally, when we finish using the `config` object, we will need to release it, as
   shown here:

```
//release this config when no longer needed.
resolver.releaseConfig(config);
```

If a config object is associated with multiple classloaders, when releasing the config object, all occurrences of it will have to be removed.

We have covered the most useful features of MicroProfile Config. To use the APIs from MicroProfile Config, you need to specify the Maven or Gradle dependencies. We will cover this in more detail in the next section.

Making the MicroProfile Config API available

MicroProfile Config API JARs can be made available for either Maven and Gradle projects. If you create a Maven project, you can directly add the following to your pom.xml:

```
<dependency>
  <groupId>org.eclipse.microprofile.config</groupId>
  <artifactId>microprofile-config-api</artifactId>
  <version>2.0</version>
</dependency>
```

Alternatively, if you create a Gradle project, you need to add the following dependency:

```
dependencies {
providedCompile org.eclipse.microprofile.config
    :microprofile-config-api:2.0
}
```

You have learned how to configure your cloud-native applications. The next step is to make your applications resilient. In the next section, we will cover details on how you can make your applications resilient using MicroProfile Fault Tolerance.

Making a cloud application resilient using MicroProfile Fault tolerance

Why do you need to care about resilience? For mission-critical applications, a very brief downtime might cause you a huge penalty. Besides, your customer satisfaction will decrease if your applications are too fragile and aren't resilient. Therefore, you should consider building resilient applications, which means they will function under all kinds of situations with zero downtime. MicroProfile Fault Tolerance (source code at https://github.com/eclipse/microprofile-fault-tolerance) introduces several resilience policies that can help you build a resilient application. These policies can be applied to CDI beans. It also provides a way to execute method invocations asynchronously via the annotation @Asynchronous.

@Asynchronous

The annotation `@Asynchronous` can be placed on a CDI bean class or the methods of a CDI bean class. If placed on a class, it means all of the methods declared on this class will be executed on a separate thread. Methods annotated with `@Asynchronous` must return a `Future` or a `CompletionStage` value, otherwise, `FaultToleranceDefinitionException` will be thrown. The following is a code snippet to show its usage:

```
@Asynchronous
public CompletionStage<String> serviceA() {
   return CompletableFuture.completedFuture("service a");
}
```

The aforementioned example means the invocation of `serviceA()` will be executed on a different thread and then return with `CompletionStage`. If the method returns `Future`, the method call is always considered successful unless the method throws an exception. If the method returns `CompletionStage`, the method call is considered successful only if `CompletionStage` completes without any exceptions.

> **Note**
>
> When using the `@Asynchronous` annotation, it is best practice to return `CompletionStage`, which enables other Fault Tolerance policies to be invoked on an abnormal return.

But what do you do when you hit a temporary network glitch? The first instinct is to try it again, which is what this next annotation helps with.

@Retry

MicroProfile Fault Tolerance offers the retry capability via the annotation `@Retry`. When using this annotation, you can specify the following properties:

- `maxRetries`: This indicates the maximum number of retries.
- `delay`: This indicates the delays between each retry.
- `delayUnit`: This specifies the time unit for the delay.

- `maxDuration`: This indicates the maximum duration for the overall retries.
- `durationUnit`: This specifies the duration unit.
- `jitter`: This indicates the random gap per delay.
- `jitterDelayUnit`: This specifies the jitter delay unit.
- `retryOn`: This indicates the failures that cause the retries.
- `abortOn`: This specifies the failures that skip the retries.

You can add the annotation `@Retry` on any class or business method (`https://docs.jboss.org/cdi/spec/2.0/cdi-spec.html#biz_method`). Let's take a look at the following example:

```
@Retry(maxRestries=5, delay=400, maxDuaration=4000,
    jitter=200, retryOn=Exception.class, abortOn=
        IllegalArgumentException.class)
public void callService(){

    //do something
    doSomething();
}
```

In the aforementioned code snippet, the `@Retry` annotation means the following:

- An exception other than `IllegalArgumentException` will trigger the `Retry` operation.
- The maximum number of retries is 5 and the maximum duration is 4000 ms (milliseconds). The `Retry` operation will terminate when either condition is met.
- The delay between the retries is 200 ms (jitter) and 600 ms (delay+jitter).

Sometimes you may not want to keep on retrying; you might want to fail fast and return to the caller within a time constraint, for instance, if the caller only assigns a limited waiting time and can't afford to wait till a request returns. The `@Timeout annotation` was introduced to force the operation to return within the specified period.

@Timeout

The `@Timeout` annotation specifies the maximum response time. Without the specified time out, an indefinite wait might occur. With the `@Timeout` annotation, the affected operation needs to return within the specified time duration otherwise, a `TimeoutException` will be thrown. This annotation can be used on a class or any business method. Let's take a look at the following code example:

```
@Timeout(700)
public String getServiceName() {
    //retrieve the backend service name
}
```

In the aforementioned code snippet, the `getServiceName()` operation will either return within `700` ms or throw a `TimeoutException` if the operation takes more than `700` ms to compute.

If a service is not working, you might not want to wait for the specified timeout and then get a `TimeoutException` repeatedly. It would be good to fail fast after a certain amount of failure time. Failing fast provides time for the backend to recover and the request can get feedback immediately. This is what `@CircuitBreaker` does.

@CircuitBreaker

The **Circuit Breaker** pattern helps an invocation fail fast and provides time for the backend to recover by preventing requests from reaching the backend. How does the Circuit Breaker pattern work? It is very simple. The circuit in the Circuit Breaker pattern is like an electrical circuit. If the circuit is open, there will be no electricity. A closed circuit means normal service. A circuit breaker has three states:

- **Closed**: In this state, any requests will be routed to the backend. The circuit breaker records the success or failure rate for each request. If the failure ratio reaches the configured `failureRatio` within a number of consecutive requests or rolling window, called `requestVolumeThredshold`, the circuit breaker will trip. The circuit breaker will transition its state from closed to open.

- **Open**: In this state, any calls will be returned immediately with `CircuitBreakerOpenException`. After a specified delay period, the circuit breaker will transition to the half-open state.

- **Half-open**: This is a transit state from open to closed. In this state, many requests are allowed to go through. If the consecutive success number reaches the configured `successThreshold`, the circuit breaker will transition to the **Closed** state.

The circuit breaker has the following parameters:

- `requestVolumeThreshold` specifies the size of the rolling window where the circuit breaker will be assessed. If the value of `requestVolumeThreshold` is 10, it means the circuit breaker will only be checked after 10 requests.

- `failureRatio` controls the failure rate within the rolling window. If the failure rate is equal to or above the `failureRatio` parameter, the circuit breaker will trip open.

- `successThreshold` specifies the criteria when the circuit breaker transitions from half-open to closed. If the value of `successThreshold` is 2, it means after 2 successful requests, the circuit breaker will transition from half-open to closed.

- `delay` and `delayUnit` indicate how long the circuit breaker stays open. The circuit breaker will not stay open forever.

- `failOn` specifies the exceptions that are considered to be failures.

- `skipOn` states the exceptions that are excluded from contributing towards the circuit breaker.

The Circuit Breaker pattern can be specified via the `@CircuitBreaker` annotation. The `@CircuitBreaker` annotation can be placed on a class or a business method to avoid repeated failures. You can configure the parameters on the annotation, as follows:

```
@CircuitBreaker(requestVolumeThreshold = 10,
    failureRatio=0.5, successThreshold = 3, delay = 2,
        delayUnit=ChronoUnit.SECONDS, failOn={ExceptionA.class,
            ExceptionB.class}, skipOn=ExceptionC.class)
```

In the aforementioned code snippet, it means the circuit breaker will trip to open if there are 5 or more (10*0.5) failures among 10 (`requestVolumeThreshold`) consecutive requests. After 2 seconds, specified by the parameters `delay` and `delayUnit`, the circuit will transition to half-open. After 3 (`successThreshold`) consecutive successes, the circuit breaker will transition to close.

When deciding whether an invocation should be treated as a failure or not, the criteria is that the exception from the invocation must be assignable to `ExceptionA` or `ExceptionB` but not assignable to `ExceptionC`. If an exception is assignable to `ExceptionC`, this execution will be treated not as a failure but as a success when counting towards a circuit breaker.

> **Success in Circuit Breaker**
>
> The success marked by the annotation `@CircuitBreaker` does not mean the operation returns normally. It only means that the return is treated as a success by Circuit Breaker. For instance, if a returned exception is assignable to any of the `skipOn` exceptions, the exception does not count as a failure but counts as a success instead.

The scope of `@CircuitBreaker` annotation is per class per method, which means all instances for a particular class share the same circuit breaker for the same method. When applying `@CircuitBreaker` annotation on a CDI bean, it is irrelevant what CDI scope the bean has. All invocations for a particular method share the same circuit breaker.

In a mission-critical service, it is important to ensure that the service has fault isolation capabilities, preventing faults in one part of the system cascading to the entire system. This is known as **the Bulkhead pattern**.

The Bulkhead pattern

The Bulkhead pattern is to prevent one failure from cascading, which then brings down the whole application. The Bulkhead pattern is achieved by limiting the number of concurrent requests accessing a resource. There are two different types of bulkhead: **Semaphore** isolation and **Thread Pool** isolation.

Semaphore isolation

Semaphore isolation limits the number of concurrent requests to a specified number. You can directly use `@Bulkhead(n)` to limit the maximum requests where n is the number of concurrent requests. The extra request n+1 will fail with `BulkheadException`.

However, sometimes you might want to have a waiting queue for the extra requests to queue. For this requirement, you will need to use Thread Pool isolation.

Thread Pool isolation

Thread Pool isolation also limits a certain number of concurrent requests. It dispatches a new thread for method execution. In addition, it also has a waiting queue to store the extra requests. Only when the waiting queue is full, `BulkheadException` will be thrown.

To define Thread Pool isolation, you need to use `@Bulkhead` together with `@Asynchronous` as shown here:

```
@Asynchronous
@Bulkhead(value=5, waitingTaskQueue=6)
```

```
public CompletionStage<String> serviceA() {

}
```

The aforementioned code snippet means the size of the bulkhead is 5, which allows 5 concurrent requests accessing the method `serviceA()`. The extra requests will be queued in the waiting queue. When the waiting queue is full, the extra requests will cause `BulkheadException` to be thrown.

Similar to the `@CircuitBreaker` annotation, the scope of `@Bulkhead` annotation is per class per method, which means all instances for a particular class share the same bulkhead for the same method. When applying a `@Bulkhead` annotation on a CDI bean, it is irrelevant what CDI scope the bean has. All invocations for a particular method share the same bulkhead.

Apart from Retry, the Fault Tolerance policies we have covered so far are about failing gracefully. However, sometimes, you want to return a reasonable response to your caller. In these circumstances, you should provide an alternative answer. This is what the Fallback policy is for.

Fallback

The **Fallback** policy provides a way to specify a backup action, which will be executed if the current operation fails. The way to apply the Fallback policy is to apply the `@Fallback` annotation. The `@Fallback` annotation has the following parameters:

- `value`: This specifies a class that implements the `FallbackHandler` interface.
- `fallbackMethod`: This method specifies the fallback method name. The fallback method must be defined in the same class as the method applying the `@Fallback` annotation.
- `applyOn`: This defines the criteria when the Fallback policy should be applied.
- `skipOn`: This defines the criteria when the Fallback policy should be skipped.

The `value` and `fallbackMethod` parameters are mutually exclusive. If you specify both on the `@Fallback`, annotation `FaultToleranceDefinitionException` will be thrown. To specify the backup operation, you need to either define the `fallbackMethod` or `value` parameter.

The `fallbackMethod` signature and return type must match the method that defines the Fallback policy. The `value` parameter should be used if you would like to define a handler to handle multiple Fallback policies.

You can use `skipOn` or `applyOn` to specify what exception should trigger the fallback operation. As the name says, all exceptions and the subclasses listed under `skipOn` will bypass fallback while the exception and their subclasses listed by `applyOn` should trigger the fallback operation. When `skipOn` and `applyOn` are used together, `skipOn` takes precedence.

Let's look at the following code snippet for an example of the Fallback policy:

```
@Fallback(fallbackMethod="myFallback",
   applyOn={ExceptionA.class, ExceptionB.class},
     skipOn={ExceptionAsub.class})
public String callService() {
...
}
public String myFallback() {
...
}
```

In the aforementioned code snippet, if the method `callService()` throws an exception and if this exception is assignable to `ExceptionAsub`, the exception will be rethrown and the fallback method `myFallback` will not be executed. However, if the thrown exception is not assignable to `ExceptionAsub` and assignable to `ExceptionA` or `ExceptionB`, the fallback method `myFallback` will be triggered.

We have covered all of the Fallback policies so far. You might have realized that all of the policies are annotations. Actually, these annotations are CDI interceptor bindings, which means they only work on business method invocations on CDI beans, as explained at `https://jakarta.ee/specifications/cdi/2.0/cdi-spec-2.0.html#biz_method`.

CDI interceptors have a priority. In Fault Tolerance, some implementations provide one interceptor for all the interceptor bindings while others might provide multiple interceptors. The Fault Tolerance specification declared the base priority to be `Priority.PLATFORM_AFTER` (4000)+10, which is 4010. If multiple interceptors are provided by an implementation, the priority range should be between base priority and base priority + 40 so that other application interceptors can define their priorities accordingly based on whether they want to be invoked before or after Fault Tolerance interceptors. You can update the base priority via the property mp.fault.tolerance. interceptor.priority.

A method annotated with Fault Tolerance annotations may also specify any other **Interceptor Bindings**. The invocation order on the interceptors will be determined by the priority of the interceptors.

So far, we have covered all Fault Tolerance annotations. You might be wondering whether you could use these annotations together. Yes, of course. We will discuss this in more detail in the next section.

Using Fault Tolerance annotations together

It is fine to use annotations together to achieve multiple Fault Tolerance capabilities such as setting up for `Retry` and `Timeout` together. Let's take a look at the following example:

```
@GET
@Path("/{parameter}")
@Asynchronous
@CircuitBreaker
@Retry
@Bulkhead
@Timeout(200)
@Fallback(fallbackMethod = "myFallback")
public CompletionStage<String> doSomething(@PathParam
    ("parameter") String parameter) {
//do something
}
```

The aforementioned code snippet means that the operation `doSomething()` applies all of the Fault Tolerance policies. If this method throws an exception, the following Fault Tolerance policies will be applied in this order:

1. Check whether the `CircuitBreaker` is open.
2. If it is not open, the timer will start recording the time duration.
3. Try to get a slot in `Bulkhead`.
4. If there are 10 running tasks already, it will queue up in the waiting queue, which has 10 slots. However, if there is no free slot in the waiting queue, a `BulkheadException` exception will be thrown. If there is a slot in the waiting queue, it will wait to be scheduled. During the waiting, if the timeout duration exceeds `200` milliseconds, `TimeoutException` will be thrown. The thrown exception will be recorded in the `CircuitBreaker` record and then trigger `Retry`. Go back to *step 1* for `Retry`.

After `Retry` has been exhausted, the Fallback policy will be triggered.

You might have noticed that the parameters on each annotation have default values. You can also specify values on the annotations. Are you wondering whether the values are configurable? Let's discuss this in the next section!

Fault Tolerance configuration

The good news is that all of the parameters on the annotations are configurable. The values can be overridden either globally or individually. This is achieved via **MicroProfile Config**. All of the parameters are properties. Their values can be specified in any configured config source.

Overriding parameter values

To override individual annotation parameters, you can use method-level configuration, class-level configuration, or global configuration as explained here:

- **Method-level configuration**: It is specified using the format *<fully.qualified.class. name>/<method.name>/<annotation.name>/<parameter.name>*.

- **Class-level configuration**: It is specified using the format *<fully.qualified.class. name>/<annotation.name>/<parameter.name>*.

- **Global configuration**: It is specified using the format *<annotation. name>/<parameter.name>*.

Let's take a look at an example to explain further:

```
package cloudnative.sample.fault.tolerance;
public class FaultToleranceDemo {
    @Timeout(500)
    @Retry(maxRetries = 6)
    @GET
    public String invokeService() {
        //do something
    }
}
```

This code snippet sets the `Timeout` to be `500` milliseconds with at most `6` retries. To set `Timeout` to `300` milliseconds and at most `10` retries, you can specify the following method-level config properties in any config sources:

```
cloudnative.sample.fault.tolerance.FaultToleranceDemo/
invokeService/Timeout/value=300
```

```
cloudnative.sample.fault.tolerance.FaultToleranceDemo/
invokeService/Retry/maxRetries=10
```

Alternatively, if you would like to update all of the timeout and the maximum of retries for this class, you can just omit the method names, which means the configurations are appliable to all of the methods with the corresponding annotations specified. Then, specify the following class-level configuration in a configured config source:

```
cloudnative.sample.fault.tolerance.FaultToleranceDemo/Timeout/
value=300
```

```
cloudnative.sample.fault.tolerance.FaultToleranceDemo/Retry/
maxRetries=10
```

Sometimes, you might want to specify the same timeout value for all of the classes under one application. It is simple. Just omit the fully qualified class name. Therefore, you can use the following global configuration to achieve that:

```
Timeout/value=300
Retry/maxRetries=10
```

Sometimes, your cloud infrastructure, such as **Istio**, which we will discuss in *Chapter 7, MicroProfile Ecosystem with Open Liberty, Docker, and Kubernetes*, provides some Fault Tolerance capabilities. However, cloud infrastructure will not be able to provide fallback capabilities as the infrastructure needs business knowledge. If you prefer to use the Fault Tolerance capabilities provided by Istio, you might want to turn off some MicroProfile Fault Tolerance capabilities. If you don't, you will get both Fault Tolerance functionalities and they will interfere with each other.

Disabling Fault Tolerance policies

If you want to use the Fault Tolerance policies provided by Istio, you can specify the following property to turn off all of Fault Tolerance policies except `Fallback`:

```
MP_Fault_Tolerance_NonFallback_Enabled=false
```

To disable a particular policy on a method, specify the following method-level property:

```
<fully.qualified.class.name>/<method.name>/<annotation>/
enabled=false
```

In the previous example, in order to turn off `Timeout` on the method `invokeService()`, specify the following method-level configuration:

```
cloudnative.sample.fault.tolerance.FaultToleranceDemo/
invokeService/Timeout/enabled=false
```

Alternatively, in order to turn off `Timeout` on the class, specify the following class-level configuration.

```
cloudnative.sample.fault.tolerance.FaultToleranceDemo/Timeout/
enabled=false
```

To disable the `Timeout` capability for your cloud-native application, specify the following property:

```
Timeout/enabled=false
```

If multiple configurations are specified, the configuration specified on the method level has a higher priority, followed by class-level configuration and then global configuration.

So far, you have learned how to apply Fault Tolerance policies to some operations and configure the policies. However, these policies are there to be triggered under some criteria. It is very possible that none of the policies are utilized. You might be keen to find out whether any Fault Tolerance policies are activated. In response to this need, we have Fault Tolerance metrics. Let's take a look at them in the next section.

Fault Tolerance metrics

MicroProfile Fault Tolerance, when used together with MicroProfile Metrics, is able to emit some useful metrics for the Retry, Timeout, CircuitBreaker, Bulkhead, and Fallback policies. In the following tables, I have listed all of the relevant metrics.

The following table shows the general metrics whenever Fault Tolerance is applied:

Name	Metric Tags
ft.invocations.total	method – fully qualified method name result= [valueReturned|exceptionThrown] fallback= [applied|notApplied|notDefined]

Table 5.1 – Method invocation metrics

If @Retry is used, the metrics for retry will be provided:

Name	Metric Tags
ft.retry.calls.total	method – fully qualified method name retried = [true|false] retryResult =
ft.retry.retries.total	method – the fully qualified method name

Table 5.2 – Retry metrics

If @Timeout is used, the following metrics will be provided:

Name	Metric Tags
ft.timeout.calls.total	method – fully qualified method name timedOut = [true|false]
ft.retry.retries.total	method – fully qualified method name

Table 5.3 – Timeout metrics

If `@CircuitBreaker` is used, you will see the following metrics:

Name	Metric Tags
ft.circuitbreaker.calls. total	method – fully qualified method name circuitBreakerResult = [success|failure|circuitBreakerOpen]
ft.circuitbreaker.state. total	method – fully qualified method name state = [open|closed|halfOpen]
ft.circuitbreaker. opened.total	method – fully qualified method name

Table 5.4 – CircuitBreaker metrics

If `@Bulkhead` is used, you will be able to see the following metrics:

Name	Metric Tags
ft.bulkhead.calls.total	method – fully qualified method name bulkheadResult = [accepted|rejected]
ft.bulkhead. executionsRunning	method – fully qualified method name
ft.bulkhead. executionsWaiting	method – fully qualified method name
ft.bulkhead. runningDuration	method – fully qualified method name
ft.bulkhead. waitingDuration	method – fully qualified method name

Table 5.5 – Bulkhead metrics

You have learned about all of the functionalities of Fault Tolerance. You might be wondering how to start using the APIs provided by Fault Tolerance. We will discuss this in the next section.

Making the MicroProfile Fault Tolerance API available

MicroProfile Fault Tolerance API JARs can be made available for either Maven and Gradle projects. If you create a Maven project, you can directly add the following to your pom.xml:

```
<dependency>
  <groupId>
    org.eclipse.microprofile.fault.tolerance
  </groupId>
  <artifactId>microprofile-fault-tolerance-api</artifactId>
  <version>3.0</version>
</dependency>
```

Alternatively, if you create a Gradle project, you need to add the following dependency:

```
dependencies {
providedCompile org.eclipse.microprofile.fault.tolerance:
  microprofile-fault-tolerance-api:3.0
}
```

You have now learned how to make your cloud-native applications resilient. The next step is to document your applications. You will learn how to document your applications using MicroProfile OpenAPI in the next section.

Documenting cloud native applications using MicroProfile OpenAPI

As mentioned in *Chapter 2*, *How Does MicroProfile Fit into Cloud-Native Applications?*, you might have difficulties remembering what functionalities a particular cloud-native application has when you have tens or hundreds of cloud-native applications to manage. You will need to provide documentation for them. With documented endpoints, some clients can discover and invoke them.

MicroProfile OpenAPI (source code at `https://github.com/eclipse/microprofile-open-api/`) provides a set of annotations and programming models that enable you to document cloud-native applications and then produce documents conforming to the **OpenAPI** v3 specification (`https://github.com/OAI/OpenAPI-Specification`). The OpenAPI v3 specification defines a set of interfaces for documenting and exposing RESTful APIs. MicroProfile OpenAPI adopts the OpenAPI Specification and further simplifies the OpenAPI model so that it is much easier for Java developers to document their cloud-native applications.

MicroProfile OpenAPI offers three ways to document cloud-native applications:

- By applying **MicroProfile OpenAPI** annotations on JAX-RS operations
- Using the programming model from **MicroProfile OpenAPI** to provide an **OpenAPI** model tree
- Using pre-generated **OpenAPI** documents

In the next section, we will cover these three mechanisms in more detail.

Applying MicroProfile OpenAPI annotations on JAX-RS operations

The simple way to produce documentation for your JAX-RS operations is to add MicroProfile OpenAPI annotations. A few useful and widely used annotations are listed here:

Annotation	Description
`@APIResponse`	This describes a single response from an API operation
`@APIResponses`	This indicates the number of API responses
`@APIResponseSchema`	The schema describing an API response
`@Content`	This provides a schema and media type for the enclosed API response
`@Schema`	Describes the data types
`@Operation`	Provides some information on an API operation
`@Parameter`	Describes an operation parameter

Table 5.6 – MicroProfile OpenAPI annotations

The following is an example of using OpenAPI annotations to document an operation in the IBM StockTrader app **Trade-History**:

```
@APIResponses(value = {
        @APIResponse(
            responseCode = "404",
            description = "The Mongo database cannot be
              found. ", content = @Content(
                        mediaType = "text/plain")),
        @APIResponse(
            responseCode = "200",
            description = "The latest trade has been
              retrieved successfully.",
            content = @Content(mediaType = "application/json",
                      schema = @Schema(implementation =
                        Quote.class)))})
    @Operation(
        summary = "Shows the latest trade.",
        description = "Retrieve the latest record from the
          mongo database."
    )
public String latestBuy() {
. . .
}
```

The aforementioned code snippet documents two responses with the annotation @APIResponse: 404 and 200. The annotation @Operation documents the purpose of the operation. The OpenAPI document generated with the preceding annotations is detailed here:

```
---
openapi: 3.0.3
info:
  title: Generated API
  version: "1.0"
servers:
```

```yaml
  - url: http://localhost:9080
  - url: https://localhost:9443
paths:
  /data/latestBuy:
    get:
      summary: Shows the latest trade.
      description: Retrieve the latest record from the
        mongo database.
      responses:
        "404":
          description: 'The Mongo database cannot be found'
          content:
            text/plain: {}
        "200":
          description: The latest trade has been retrieved
            successfully.
          content:
            application/json:
              schema:
                $ref: '#/components/schemas/Quote'
components:
  schemas:
    Quote:
      type: object
      properties:
        date:
          type: string
        price:
          format: double
          type: number
        symbol:
          type: string
        time:
          format: int64
          type: integer
```

In the aforementioned document, the endpoint path and the `get` operation description were explained with the information from the annotation `@Operation`. Further on, the responses for `200` and `404` were described from the information provided by the `@APIResponse` annotation. As for the response for the return code `200`, the schema `Quote` was referenced by the annotation `@Schema`, so `$ref: '#/components/schemas/Quote` was displayed as the schema reference. The reference points to the section `components/ schemas/Quote`, which displays the details of the schema `Quote`.

Without using any MicroProfile OpenAPI annotations, MicroProfile OpenAPI still generates an OpenAPI document for all of the JAX-RS endpoints with minimum information. The following is the example for the endpoint `latestBuy` if no OpenAPI annotations are applied. It only lists the minimum information on the successful return code `200`:

```
---
openapi: 3.0.3
info:
  title: Generated API
  version: "1.0"
servers:
- url: http://localhost:9080
- url: https://localhost:9443
paths:
  /data/latestBuy:
    get:
      responses:
        "200":
          description: OK
          content:
            application/json:
              schema:
                type: string
```

Apart from using MicroProfile OpenAPI annotations, you can use a programming model to generate documents. We will discuss this in the next section.

Using a programming model to generate documentation

Sometimes, it might not be possible to put MicroProfile OpenAPI annotations on JAX-RS operations. In this case, you can provide your own implementation of **OASModelReader** from MicroProfile OpenAPI. The OASModelReader API provides a way for an OpenAPI document to be built from scratch. Follow the steps mentioned to build an OpenAPI model tree:

1. Implement the `org.eclipse.microprofile.openapi.OASModelReader` interface. You can see an example here: `https://github.com/eclipse/microprofile-open-api/wiki/OASModelReader-Samples`.

2. Register the implementation using the `mp.openapi.model.reader` configuration key and store the configuration in a config source.

3. If providing a complete OpenAPI model tree, set the configuration `mp.openap.scan.disabled=true`.

The link `https://github.com/eclipse/microprofile-open-api/wiki/OASModelReader-Samples` provides an example of implementing `OASModelReader`. In *step 2* and *step 3*, you can specify the properties under `META-INF/microprofile-config.properties` or as system properties.

Using pre-generated OpenAPI documents

Sometimes, you will write OpenAPI documents first by using an editor such as the Swagger Editor (`https://editor.swagger.io/`). Documents must be named `openapi` with a `yml`, `yaml`, or `json` file extension and be placed under the `MEAT-INF` directory. If the document is complete, you can set the property `mp.openap.scan.disabled=true`. Otherwise, the scan operation will be performed to discover any MicroProfile OpenAPI annotations.

So far, we have briefly introduced the three ways to create OpenAPI documents. The documents can be viewed using the URL `http://host_name/port_number/openapi`. Open Liberty, which will be discussed in *Chapter 7, MicroProfile Ecosystem with Open Liberty, Docker, and Kubernetes*, has the Swagger UI integrated, so you can visit `http://host_name/port_number/openapi/ui` for a GUI view, where you can supply parameters and then directly invoke the individual endpoints. More information on this UI will be covered in *Chapter 9, Deployment and Day 2 Operations*.

Cloud-native application developers may wish to remove or update certain elements of the OpenAPI document. This is done via a filter, which is invoked once the OpenAPI document is created. We will discuss filters in the next section.

Applying filters to the OpenAPI document

If you want to add some information to the OpenAPI document, you can create a filter. The filter needs to implement the OASFilter interface, which provides a way to update an OpenAPI document. Let's look at the following filter:

```
public class MyOASFilter implements OASFilter {
  @Override
  public void filterOpenAPI(OpenAPI openAPI) {
    openAPI.setInfo(OASFactory.createObject(Info.class)
      .title("Stock App").version("1.0").description
        ("App for displaying stocks.").license
          (OASFactory.createObject(License.class)
            .name("Apache License 2.0").url
              ("https://www.apache.org/licenses/
                LICENSE-2.0"))); //1
    openAPI.addServer(OASFactory.createServer()
      .url("http://localhost:{port}").description
        ("Open Liberty Server.").variables(Collections
          .singletonMap("port",OASFactory
            .createServerVariable().defaultValue("9080")
              .description("HTTP port.")))); //2
  }
}
```

In the aforementioned code snippet, the `filterOpenAPI()` method filters the OpenAPI element. This method is called only once as the last method for a particular filter. It provides the `info` and the `servers` elements of the OpenAPI document.

After you have created a filter class, the next step is to specify the configuration `mp.openapi.filter=com.acme.MyOASFilter` in a config source, such as `microprofile-config.properties`.

A MicroProfile OpenAPI implementation generates the documents in the following sequence:

1. The implementation fetches configuration values with the prefix of `mp.openapi`.
2. It then invokes `OASModelReader`.
3. It fetches static OpenAPI files with the name of `openapi.yml`, `openapi.yaml`, or `openapi.json`.

4.   It processes MicroProfile OpenAPI annotations.

5.   Finally, it filters the OpenAPI documentation via `OASFilter`.

As mentioned in *step 1*, several configurations with the prefix of `mp.openapi` can be defined by MicroProfile OpenAPI. We will go through the configurations in the next section.

MicroProfile OpenAPI configuration

MicroProfile OpenAPI provides some flexibility for application developers to configure the process when generating OpenAPI documents. The configurations are listed in the following table:

Configuration Name	Description
`mp.openapi.model.reader`	Specifies the fully qualified name of the `OASModelReader` implementation.
`mp.openapi.filter`	Specifies the fully qualified name of the `OASFilter` implementation.
`mp.openapi.scan.disable`	Specifies whether to disable the scanning or not. The default value is false.
`mp.openapi.scan.packages`	Specifies the list of packages to scan.
`mp.openapi.scan.exclude.packages`	Specifies the list of packages not to scan.
`mp.openapi.scan.classes`	Specifies the list of fully qualified classes to scan.
`mp.openapi.scan.exclude.classes`	Specifies the list of fully qualified classes not to scan.
`mp.openapi.servers`	Specifies the list of global servers, separated by a comma.
`mp.openapi.servers.path.`	Specifies an alternative list of servers that service all operations in a path.
`mp.openapi.servers.operation.`	Specifies an alternative list of servers that service the specified operation.
`mp.openapi.schema.`	Specifies a schema for the specified class.

Table 5.7 – MicroProfile OpenAPI configurations

Now we have covered how **MicroProfile OpenAPI** works. The implementation of MicroProfile OpenAPI will generate an OpenAPI document based on MicroProfile OpenAPI policies. Where can you view the fully processed OpenAPI document? In the next section, we will discuss where the OpenAPI document can be accessed.

Viewing an OpenAPI document

The fully processed OpenAPI document must be available at the root URL /openapi, as an HTTP Get operation, such as http://localhost:9080/openapi. The default format of the document is YAML. Support for the JSON format is required if the response contains a Content-Type header with a value of application/json. Open Liberty supports the query parameter format, which allows you to specify whether you want YAML or JSON format. For instance, the endpoint http://localhost:9080/openapi?format=JSON displays the OpenAPI document in JSON format, while the endpoint http://localhost:9080/openapi?format=YAML displays an OpenAPI document in YAML format.

Open Liberty provides a UI for OpenAPI documents, where you can invoke the endpoints included. The UI is available at the root URL /openapi/ui.

You have learned how MicroProfile OpenAPI works and where to find the OpenAPI documents. Now, you are ready to use MicroProfile OpenAPI. In the next section, we will discuss how to make the APIs available to your Maven and Gradle projects.

Making MicroProfile OpenAPI APIs available

To use MicroProfile OpenAPI APIs, you need to make these APIs available to your application. If you create a Maven project, you can directly add the following to your pom.xml:

```
<dependency>
  <groupId>org.eclipse.microprofile.openapi</groupId>
  <artifactId>microprofile-openapi-api</artifactId>
  <version>2.0</version>
</dependency>
```

Alternatively, if you create a Gradle project, you need to add the following dependency:

```
dependencies {
providedCompile org.eclipse.microprofile.openapi:
  microprofile-openapi-api:2.0
}
```

With this, you have learned how to document your cloud-native application. The next step is to secure your applications. We will learn how to secure your applications with the help of MicroProfile JWT (https://github.com/eclipse/microprofile-jwt-auth).

Securing cloud-native applications using MicroProfile JWT

MicroProfile JWT utilizes **JSON Web Token** (**JWT**) with some additional claims for role-based access control of an endpoint to help with securing cloud-native applications. Securing cloud-native applications is often the must-have feature. It is often the case that cloud-native applications supply sensitive information, which should only be accessible to a particular group of users. Without securing cloud-native applications, everyone would be able to access the information. **Jakarta Security** (source code at https://github. com/eclipse-ee4j/security-api), a specification (https://jakarta.ee/ specifications/security/) under Jakarta EE, can be used to secure cloud-native applications.

In the following example, the method checkAccount is secured via the Jakarta Security API @RolesAllowed. This method can only be invoked by clients with the access group StockViewer or StockTrader. All other users are denied as shown here:

```
@RolesAllowed({ "StockViewer", "StockTrader" })
@GET
public String checkAccount() {
    return "CheckAccount";
}
```

Alternatively, you can use web.xml configuration to directly secure the end point. In the following code snippet, it defines two roles, StockViewer and StockTrader, and they can access all GET operations, where StockViewer can only access read-only operations and StockTrader can access all operations:

```
<security-role>
        <description>Group with read-only access to stock
          portfolios</description>
        <role-name>StockViewer</role-name>
    </security-role>
    <security-role>
        <description>Group with full access to stock
```

```
            portfolios</description>
        <role-name>StockTrader</role-name>
    </security-role>
<security-constraint>
        <display-name>Account read-only security</display-name>
        <web-resource-collection>
            <web-resource-name>Account read-only
                methods</web-resource-name>
            <description>Applies to all paths under the
                context root (this service specifies the
                account as a path param)</description>
            <url-pattern>/*</url-pattern>
            <http-method>GET</http-method>
        </web-resource-collection>
        <auth-constraint>
            <description>Roles allowed to access read-only
                operations on accounts</description>
            <role-name>StockViewer</role-name>
            <role-name>StockTrader</role-name>
        </auth-constraint>
    </security-constraint>
```

After the endpoint is secured, we then need to work out how to get the client to invoke the secured backend. To answer this question, we'll first discuss the unique aspect of application security for cloud-native applications.

Cloud-native application security is different from traditional applications as cloud-native applications are often stateless and the server side might not be able to persist any states on the clients. Besides, there might be different instances of the backend and each subsequent client request might not hit the same backend instance. As you can see, storing client data on the backend is problematic. Therefore, the recommended approach is to pass on the security-related info via each request.

The backend service will then create a security context for each request and perform both authentication and authorization checks. This means that the security-related info needs to include both authentication and authorization details. In the next section, we will look at the technologies used to achieve this goal.

What technologies do we use to secure cloud-native applications?

The technologies used for cloud-native application security are based on **OAuth2**, **OpenID Connect**, and **JSON Web Token** (**JWT**) standards:

- **OAuth2**: An authorization framework that controls authorization to a protected resource such as a cloud-native application. OAuth2 is about user authorization.

- **OpenID Connect (OIDC)**: An authentication framework that builds on top of the OAuth 2.0 protocol. It allows third-party applications such as Google or Facebook to verify the identification of an end user and to obtain some user information. OIDC is about user authentication.

- **JWT**: A compact, URL-safe way to transfer claims between two parties. It contains a set of claims, represented as a JSON object, which is base64url-encoded, digitally signed (**JWS**), and optionally encrypted (**JWE**).

JWT format

JWT can be used to propagate ID for authentication and user entitlement for authorization. It is used by both OAuth2 and OpenID Connect. The most important feature of JWT is that the data itself is self-described and verifiable. It provides a tamper-resistant way to pass information around. At JWT creation time, the **Issuer** signs the JWT with its **Private Key**. Upon receiving the JWT, **Receivers** can then use the matching **Public Key** to verify the JWT to ensure that the JWT has not been tampered with.

JWT is a general abstract term. It can be either **signed JWT** or **encrypted JWT**. A signed JWT is known as a **JWS (JSON Web Signature)** while an encrypted JWT is known as **JWE (JSON Web Encryption)**. A **JSON Web Key (JWK)** is a JSON object that represents a cryptographic key and is used to decrypt a JWE or JWS to validate the signature.

After a security token – JWT – has been generated, **Token-Based Authentication** is normally used to allow systems to make authentication and authorization decisions based on a security token. For cloud-native applications, a token-based authentication mechanism offers a lightweight way for security controls and security tokens to propagate user and entitlement info across cloud-native applications. Since the JWT token is used for authentication and authorization purposes, two new claims are introduced to the MicroProfile JWT:

- **upn**: This claim specifies the user principal.

- **groups**: This claim lists the group names.

There can be many claims included in a JWT. The following claims are required for MicroProfile JWT, while the claim for groups are optional from MicroProfile JWT Propagation version 1.2 onwards:

- `iss`: This claim specifies the token issuer.
- `iat`: This claim specifies the time when the token was issued.
- `exp`: This claim indicates the expiration time of the token.
- `upn` (or `preferred_username` or `sub`): This claim specifies the principal name. If `upn` is not present, fall back to `preferred_username`. If `preferred_username` is not present, fall back to `sub`.

Apart from the aforementioned mandatory claims, there are some optional claims listed here:

- `aud`: The endpoint, which can be assessed by JWT.
- `jti`: The unique identifier for this JWT
- `sub`: The unique identifier of the principal of this JWT.
- `preferred_user_name`: The preferred username of this JWT.

As mentioned earlier, there are two different types of JWT: JWS and JWE. JWS is very popular. We will discuss it in more detail.

JWS in more detail

JWS is a prominent format of JWT. A JWS has three parts, which are separated by a dot. The following is an example of JWS, where you can find the first dot on the first line and the second dot on the seventh line:

```
eyJ0eXAiOiJKV1QiLCJhbGciOiJSUzI1NiJ9.
eyJpc3MiOiJodHRwczovL3NlcnZlci5leGFtcGxlLmNvbSIsImF1ZCI6ImNsb3V
kLW5hdGl2ZS1hcHAiLCJqdGkiOiIwZmQwODljYi0xYzQ1LTRjMzAtOWIyMy02YW
E0ZmQ1ZTcwYjUiLCJleHAiOjE2MTk2OTk5MDYsImlhdCI6MTYxOTY5OTg3Niwic
3ViIjoiRW1ppbHkiLCJ1cG4iOiJFbWlseSIsInByZWZlcnJlZF91c2VybmFtZSI6
bnVsbCwiYm9vayI6I1ByYWN0aWNpYWwgTWljcm9Qcm9maWxlIiwiZ3JvdXBzIjp
bInVzZXIiLCJwcm90ZWN0ZWQiXX0.d0BF1qTrjlQPnb5tppM4LP1T2QWvs9sh6Q
lsXcKbFUsHvdzXGDSXkkZTqZl67EkJcUBPy9-I4i5913r9LTBbLIR_bataTVSL9
AcMsSY6tk_B4IU69IjV1GRohGf_LXHyFu_iWGfSWO7TV3-tX43E5Yszvik5sial
OrqgVF9uYUy_UaOOY7TEQynpHv4oCTwNKg48-Nlw15Yfz__i7CaOmiRNROp6_cD
Zhn1t_aFndplxv4Q-A-p_j2gPpsEldl5mbnBi73-cQvuImawBxAlsrRYQSj6aAK
JDCBcCj4wh338Nb93161_PxET8_blXZywJszmLQllJfi2SeR3WucxJ3w
```

The three dot-separated parts are the header, payload, and signature. You can paste the preceding encoded form in `https://jwt.io/` to retrieve the three parts in human-readable text. We are going to review the three parts in more detail here:

- **Header**: The header normally contains `alg` (RS256 or ES256), `enc` (a cryptographic algorithm to encrypt the claims), `typ` (JWT), and `kid` (the key that was used to secure the JWT). Here is an example of the header. It means `JWT` as the `typ` and `RS256` as the `alg`:

```
{
    "typ": "JWT",
    "alg": "RS256"
}
```

- **Payload**: This contains a number of claims. Here is an example of the payload:

```
{
    "iss": "https://server.example.com",
    "aud": "cloud-native-app",
    "jti": "0fd089cb-1c45-4c30-9b23-6aa4fd5e70b5",
    "exp": 1619699906,
    "iat": 1619699876,
    "sub": "Emily",
    "upn": "Emily",
    "preferred_username": null,
    "book": "Practicial MicroProfile",
    "groups": [
      "user",
      "protected"
    ]
}
```

- **Signature**: The signature is used to verify that the messages weren't changed during the transmission. It is created using an encoded header, an encoded payload, a secret, the algorithm specified in the header, and then signed. The following is an example of verifying a signature, which computes the signature based on the header and payloader and then compares it with the passed-in signature. If they match, it means the token has not been tampered with during transmission:

```
RSASHA256(
  base64UrlEncode(header) + "." +
  base64UrlEncode(payload), <paste-public-key>
  , <paste-private-key>
)
```

In the next section, we are going to discuss how MicroProfile JWT works.

How does MicroProfile JWT work?

We have learned what MicroProfile JWT looks like together with the basic concept of MicroProfile JWT. To use JWT, we need to first create a token.

Issuing a MicroProfile JWT token

A MicroProfile JWT token can be issued by runtimes that support the creation of MicroProfile JWT or trusted OpenID Connect providers. MicroProfile JWT can be self-issued by a trusted server, where a set of token-issuing APIs are provided. Open Liberty, Eclipse Vert.x, and other runtimes have such APIs available. The following is an example of using the Open Liberty API to create a JWT token:

```
import com.ibm.websphere.security.jwt.JwtBuilder;
import com.ibm.websphere.security.jwt.Claims;
private String buildJwt(String userName, Set<String> roles)
  throws Exception {
        return JwtBuilder.create("jwtBuilder")
                        .claim(Claims.SUBJECT, userName)
                        .claim("upn", userName)
                        .claim("groups", roles.toArray(new
                          String[roles.size()]))
                        .buildJwt()
```

```
                            .compact();

    }
```

This JWT token contains the claims sub (Claims.SUBJECT), upn, and groups. In production, it is common that MicroProfile JWTs are issued by some trusted OpenID Connect providers such as Auth0, Keycloak, Azure, Okta, and so on.

The only supported JWT algorithms are RS256 and ES256. The token will be rejected if other algorithms are used.

> **JWT generation**
>
> Since MicroProfile JWT has two more claims over JWT, these claims need to be manually added as custom claims in the OpenID Connect providers such as Keycloak, Okta, and others.

Transferring MicroProfile JWTs from a client to a server

MicroProfile JWTs are transferred over a HTTP request. They can be passed either via an HTTP Authorization header or an HTTP cookie:

- **Passing JWTs as an HTTP Authorization header**: When passing a JWT as an HTTP Authorization header, the configuration mp.jwt.token.header can be used to store the JWT in the following format:

```
mp.jwt.token.header=Bearer as14efgscd31qrewtadg
```

- **Passing JWTs as cookies**: When passing a JWT as a cookie, the configuration mp.jwt.token.cookie can be used to store the JWT in the following format:

```
mp.jwt.token.cookie=Bearer= as14efgscd31qrewtadg
```

Validating MicroProfile JWTs by the server

MicroProfile JWTs must be signed (JWSes). To decode JWSes, the corresponding public key must be specified. The location to the public key can be provided via the property mp.jwt.verify.publickey.location. Alternatively, the public key itself can be provided via the property mp.jwt.verify.publickey. The two properties are not allowed to be specified together. Otherwise, a DeploymentException will be thrown.

The signed JWTs can be further encrypted (JWE). When the server receives MicroProfile JWTs, it will validate the JWTs. If the JWT is a JWE, it will need to use the corresponding private key to decrypt the JWE. The location of the private key can be specified in the property mp.jwt.decrypt.key.location. If this property is present, the received JWTs must be a JWE. Otherwise, the JWTs will be rejected.

After the signature of a JWT has been verified or the token has been decrypted, some further validations can be performed, such as iss and aud validation. The mp.jwt.verify.issuer property specifies the expected iss value while the property mp.jwt.verify.audiences specifies the aud value.

After the JWTs have been verified, the object JsonWebToken is made available to the cloud-native application as a backend.

Some MicroProfile JWT implementation might also provide additional validation mechanisms. In Open Liberty, you can specify the following line in your server.xml to validate against the issuer and audiences if the corresponding properties are absent:

```
<mpJwt id="stockTraderJWT" audiences="${JWT_
AUDIENCE}" issuer="${JWT_ISSUER}" keyName="jwtSigner"
ignoreApplicationAuthMethod="false" />
```

This mechanism will be used by the **Stock Trader** application, which will be covered in more detail in *Chapter 8, Building and Testing Your Cloud-Native Application*.

In the preceding example, when a JWT is received and decoded, its aud and iss claim will be compared with audiences defined in ${JWT_AUDIENCE} and ${JWT_ISSUER} correspondingly. If they match, the JWT will be accepted and then perform further authentication and authorization checks.

Accessing JsonWebToken

Cloud-native applications can access JsonWebToken via the following ways:

- Access JsonWebToken via SecurityContext. The following code snippet demonstrates how to retrieve a JsonWebToken object from the injected SecurityContext:

```
@GET
@Path("/getAud")
public Set<String> getAudience(@Context
    SecurityContext sec)
```

```
            Set<String> auds = null;
            Principal user = sec.getUserPrincipal();
            if (user instanceof JsonWebToken) {
                JsonWebToken jwt = (JsonWebToken) user;
                auds = jwt.getAudience();
            }
            return auds;
    }
```

> **Note**
>
> JsonWebToken contains all claims. JsonWebToken is a subclass of
> Principal.

- You can use CDI injection to inject the whole JsonWebToken:

  ```
  @Inject private JsonWebToken jwt;
  ```

- You can use CDI injection to inject a particular claim. The following example
  demonstrates assigning the claim raw_token string to the rawToken
  variable:

  ```
  @Inject @Claim(standard= Claims.raw_token) private String
  rawToken;
  ```

  This line is to inject the claim iat with the type of Long to the dupIssuedAt
  variable:

  ```
  @Inject @Claim("iat") private Long dupIssuedAt;
  ```

- The following line injects the claim sub with the type of ClaimValue to the
  optSubject variable. This lookup is dynamic:

  ```
  @Inject @Claim("sub") private ClaimValue<Optional<String>>
  optSubject;
  ```

> **Note**
>
> ClaimValue is a representation of a claim in a `JsonWebToken`, which is a wrapper class for the specified claim.

Since the JWT is attached to a particular request, it is expected that the token is bound to a lifecycle of `RequestScoped`. When injecting `JsonWebToken` or `Claims` into a scope with a lifecycle greater than `RequestScoped`, such as `ApplicationScoped`,or `SessionScoped`, you should use the type of `Provider`, `Instance`, or `ClaimValue` as these are wrappers and will always retrieve the JWTs dynamically for the specified request. Generally speaking, you can use the following code snippet to retrieve a specified claim, `a_claim`:

```
@Inject @Claim("a_claim") <Claim_Type> private myClaim;
```

`<Claim_Type>` can be `String`, `Long`, `long`, `Boolean`, `Set<String>`, `JsonValue.TRUE`, `JsonValue.FALSE`, `JsonString`, `JsonNumber`, `JsonArray`, or `JsonObject`. It can be optional wrapper of the listed types or `ClaimValue` of the types, including `Optional`.

MicroProfile JWT can be propagated to downstream services if the invocation is via the MicroProfile Rest Client (MicroProfile Rest Client has been discussed in great detail in *Chapter 4, Developing Cloud-Native Applications*.). The propagation will be automatically handled by setting the following configuration:

```
org.eclipse.microprofile.rest.client.propagateHeaders=
   Authorization/Cookie
```

If the JWT is specified as an authorization header, the value will be `Authentication`. If the JWT is specified as a cookie, the value will be `Cookie`.

Where to find the public key and private key

When it comes to security, you will immediately think about keys. There is no exception here. In MicroProfile JWT, you will need a public key to decode a JWS and a private key to decrypt JWE. If you received JWE, you will need to use your private key to decrypt it first. After the decryption, you will get a JWS. Then you will need to use your public key to decode the JWS to verify the signature. MicroProfile JWT provides the following configuration for you to retrieve the keys:

Property	Description
`mp.jwt.token.header`	The header that contains a JWT token. `Cookie` or `Authorization` (default) are valid values.
`mp.jwt.verify.publickey`	The public key text itself.
`mp.jwt.verify.publickey.location`	The location of the public key. The value is either a relative path or a URL.
`mp.jwt.verify.publickey.algorithm`	Decode algorithm, which is either RS256 or ES256.
`mp.jwt.decrypt.key.location`	The location of the private key. The value is either a relative path or a URL.

Table 5.8 – MicroProfile JWT configuration

If the `mp.jwt.decrypt.key.location` property is set and either `mp.jwt.verify.publickey.location` or `mp.jwt.verify.publickey` are set, only encrypted JWTs can be accepted.

The properties mentioned in the preceding table are regular MicroProfile configurations. They can be specified in any of the config sources, such as *META-INF/microprofile-config.properties*, *system properties*, *environment variables*, or other custom config sources.

We have covered how MicroProfile JWT works. In the next section, we will discuss how to make the APIs available to your Maven or Gradle projects.

How to make MicroProfile JWT available to applications?

To use MicroProfile JWT APIs, you need to make these APIs available to your application. If you create a Maven project, you can directly add the following to your `pom.xml`:

```
<dependency>
    <groupId>org.eclipse.microprofile.jwt</groupId>
    <artifactId>microprofile-jwt-auth-api</artifactId>
    <version>1.2</version>
</dependency>
```

Alternatively, if you create a Gradle project, you need to add the following dependency:

```
dependencies {
providedCompile org.eclipse.microprofile.jwt:
  microprofile-jwt-auth-api:1.2
}
```

Summary

In this chapter, we have learned about MicroProfile Config, which enables you to externalize your configuration to achieve a flexible and efficient cloud-native architecture, which is also highly recommended by the twelve-factor app.

We then went forward to explore how to create a resilient cloud-native application using MicroProfile Fault Tolerance so that application developers can concentrate on their business logic, where MicroProfile Fault Tolerance handles possible failures and then performs retries or limits resource consumption, and so on, via simple Fault Tolerance annotations.

After we covered Fault Tolerance, we then dived into MicroProfile OpenAPI to learn how to document your cloud-native applications using MicroProfile OpenAPI. We discussed a few ways to generate OpenAPI documents. Some MicroProfile OpenAPI implementation, such as Open Liberty, also provides UI integration for you to access endpoints directly via the UI.

Finally, we learned about the topic of securing cloud-native applications using MicroProfile JWT. We discussed, in general, the unique requirements for securing cloud-native applications and then explained how to use MicroProfile JWT to facilitate securing cloud-native applications in a portable and interoperable way.

Up to now, you have learned about quite a few technologies you need to develop your cloud-native applications. The next task is to consider how to improve your day 2 operation experience by building a smart and intelligent cloud-native application, which means the application can communicate automatically with cloud infrastructures when it is ready to receive requests and so on. It will also be beneficial if the application can provide some metrics so that day 2 operations can take some precautions before it is too late. We all know faults cannot be eliminated completely. If something goes wrong, day 2 operations will offer an easy and simple diagnosis to identify the failure straightaway. MicroProfile Health, MicroProfile Metrics, and MicroProfile OpenTracing are the technologies to fulfill these requirements.

In the next chapter, we will discuss why and how you should use MicroProfile Health, MicroProfile Metrics, and MicroProfile OpenTracing to help with day 2 operations.

6

Observing and Monitoring Cloud-Native Applications

In the previous two chapters, we discussed and explained the varying capabilities of the MicroProfile 4.1 platform for building and enhancing your cloud-native application. At this point, your cloud-native application is built on a strong fundamental core with much credit due to the tried and true components of the Jakarta EE platform. On top of that, you've added a few bells and whistles to make your application more resilient, secure, configurable, and documentable. For all intents and purposes, you have yourself a fully capable cloud-native application that's ready for deployment. But as the savvy developer that you are, you know that the story of your cloud-native application is not complete once you deploy it. Nothing is truly perfect and, depending on the complexity of your application ecosystem, letting your applications run wild can be disastrous.

This brings forth the important task of monitoring your applications. You, your team, or your operations team will need to be able to monitor the activity and performance of your applications to identify any potential problems. Effective monitoring can be used as an early warning for impending trouble, shedding light on areas that may need optimizing, or aiding in the post-mortem analysis to see what might have gone wrong. Alternatively, from a more optimistic perspective, effective monitoring can simply provide beautiful data on the performance of your application.

This leads us to this chapter, where we will cover the last three specifications that are included in the MicroProfile platform's release scope. For observing and monitoring your cloud-native applications, the MicroProfile platform provides the **MicroProfile Health**, **MicroProfile Metrics**, and **MicroProfile OpenTracing** technologies.

In particular, we will cover the following topics:

- Determining the health of your cloud-native application using MicroProfile Health
- Instrumenting and using metrics on your cloud-native application using MicroProfile Metrics
- Tracing your cloud-native application using MicroProfile OpenTracing

Technical requirements

To build and run the samples mentioned in this chapter, you will need a Mac or PC (Windows or Linux) with the following software:

- Java Development Kit, version 8 or higher: `https://adoptium.net/`
- Apache Maven: `https://maven.apache.org/`
- A Git client: `https://git-scm.com/`

All the source code used in this chapter is available on GitHub at `https://github.com/PacktPublishing/Practical-Cloud-Native-Java-Development-with-MicroProfile/tree/main/Chapter06`.

Once you have cloned the GitHub repository, you can start the Open Liberty server that these code samples will execute in, by entering the ch6 directory and entering the following command from the command line:

```
mvn clean package liberty:run
```

You can then stop the server in the same command window by pressing *Ctrl* + *C*.

The application that's deployed to the Open Liberty server will be given a context root of ch6. For example, the full URL to a JAX-RS resource would be `http://localhost:9080/ch6/path/to/resource`. This will be reflected in the code samples in this chapter that illustrate sending requests to an endpoint.

Determining the health of your cloud-native application using MicroProfile Health

To begin our three-part journey of looking at the MicroProfile observability toolkit, we'll examine the MicroProfile Health technology. We chose to examine this technology first as its benefits and use cases are much broader in scope compared to the other two technologies in this chapter. The MicroProfile Health technology reports information regarding the health, or status, of your microservice. The expected health status is either *UP* or *DOWN*.

The importance of MicroProfile Health in a cloud-native application

We now know what the MicroProfile Health technology can do. But what purpose does it serve? To find out, we must take a step back. The driving force for developing applications with the MicroProfile technologies is that they will be cloud native. And if you recall *Chapter 1, Cloud-Native Application*, the important distinction between a cloud-native application and a non-cloud-native application is its ability to take advantage of the capabilities provided by the cloud. The MicroProfile Health technology is a perfect example of this.

At its very core, the MicroProfile Health technology strives to report the health of your application to some external observer. Since we are developing a cloud-native application, the application will live its life in a container that's been deployed on your cloud platform. Whether its tenure is short-lived or not is what the health statuses serve to dictate. In effect, these health statuses report the health of your container to your cloud platform. Using the status report of the container, the cloud platform's monitor service can use that data to make decisions to terminate and replace any troublesome containers. The circumstances of when your containers are terminated and restarted ultimately dependent on you, the developer. Your cloud platform may have rules on what to do, given the health of a container, but the context of how these health statuses are reported depends on how the MicroProfile Health technology is used throughout your application.

Later in this chapter, we will examine a sample scenario of using the health status of your application/container with **Kubernetes**. Kubernetes is an open source project that provides a container orchestration solution for deploying, scaling, and managing your containers. As one of the more well-known container orchestration platforms, it will provide an excellent vehicle for demonstrating the benefits of using the MicroProfile Health technology. Kubernetes, along with other cloud infrastructure topics, will be covered in more detail in *Chapter 7, MicroProfile Ecosystem with Open Liberty, Docker, and Kubernetes*.

MicroProfile Health technology overview

MicroProfile Health provides three types of health, or status, checks. They are the **liveness**, **readiness**, and **startup** health checks. We will explain these health checks in detail shortly, but for now, know that their purpose is to report whether an application is alive, ready, or if it has even completed starting up. The instrumentation and existence of a health check in an application is defined as a **procedure**. This procedure is called upon to check if the application has started, as well as its liveness or readiness for the instrumented components of the application. Moving forward, we will refer to health checks as either a health check, a procedure, or a combination of both.

Health check procedures can be instrumented throughout your microservice and will return an *UP* or *DOWN* status to indicate the liveness or readiness of the various components of your application, as well as if the application has completed initialization. The liveness, readiness, and startup health checks will be reported through the `http://host:port/health/live`, `http://host:port/health/ready`, and `http://host:port/health/started` endpoints, respectively. An overall status is provided for each endpoint and is the logical conjunction of all procedures. If there are five readiness procedures instrumented in your application and all but one procedure returns *UP*, then the overall readiness of your application is *DOWN*. There is also the `http://host:port/health` endpoint, which provides an overall status of the whole application from the conjunction of the health check procedures for the liveness, readiness, and startup health checks. When using the `http://host:port/health` endpoint, there is no distinction between liveness, readiness, or startup health checks. All health check procedures, regardless of their type, must return *UP* for the `http://host:port/health` endpoint to return *UP*. It should be noted that the order in which procedures are invoked is arbitrary, so they can be invoked in any order. Moving forward, when referring to the health endpoints, we will omit `http://host:port` for brevity.

Before we move on, let's learn a little bit more about these three types of health checks.

Liveness health check

The purpose of the liveness health check procedure, as its name suggests, is to report whether the application is alive. In a cloud environment, this status can be used by the monitoring service to determine if the application is running as expected. Failing this health check may prompt your cloud platform's monitoring service to terminate the application's container. Depending on the policy that you've configured, this may cause the application's container to be restarted.

Note that a failing liveness procedure does not mean that the application is no longer running. Instead, it means that the strategy that's been employed for instrumenting the check has deemed that the application has suffered or is suffering from a deterioration of service and can no longer be considered operationally effective. For example, a liveness procedure can be used to detect a memory leak in the JVM and at the rate of memory loss, so it would be prudent to terminate this container now instead of later. As a result, a *DOWN* status will be returned.

Startup health check

The purpose of the startup health check is to provide an intermediary check that is a precursor to the liveness health check. In a container environment, not all containers are made equal. Understandably, certain containers may be slow to start and initialize due to the complexity of the application that is running within them. In a compatible cloud environment, the startup check can be carried out for an *UP* before liveness checks are carried out.

Readiness health check

The purpose of a readiness health check procedure is to allow external observers (for example, the cloud monitoring service) to identify if the application is ready to receive and conduct business logic. The application may have effectively started and be alive and running with no issues, as indicated by the liveness checks, but it isn't quite ready to receive traffic yet. This could be because the application is still attempting to initialize a resource or connect to another application that it depends on. The readiness check will report *DOWN* as it continues its attempt to secure a connection.

> **Special Note About Default Health Checks**
>
> Depending on your underlying MicroProfile runtime, your runtime may provide **default health check procedures**. For example, a default liveness procedure may be provided to indicate that the MicroProfile Health component of the runtime is running and *alive*. This may have been a very contrived example, but any default procedure, whether it's useful or not, can be disabled. You can disable default procedures by using the MicroProfile `mp.health.disable-default-procedures` Config element and setting its value to `true`.

Instrumenting health check procedures

A health check procedure is called upon by the MicroProfile runtime to find out the health of a particular component of an application, whether it be a liveness, readiness, or startup procedure. But it can also be the case that the health check reports on the liveness, readiness, and startup procedures simultaneously. This is due to how the MicroProfile Health runtime operates under the hood. Like the other MicroProfile technologies, MicroProfile Health is intrinsically integrated with **Context Dependency Injection** (**CDI**), a technology we covered in *Chapter 4, Developing Cloud-Native Applications*. To identify what type of health checks a procedure reports on, we must use the @Liveness, @Readiness, and @Startup qualifier annotations. Using any of these annotations lets the MicroProfile Health runtime know what health statuses are being reported. But before we get too ahead of ourselves, what exactly is a health check in the application code?

The basis for every health check procedure is the functional interface, called HealthCheck. This consists of a single function, call(), that returns a HealthCheckResponse. In an application, the HealthCheck implementation is annotated with at least one of the @Liveness, @Readiness, or @Startup annotations. Remember that MicroProfile Health's integration with CDI means that every health check procedure (that is, the HealthCheck implementation) is a CDI bean and has a place in the application's life cycle context. It would be prudent to also define a CDI scope for your health check procedure. We will be using @ApplicationScoped in our examples.

The following code snippet demonstrates how to instrument the liveness, readiness, and startup health checks in the same procedure. You can instrument a singular health check by using one annotation instead:

```
@ApplicationScoped
@Liveness
@Readiness
@Startup
public class LivenessCheck implements HealthCheck {

    public HealthCheckResponse call() {
        [...]
    }
}
```

So, now that we know how to create and define the different types of health checks, we can learn how to build the health check response, whose data will be consumed by an external observer through one of the /health/* endpoints.

As we mentioned earlier, we will be returning a `HealthCheckResponse` object. This data object contains all the information we need for uniquely identifying the health check and, most importantly, the health of your cloud-native application.

`HealthCheckResponse` consists of three fields:

- **Name**: This is a `String` field that distinguishes this health check procedure from other health check procedures.
- **Status**: This is an `enum` field with either an *UP* or *DOWN* value.
- **Data**: This is an optional field and holds a `Map<String, Object>`. When **instrumenting** a procedure, you can choose to provide additional information in key-value format. This map serves to provide additional contextual information about the procedure. The map holds a `String` key and its value can be either `String`, `long`, or `boolean`.

Now, let's look at the different ways of constructing health check procedures.

Using HealthCheckResponseBuilder

To create a `HealthCheckResponse`, you can call one of two static methods in `HealthCheckResponse` that will return a `HealthCheckResponseBuilder`. These two methods are `builder()` and `named(String name)`. The latter creates a `HealthCheckResponseBuilder` with a name that's already specified, whereas the former provides a *clean* instance.

`HealthCheckResponseBuilder` provides a builder pattern for constructing a `HealthCheckResponse` containing the required and optional fields. This is the preferred method if you intend to provide optional data.

The following code example shows a scenario where we are performing a liveness health check based on the heap memory usage of the JVM.

The full source code for `LivenessCheck` can be found at `https://bit.ly/2WbiVyV`:

```
@ApplicationScoped
@Liveness
public class LivenessCheck implements HealthCheck {

    public HealthCheckResponse call() {

        //Percentage value from 0.0-1.0
```

```
        Double memoryUsage = getMemUsage();
    HealthCheckResponseBuilder builder =
        HealthCheckResponse.named("LivenessCheck");
    if (memoryUsage < 0.9) {
        builder.up();
    } else {
        builder.down();
    }
    builder = builder.withData("MemoryUsage",
        memoryUsage.toString());
    return builder.build();
    }
}
```

In this example, we used the named(String name) static method to provide the health check with a name. We then used the HealthCheckResponseBuilder class's up(), down(), and withData(String key, String value) methods to specify the status of the health check and to provide any additional contextual data. The withData(...) method is an overloaded method and can accept String, long, and boolean values. In this example, if the memory usage is less than 90% (that is, a value less than 0.9 is returned by the getMemUsage() method), we will return an *UP* status. Otherwise, we will return a *DOWN* status.

Alternatively, if you're using HealthCheckResponse.builder() instead, you will need to use the HealthCheckResponseBuilder class's name(String name) to provide a name for the health check.

Now, instead of having a bulky if-else block, we can use HealthCheckResponseBuilder.status(boolean status) in one line:

```
    return HealthCheckResponse.builder()
        .name("LivenessCheck")
        .status(memoryUsage < 0.9)
        .withData("MemoryUsage", memoryUsage
        .toString()).build()
```

As you can see, we've reduced eight lines of code to one line!

Using HealthCheckResponse

Instead of using `HealthCheckResponseBuilder`, we can also use the `HealthCheckResponse` class's two static methods, which conveniently create an *UP* or *DOWN* `HealthCheckResponse`, as illustrated in the following example.

The full source code for `ReadinessCheck` can be found at `https://bit.ly/3iV3WBP`:

```
@ApplicationScoped
@Readiness
public class ReadinessCheck implements HealthCheck {

    public final String NAME = "evenNumberPhobic";

    public HealthCheckResponse call() {
        long time = System.currentTimeMillis();

        if (time % 2 == 0)
            return HealthCheckResponse.down(NAME);
        else
            return HealthCheckResponse.up(NAME);
    }
}
```

The methods that are being used here are aptly named `up(String name)` and `down(String name)` and accept a `String` parameter that defines the name of the health check. This approach assumes that there is no additional optional data to be incorporated with this health check procedure. In the following example, we will retrieve the current system time and if it is an even number, we will return a *DOWN* status (otherwise, it will be an *UP* status).

CDI producers

With MicroProfile Health's implicit reliance on CDI, health checks procedures can also be instrumented using a CDI method producer. You can instrument multiple health check procedures in one class by using CDI method producers. The following example shows the liveness, readiness, and startup health check procedures being instrumented as CDI method producers.

The full source code for `CDIMethodProducerCheck` can be found at `https://bit.ly/3k9GrUT`:

```
@ApplicationScoped
public class CDIMethodProducerChecks {

    @Produces
    @Liveness
    HealthCheck livenessCDIMethodProducer() {
        return () -> HealthCheckResponse.named("cdiMemUsage")
            .status(getMemUsage() < 0.9).build();
    }

    @Produces
    @Readiness
    HealthCheck readinessCDIMethodProducer() {
        return () -> HealthCheckResponse.named("cdiCpuUsage")
            .status(getCpuUsage() < 0.9).build();
    }

    @Produces
    @Startup
    HealthCheck startupCDIMethodProducer() {
        return () -> HealthCheckResponse.named
            ("cdiStartStatus").status(getStatus()).build();
    }

}
```

The liveness procedure that's encapsulated by the `livenessCDIMethodProducer` method will return *UP* if the memory usage is below 90% (that is, a value less than 0.9 is returned by the `getMemUsage()` method). The readiness procedure that's encapsulated by the `readinessCDIMethodProducer` method will return *UP* if the CPU usage is below 90% (that is, a value less than 0.9 is returned by the `getCpuUsage()` method). The startup procedure that's encapsulated by the `startupCDIMethodProducer` method will execute the `getStatus()` business method to evaluate the condition of the application's startup state, and will return either `true` or `false` to invoke an *UP* or *DOWN* status, respectively.

Retrieving health check data

As we mentioned previously, we can view the data through the /health, /health/ liveness, /health/readiness, and /health/started endpoints. Due to this, these health checks can be consumed by requests over HTTP/REST. Through an HTTP/REST call, the health check procedures are presented in JSON format. The root level contains the overall health status with a status field, and it is calculated from the conjunction of all health check procedures defined in the checks JSON list.

The overall status dictates the HTTP response code. An *UP* status returns HTTP 200, while a *DOWN* status returns HTTP 500. Any failures or errors that are encountered by the health check procedure will result in an HTTP 503 return code, which equates to a *DOWN* status. Remember that if any health check reports are down, then the overall status is *DOWN*. Each health check JSON object in the list displays the contents of HealthCheckReponse (that is, its name, status, and optional key-value map). If there a no health check procedures, then an automatic *UP* (that is, HTTP 200) is returned. The formatting structure and behaviors listed previously apply to all four endpoints. The use of response codes is important as this may be the method in which the external observer is determining the health of your application (that is, the cloud platform).

The following example output can be applied to any of the four health endpoints, so we will not define which endpoint it is from:

```
{
    "status": "DOWN",
    "checks": [
        {
            "name": "goodCheck",
            "status": "UP"
        },
        {
            "name": "questionableCheck",
            "status": "DOWN",
            "data": {
                "application": "backend",
                "locale": "en"
            }
        }
    ]
}
```

The output reports that we have a health check procedure named `"goodCheck"` that reports *UP*. We also have a procedure named `"questionableCheck"` that is reporting *DOWN*. This causes the overall status to report *DOWN* and will result in an HTTP 500 error being returned. As shown in the output, the `"questionableCheck"` procedure has incorporated the additional contextual map data; that is, `"application":` `"backend"` and `"locale": "en"`.

Special Note About Default Readiness and Startup Procedures

The MicroProfile Health runtime provides a configuration value (through MicroProfile Config) called `mp.health.default.readiness.` `empty.response`. Its value can be either *UP* or *DOWN*. The default value is *DOWN*. This value is used to report the readiness of your microservice if the application is still starting up and the readiness procedures cannot be called yet. This is not applicable if no readiness health check procedures have been defined in the application code. If that is the case, then the default behavior for no health check procedures is to return an HTTP 200 response with an *UP* status on the `/health/readiness` endpoint.

There is also a configuration value that exists for the startup health check called `mp.health.default.startup.empty.response`. If there are no startup health checks at all, then the default *UP* status is returned on the `/health/started` endpoint.

Liveness checks, on the other hand, do not have configurable values. They follow the simple rule of returning an HTTP 200 response with an *UP* status if the application is still starting, and the liveness checks are not ready to be invoked yet.

Other connections and payload formats

Depending on the runtime you chose, it may be the case that the results of the health check procedures can be obtained through additional means (for example, TCP or JMX). We're using the word *additional* here because, at the very minimum, a MicroProfile Health runtime must support an HTTP/REST request. However, as a cloud-native technology, MicroProfile Health understands that other strategies for obtaining the data may be preferred. The MicroProfile Health specification defines a set of protocols and wire format rules for how the data can be consumed and presented. Health check data should be presented in JSON format whenever possible. But failing that, the same payload of data must be made available.

This book will not discuss the intricacies of the protocol and the wire format semantics defined in the MicroProfile Health specification. You can review the MicroProfile Health specification for such information at `https://bit.ly/3ecI6Gz`.

MicroProfile health checks with Kubernetes' liveness, readiness, and startup probes

We will now look at how the health check data that's reported by health check procedures can be consumed in a real-life scenario. To do this, we will be using Kubernetes. As this is one of the more well-known cloud container orchestration platforms, this will serve as an excellent vehicle of demonstration. We will be using Kubernetes terminology and will try our best to describe these terms in this section. We will explore Kubernetes and the cloud infrastructure in more depth in *Chapter 7, MicroProfile Ecosystem with Docker, Kubernetes, and Istio.*

In a cloud environment, the containers you deploy exist on an interconnected web of physical or virtual machines. Kubernetes serves to seamlessly manage and integrate your container deployments that reside in Kubernetes' **Pods**. Pods can contain one or more containers. To get a pulse on the activity of the Pods in this network (that is, your cloud), a **kubelet** is present on each machine. This acts as a node agent that manages the Pods on the machine and communicates with the central Kubernetes management facilities. As part of its duties, it can determine when the containers within these Pods are stale or broken, and it has the power to stop and restart them if the need arises. Kubelets are also given the task of evaluating when a container is ready to receive traffic or not. And, most fundamentally, they can check if the container has completed initializing. They accomplish these tasks by checking the liveness, readiness, and startup statuses of the containers within the Pods using liveness, readiness, and startup probes.

This behavior is container-specific in that it must be enabled on a per-container basis. This is achieved when configuring the container in the Pod's configuration YAML file. The following example uses a snippet from the `broker.yaml` file, which configures the Broker microservice from the StockTrader application that we introduced in *Chapter 3, Introducing the IBM Stock Trader Cloud-Native Application*, and will look at again in *Chapter 8, Step-by-Step Stock Trader Development*. The YAML file contains a Kubernetes `Deployment` definition, which provides the configuration needed to deploy the container(s) onto a Pod, including the container image to use, environment variables, and, of course, the liveness, readiness, and startup probes, which can be configured for each container that is defined. We've omitted the other parts of the file to only show the configuration of the liveness, readiness, and startup probes.

The full source code for `broker.yaml` can be found at `https://bit.ly/3sEvHAa`:

```
apiVersion: apps/v1
kind: Deployment
[...]
spec:
```

```
[...]
readinessProbe:
  httpGet:
    path: /health/ready
    port: 9080
  initialDelaySeconds: 60
  periodSeconds: 15
  failureThreshold: 2
livenessProbe:
  httpGet:
    path: /health/live
    port: 9080
  periodSeconds: 15
  failureThreshold: 3
startupProbe:
  httpGet:
    path: /health/started
    port: 9080
  periodSeconds: 30
  failureThreshold: 4

[...]
```

The liveness, readiness, and startup endpoints are defined in the livenessProbe, readinessProbe, and startupProbe sections, respectively. The probes are configured to use HTTP/S with httpGet. In our example, we will be using an unsecured HTTP endpoint. You will need to add a new field under httpGet named scheme and set the value to HTTPS if you want a secure connection. We specify /health/live, /health/ready, and /health/started with the path field and the port to reach it on with port. An initial delay of 60 seconds is configured with the initialDelaySeconds field for the readiness probe. This prevents the readiness probe from firing until this time has elapsed, to allow the container and its application to start up. When the probes are firing, requests will be sent every 15 seconds for the readiness and liveness probes and 30 seconds for the startup probe, as configured through periodSeconds. However, what's not defined in this example is the timeoutSeconds field. By default, the value is 1 second and it defines the period in which the kubelet should wait before it times out. failureThreshold defines how many times the probes will retry before it is considered a failure.

You may notice that the liveness probe does not specify the `initialDelaySeconds` field. You can do so, but this is unnecessary as we are using `startUpProbe`. Remember that (if defined) the startup probe will be queried first until it provides the *UP* status, and then the liveness probe will be checked. This is the behavior that Kubernetes provides.

If any of the probes fail completely, as in all attempts have transpired, then the container is subject to being restarted.

It should be of no surprise now that the MicroProfile Health technology had the Kubernetes platform in mind with its availability of liveness, readiness, and startup endpoints, all of which match the specific Kubernetes liveness, readiness, and startup probes. However, the existence of the simple `/health` endpoint allows it to be used by other platforms that only care about a single health endpoint. But remember that when using the `/health` endpoint, the concept of liveness, readiness, and startup maybe no longer be applicable. On top of that, MicroProfile Health's straightforward protocol and wire format rules allow its health check data to be easily consumed by any external observer, sentient or not.

We've now come to the end of the MicroProfile Health section. As we mentioned earlier, in the introduction to MicroProfile Health, this technology serves to satisfy a broad monitoring scope. In the next section, we'll start to cover a more detailed monitoring scope with MicroProfile Metrics.

Instrumenting metrics on your cloud-native application using MicroProfile Metrics

This is the second part of our MicroProfile observability trilogy, where we find ourselves in the thick of things with MicroProfile Metrics. The previous technology we discussed – MicroProfile Health – strived to report on the overall health of your cloud-native application by allowing you, the developer, to strategically place health checks throughout your application. MicroProfile Metrics, on the other hand, strives to report on the performance and inner workings of the application and its environment using metrics instrumented in the application by you, as well as metrics provided by the MicroProfile Metrics runtime. This provides real-time statistics that can be recorded and/or aggregated to be analyzed with specialized monitoring tools. To accomplish this, the MicroProfile Metrics technology comes well-equipped with seven types of metrics that range in complexity and functionality. As we progress through this section of this chapter, we will come to know them very well.

The importance of MicroProfile Metrics in a cloud-native application

Being able to monitor the statistics and performance data of specific components throughout your application is not a cloud-native, development-specific idea. This should be a healthy practice, regardless of whether your endeavors are on the cloud. However, being able to monitor your microservices is critical when we're talking about a topology of highly scalable and diverse applications. Even if you don't command a sprawl of applications, but rather a few applications, the benefits of gathering metrics are indisputably invaluable. This is a way for your microservice to talk to you and tell you how it's feeling. This provides you with the opportunity to identify any patterns of concern before your application's liveness health checks unexpectedly decrees that it is *DOWN*. For example, in the previous section, we demonstrated a scenario where the liveness health check procedure was dependent on how much memory was being used. After it surpassed a certain threshold, it would fail and report *DOWN*. By just using MicroProfile Health, we wouldn't know anything was wrong until it was too late and by then, your cloud platform would have already restarted the container. And perhaps you may be blissfully unaware that anything has happened at all.

Having MicroProfile Metrics report on such statistics allows you to anticipate such disasters ahead of time and to understand the performance of your application. As another example, we can have metrics reporting on the number of requests that have been made to the REST endpoints in your microservice and how long it took, on average, for the requests to be fulfilled. This metric information can shed light on how popular your microservice is and how well – or how poorly – your microservice is performing. This can then prompt the necessary steps for revising and modifying the deployment environment or even the application itself.

However, MicroProfile Metrics can only report on the instantaneous value of the metrics. To properly harness this stream of information, we need to aggregate the metric data over time and, in effect, transform it into a **time series metric**. Neither MicroProfile Metrics itself, nor any other MicroProfile technology, serves to accomplish this task. MicroProfile Metrics is only here to provide a seamless and effective way of instrumenting metrics into your microservices. There is already an established ecosystem of tools and platforms that specializes in aggregating metrics and visualizing them. A popular monitoring stack to use is one that utilizes **Prometheus** and **Grafana**.

Prometheus is an open source monitoring solution for gathering, storing, and querying time series metrics. Prometheus is often combined with the use of another tool, called Grafana. Grafana is another open source monitoring solution that serves to display and visualize time series metrics through graphs, tables, and other types of visualizations by using customized queries that have been made to the time series database (for example, Prometheus). This can provide you or your operations team with the ability to monitor the performance of your microservices through meaningful visualizations in a human-friendly way.

At the end of this section, we will demonstrate how to use Grafana to visualize the metric data that's been gathered by the MicroProfile Metrics runtime. Being able to strategically instrument metrics to provide meaningful information is half the battle; effectively using that information is how the battle is won.

MicroProfile Metrics technology overview

You may have noticed that, in the introduction to this section, we mentioned that metrics can come from the application or the runtime itself. Just like MicroProfile Health, where default health checks may be provided, the MicroProfile Metrics runtime can provide default out-of-the-box metrics as well. The runtime must provide, for the most part, a certain set of metrics on top of any optional metrics that it wishes to provide. These metrics are referred to as **base metrics** and **vendor metrics**, respectively. However, not all base metrics are strictly required, and we will explain this shortly. The metrics that are instrumented in the application by the developer are referred to as **application metrics**. All these different sets of metrics live separately, agnostic of each other, under different **metric registries**. The metric registry is the control center and the heart of the MicroProfile Metrics technology. The metric registry is where metrics are registered, stored, retrieved, and deleted. This logical grouping of the different types of metrics into their own unique metric registries simplifies handling different scopes of metrics and, most importantly, avoids any metric name collisions that could occur if they resided together in one single metric registry.

To retrieve the metric data, the MicroProfile Metrics runtime provides four HTTP/REST endpoints. The first one is a general `http://host:port/metrics` endpoint, which displays all the metrics from all the scopes and registries. Metrics are prefixed with the name of their respective metric registries to avoid confusion. The other three endpoints are sub-resources of the `http://host:port/metrics` endpoint, and they report on the metrics in each specific registry. They are the `http://host:port/metrics/base`, `http://host:port/metrics/vendor`, and `http://host:hort/metrics/application` HTTP/REST endpoints. Metrics can be reported in either JSON or Prometheus exposition format. We will cover these two formats in detail later. Moving forward, when referring to the metrics endpoints, we will omit `http://host:port` for brevity.

In summary, the following diagram illustrates the general flow of the metric life cycle. First, metrics are instrumented into your microservice (or provided by the runtime!). These metrics are reported on the /metrics endpoint. Some monitoring tool or platform (for example, Prometheus) is then used to retrieve the metric data and store it, thus transforming it into time series metrics. Another monitoring tool or platform (for example, Grafana) is then used to visualize that data:

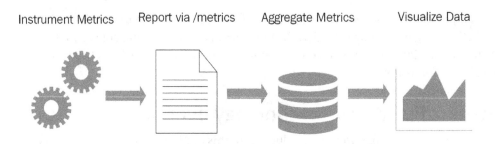

Figure 6.1 – Life cycle of a metric

We will now describe the three different metric scopes in more detail; that is, **base metrics**, **vendor metrics**, and **application metrics**.

Base metrics

Base metrics are a set of metrics that must be provided by all MicroProfile Metrics runtimes. There are, however, a few exceptions, where the metrics can be optionally implemented instead. This slight variability is due to what base metrics were meant to achieve. The list of base metrics was created in the hopes of capturing and reporting metrics that each runtime would have. Having base metrics defined and implemented by the runtime relieves the developer from the burden of having to instrument their own metrics to capture basic and/or common statistics. By providing these base metrics, they would always be available, regardless of whether they are needed.

The obvious target for base metrics would be to encompass the **Java Virtual Machine (JVM)** statistics. Base metrics cover a long list of metrics that target memory statistics, garbage collection statistics, thread usage, thread pool statistics, class loading statistics, as well as operating system statistics. However, not every JVM is made equal, and a few of these metrics are optional as the JVM under the hood may not hold such statistics. Base metrics also include optional REST metrics that track the request count, unmapped exceptions count, and time spent on each REST/JAX-RS endpoint. We encourage you to review the list of base metrics and their definitions by looking at the MicroProfile Metrics specification at https://bit.ly/3mXpL42.

The MicroProfile Metrics specification only defines the aforementioned JVM and REST metrics explicitly as base metrics, but the metrics generated by MicroProfile Fault Tolerance are classified as base metrics as well. We covered the MicroProfile Fault Tolerance metrics in the *Fault Tolerance metrics* section of the previous chapter.

Vendor metrics

Vendor metrics are metrics that are provided by the vendor for their implementation of MicroProfile Metrics. Different implementations of MicroProfile Metrics will contain different sets of vendor metrics. Vendor metrics are completely optional, and it can be the case that your chosen MicroProfile Metrics runtime does not supply any vendor metrics at all. The purpose of vendor metrics is to allow the vendor's implementation to provide any metrics that can enhance the monitoring capabilities of the end user for the specific MicroProfile Metrics runtime. For example, if the runtime you are using is also Jakarta EE compliant, then it may be possible for it to provide metrics related to components under that platform. The vendor metrics can then be exclusively accessed on the `/metrics/vendor` endpoint or combined with metrics from other scopes on the `/metrics` endpoint.

Application metrics

Application metrics are metrics that have been instrumented by you, the developer, in your application. These metrics report on statistics that interest you and your team for observing and monitoring the performance of the application. This is the metrics scope that you will be primarily interacting with when instrumenting metrics. The application metrics can then be exclusively accessed on the `/metrics/application` endpoint or combined with metrics from other scopes on the `/metrics` endpoint.

The seven metric types

Now that we understand the different scopes of the available metrics, we can list the seven types of application metrics:

- Counter
- Gauge
- Concurrent Gauge
- Histogram
- Meter
- Timer
- Simple Timer

Given the names, it's easy to deduce what the different types of metrics serve to achieve. If not, don't worry – we'll cover these metrics in detail when we cover how to instrument the different metrics later, in the *Instrumenting metrics* section.

The metric model

Now that we know what type of metrics there are, and under what scopes they may live, it's time for us to understand the underlying metric model. This may sound like a dull topic, and you may be tempted to skip this, but understanding this is crucial if you wish to know how to instrument and handle metrics effectively.

A metric, besides being one of the seven metric types, consists of a name, a set of optional key-value **tags**, and its **metadata**. These three items are used by the metric registry to identify and validate the uniqueness of any given metric. These identifying pieces of information are also made available to any observer on the `/metrics/*` endpoints.

The purpose of the name is rather obvious: it is to uniquely identify the metric from others. However, that may not be sufficient in some cases because different metrics can share the same name. This is because MicroProfile Metrics supports **multi-dimensional metrics** with key-value tags.

The combination of the metric's name and its tags is encapsulated in a `MetricID` object in the metric registry. `MetricID` is the primary identifier of a metric. It is tightly coupled with the metric instance itself in the metric registry. The use of tags for a metric is optional, and it can be the case that the metrics in your application all use distinct metric names with no tags. This results in a `MetricID` with just a name and no tags. However, you may find it useful to leverage the power of multi-dimensional metrics, if the need arises. Such a need may come if you are attempting to record the same type of data (for example, a counter to count something) from multiple similar sources. You can use the same metric name and provide a tag that uniquely identifies it from the other sources. An example of this would be if you are using metrics to count how many times the methods in a specific class are being invoked. You can name the metrics `classMethodInvocations` and provide each method with a tag, where the key is `method` and the value is the name of the method.

This use of multi-dimensional metrics is best taken advantage of when using one of the available visualization monitoring tools, such as Grafana. You can quickly retrieve and display all metrics with the same name, regardless of what their tags are, in one simple query.

The last item that is used to identify a metric is its metadata. The metadata consists of the metric's name, its type, the metric's unit of measurement (if applicable), an optional description, and an optional human-readable display name. For each unique metric name, there is only one piece of metadata. As a result, there can be multiple MetricID linked to one piece of metadata. Being able to reuse the metric's name in the metadata helps correlate the MetricIDs and the metadata as they are loosely coupled in the metric registry. The relationships described previously are illustrated in the following diagram. * denotes 0 to many:

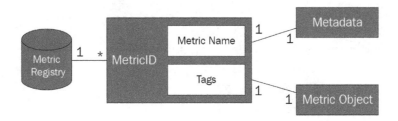

Figure 6.2 – Metric registry metric model

Retrieving metric data

Before we continue with the topic of instrumenting metrics, we will cover how metrics are made available. In the *Instrumenting metrics* section, we will be covering each metric individually and providing examples of its output, specifically its Prometheus output. Therefore, first, we must understand what we will be looking at.

As we mentioned previously, metrics are available through HTTP/REST requests to either the /metrics, /metrics/base, /metrics/vendor, or /metrics/application endpoint in either JSON or Prometheus exposition format. The metric output for a specific metric name can be retrieved by sending a request to /metrics/<scope>/<metric_name>.

JSON format

The output of the metrics in JSON format comes in two parts. We can obtain the metric and its data by invoking a GET request with the Accept header by specifying application/json. If we issue an OPTION request instead, we will be able to retrieve the metadata associated with the metrics.

Let's look at what sending a GET request to /metrics will return. Notice that the metrics from the different scopes are in their own JSON array lists. We will only show the base metrics and hide any vendor or application metrics in the sample output. We will also look at an example of multi-dimensional metrics by using the first two metrics listed in the base scope. There are two gc.total metrics whose key-value pairs are "name=scavenge" and "name=global":

```json
{
  "base": {
    "gc.total;name=scavenge": 361,
    "gc.total;name=global": 9,
    "classloader.loadedClasses.count": 9448,
    "gc.time;name=global": 33,
    "gc.time;name=scavenge": 368,
    "cpu.systemLoadAverage": -1,
    "thread.count": 73,
    "classloader.unloadedClasses.total": 0,
    "jvm.uptime": 52938,
    "cpu.processCpuTime": 23359375000,
    "memory.committedHeap": 53805056,
    "thread.max.count": 89,
    "cpu.availableProcessors": 12,
    "classloader.loadedClasses.total": 9448,
    "thread.daemon.count": 69,
    "memory.maxHeap": 536870912,
    "cpu.processCpuLoad": 0.0023284173808607016,
    "memory.usedHeap": 41412992
  },
  "vendor": {
    [..]
  },
  "application": {
    [..]
  },
}
```

To find out what the gc.total metric was meant for, we can obtain the metadata of the metrics by sending an OPTIONS request to /metrics. Since the output of this request will be lengthy, we will only show the gc.total metric and obfuscate the rest. Like the GET request, the metrics from each scope/registry are separated into their own JSON arrays:

```
{
  "base": {
    "gc.total": {
      "unit": "none",
      "displayName": "Garbage Collection Count",
      "name": "gc.total",
      "description": "Displays the total number of
        collections that have occurred. This attribute lists
          -1 if the collection count is undefined for this
          collector.",
      "type": "counter",
      "tags": [
        [
          "name=global"
        ],
        [
          "name=scavenge"
        ]
      ]
    },
    [...]
  },
  "vendor": {
    [...]
  },
  "application": {
    [...]
  }
}
```

As we can see from the metadata, the `gc.total` metric is a counter that'sused to count the number of garbage collections that have occurred in this JVM. The tags are used to identify two different garbage collectors on the system that the two metrics monitor.

A request was made to `/metrics` to demonstrate how the metrics are partitioned from different scopes. We could have also invoked `/metrics/base/gc.total` to specifically retrieve the metadata of the `gc.total` metric.

Prometheus exposition format

With the Prometheus exposition format, all metric data is provided together with a GET request to the `/metrics/*` endpoints. If `application/json` is not specified, the Prometheus format will be returned by default. As its name suggests, this format to be used directly by the Prometheus monitoring tool.

A specific template must be followed for formatting the metrics. To describe this, we'll only take a look at the output from the `gc.total` metrics. We're only using a snippet here as the full output would be too lengthy:

```
# TYPE base_gc_total counter
# HELP base_gc_total Displays the total number of collections
that have occurred. This attribute lists -1 if the collection
count is undefined for this collector.
base_gc_total{name="global"} 9
base_gc_total{name="scavenge"} 372
[...]
```

In Prometheus exposition format, metrics are organized by their metric name. The first grouping is for the `base_gc_total` metric. This corresponds to the `gc.total` metric we saw in the aforementioned JSON format examples. The true metric name is `gc.total`, but it must be transformed into `gc_total` as Prometheus formatted metrics are alphanumeric characters with underscores (`_`). The MicroProfile Metrics runtime also prepends the name of the registry scope that the metric belongs to. This is either `base_`, `vendor_`, or `application_`. Notice that the tags are appended to the end of the metric's name, within squiggly brackets.

Each unique grouping of metrics by metric name is preceded by a `# TYPE` line and a `# HELP` line. These two lines define the metric's type and a description, if available. Remember that the description is an optional field in the metric's metadata.

There are additional formatting rules for certain metrics. We will cover this in the next section.

Instrumenting metrics

The MicroProfile Metrics technology provides a rich Java API for programmatically instrumenting metrics, as well as providing CDI annotations for easily instrumenting metrics for methods, fields, and even entire classes. We will not cover all the possible scenarios of using the Java API and its annotations, particularly regarding the usage of the `MetricRegistry` class. Instead, this section will explain the main uses of the API and its annotations to allow you to understand how to use the technology with confidence. We encourage you to review the Java documentation for MicroProfile Metrics if you wish to completely master everything.

In this section, we'll cover how to instrument each metric programmatically and with annotations. This will be followed by an example of the output of the `/metrics` endpoint in Prometheus exposition format. Preceding that, we will cover the technical aspects of the metric registry, metadata, tags, and `MetricID`. They provide the fundamental knowledge needed to effectively instrument metrics.

As you may recall from the *MicroProfile Metrics technology overview* section, the metric registry is the nexus of operation for the MicroProfile Metrics runtime. Unless you are strictly using annotations to instrument metrics in your microservice, you will need to obtain a `MetricRegistry` (CDI) bean. It is through this `MetricRegistry` that we can create, register, and retrieve metrics programmatically. Even if you are strictly using annotations to instrument metrics, you will be interacting with `MetricRegistry` under the covers.

This section contains a large amount of content. The following is a summary of what we will be covering:

- Obtaining a metric registry
- Creating, registering, and retrieving metrics:

  a) Metatadata, tags, and MetricIDs

  b) Counter

  c) Concurrent gauge

  d) Meter

  e) Timer and simple timer

  f) Gauge

- The `@Metric` annotation

Let's get started!

Obtaining a metric registry

To obtain `MetricRegistry`, we can use injection, as demonstrated in the following code sample:

```
@Inject
MetricRegistry metricRegistry;
```

Remember that there are three types of metric registry scopes: the base metric registry, the vendor metric registry, and the application metric registry. By default, when you inject a `MetricRegistry` into your application, the MicroProfile Metrics runtime will provide an application registry. You can inject the other types of registries if you wish. You will need to annotate your injection with a `@RegistryType` and with an annotation parameter specifying the type of registry to inject. The following example illustrates the usage of `@RegistryType`, where we specify the type as `MetricRegistry.Type.Application`:

```
@Inject
@RegistryType(type=MetricRegistry.Type.APPLICATION)
MetricRegistry metricRegistry;
```

You can inject a base metric registry and a vendor metric registry if you specify a `@RegistryType(type=MetricRegistry.Type.BASE)` or `@RegistryType(type=MetricRegistry.Type.VENDOR)` annotation, respectively. However, in your application, you should NOT be registering metrics or manipulating the base or vendor metrics. These two metric registries should only be used to retrieve the metrics so that you can view their data.

Note About `MetricRegistry` and Annotation Usage

When using annotations to instrument metrics, you will only be interacting with the application metric registry. You will not be able to choose which `MetricRegistry` the metric annotations apply to.

Creating, registering, and retrieving metrics

Using `MetricRegistry`, you can create and register metrics using specific methods for each metric type. Each metric type, except for Gauge, will have the following method signatures. Invoking such methods from `MetricRegistry` will create, register, and return an instance of that metric if a metric with the given name, metadata, and tags does not already exist in the registry. If one does exist, then that existing metric is returned. It should be noted that using metric annotations, except for the gauge annotation, works similarly. We will demonstrate the method's signature pattern with the `Counter` metric type:

```
Counter counter(String name);
```

```
Counter counter (String name, Tag... tags);
```

```
Counter counter (MetricID metricID);
```

```
Counter counter (Metadata metadata);
```

```
Counter counter (Metadata metadata, Tag... tags);
```

The method names for the other metric types are `concurrentGauge`, `timer`, `simpleTimer`, `histogram`, and `meter`. We will demonstrate the various usages of these methods in the metric-specific sections. Gauge also has its own set of methods that `MetricRegistry` provides, but we will cover those in the *Gauge* section.

> **Note on Metric Reusability**
>
> Whether you're using `MetricRegistry` or the metric annotations to instrument your metrics, you can reuse an existing metric by specifying matching metadata or `MetricID` values.

To only retrieve metrics, you can call one of the `getMetrics()`, `getCounters()`, `getGauges()`, `getConcurrentGauges()`, `getHistograms()`, `getMeters()`, `getTimers()`, or `getSimpleTimers()` methods from `MetricRegistry`. These calls will return a map of the desired metrics, with `MetricID` as the key.

There are other methods for creating, registering, retrieving, and deleting metrics from the metric registry, some of which use a `MetricFilter`, as well as other methods concerning retrieving metadata and metric IDs. You can even create your own implementation of the metrics and register that over the instances provided by the MicroProfile Metrics runtime. However, these methods will not be covered as there a simply too many! We encourage you to review the Java documentation of the `MetricRegistry` class. The information we've provided so far regarding the use of `MetricRegistry` s is to help you understand the subsequent sections.

Metadata, tags, and MetricIDs

As you may have noticed in the previous section, metadata, tags, and MetricIDs can and will be used in your application code by the metric registry. However, we must understand how to create and use them before we can learn how to instrument and utilize the different metrics.

Every metric must contain metadata information. As you may recall, metadata information consists of its name, metric type, unit of measurement, a description, and a display name. The required fields from this set are the name and the metric type. The other metadata fields are optional. All this information is encompassed in a `Metadata` object. Every field in the `Metadata` object is a `String`. For the metric type field, you will need to specify an enum value from a `MetricType` enum. For the unit field, you will need to specify one of the static fields in `MetricUnits`.

If you are instrumenting multi-dimensional metrics, then you will also need to provide tags for your metrics. Every tag is a key-value pair of `String` values and is represented by a `Tag` object. The tag's name must match the `[a-zA-Z_] [a-zA-Z0-9_]*` regex. The value of the tag can be anything. A metric can contain 0 or more tags. This `Tag` is then set into a `MetricID` that also contains the `String` name of the metric.

Note About Configurable Tags

Using MicroProfile Config, we can define two config values for setting tag values to all the metrics in the MicroProfile Metrics runtime. `mp.metrics.appName` takes a single string value that is used to identify the application's name. This will be appended to all the metrics as a key-value tag in the form of `_app=<application_name>`. The `mp.metrics.tags` config allows a comma-separated list of key-value tags to be defined in the form of `tag1=value1,tag2=value2`. These tags will then be applied to all metrics.

Using metadata and tags programmatically

When instrumenting metrics programmatically, we need to create a `Metadata` object. To accomplish this, we need to retrieve `MetadataBuilder` by invoking the static `Metadata.builder()` method. Using this `MetadataBuilder`, we can construct a `Metadata` object using a builder pattern. At the very minimum, we will want to specify its name and metric type. In the following example, we won't be registering any metrics, so we will use the `MetricType.INVALID` metric type. When we demonstrate how to instrument each of the individual metrics in the rest of this section, we will use the appropriate `MetricType` there:

```
@Inject
MetricRegistry metricRegistry;

public void metaDataExample() {
  Metadata metadata = Metadata.builder()
  .withName("testMetadata")
  .withType(MetricType.INVALID)
  .build();
  }
```

To create a `Metadata` object with all the fields specified, you can do the following. Once again, as this example is for the sake of demonstration, we will use the `MetricUnits.NONE` value. Since the upcoming sections will not be using the unit field heavily, we encourage you to explore the available unit values available by reviewing the source file at `https://bit.ly/3ds4IDK`. The following example also includes the use of tags and a `MetricID`. Creating a `Tag` is a simple process in that you invoke the `Tag` constructor with the `String` name and value parameters. You can then construct a `MetricID` by passing the metric name and a variable-length amount of `Tag` parameters into the `MetricID` constructor.

The full source code for `MetricsResource` can be found at `https://bit.ly/2UzoczI`:

```
@ApplicationScoped
@Path("/metricsResource")
public class MetricsResource {

    @Inject
    MetricRegistry metricRegistry;
```

```
public void metadataTagMetricIDExample() {

    String metricName = "myMetric";
    Metadata metadata = Metadata.builder()
    .withName(metricName)
    .withType(MetricType.INVALID)
    .withDisplayName("Human readable display name")
    .withDescription("This metadata example"
            + " demonstrates how to create a"
            + " Metadata object")
    .withUnit(MetricUnits.NONE).build();

    Tag tag = new Tag("tagKey", "tagValue");
    Tag anotherTag = new Tag("anotherTag", "tagValue");

    MetricID metricID = new MetricID(metricName, tag,
        anotherTag);
}
}
```

Using a combination of MetricIDs, tags, and metadata, you can create, register, and retrieve metrics from `MetricRegistry`. As you may recall from the previous section, which listed the different method signatures, `MetricID` and `Metadata` are never used together as arguments. However, we know that the metric registry uses both to classify and identify the registered metrics. This is because the metric registry will be able to infer the minimum necessary data to construct the other object, whether it be `MetricID` or metadata, during processing.

Using metadata and tags with annotations

When instrumenting metrics with annotations, the metadata and tags are provided through the annotation parameters. It is possible to not have to specify any parameters at all. The MicroProfile Metrics runtime, when using CDI, can infer the necessary information. This type of annotation already provides a metric type and if no name is provided, then a name is generated using the package name, class name, and method name. Alternatively, in a situation where the annotation is used on a constructor, it will be a combination of the package name, class name, and constructor name (that is, the class name again!).

Even if a name is supplied, the full metric name is a combination of the class name and the metric name. However, this may prove undesirable. To address this, each metric annotation parameter contains an `absolute` parameter, which you can set to `true` so that the metric uses the provided metric name.

To demonstrate how to provide the metadata information with annotations, the following code snippet will use the Counter class' `@Counted` annotation:

```
@ApplicationScoped
@Path("/metricsResource")
public class MetricsResource {

    @Counted(name="sample.metric", displayName="sample
        metric", description="This sample counter metric
            illustrates how to instrument a metric annotation",
                unit=MetricUnits.NONE, absolute=true, tags=
                    {"tag1=value1", "tag2=value2")
    public void someMethod() {
        //logic
    }
}
```

As we can see, `name`, `displayName`, and `description` parameters exist that accept `String` values. The `absolute` parameter accepts a `Boolean` value. The unit accepts a static field from `MetricUnits`, and tags are accepted as a list of `String` values in *key-value* format.

Counter

We've finally arrived at our first metric: the counter. The counter metric, as its name suggests, is a metric that keeps count of the metrics. The counter can only monotonically increase. You can use this to keep track of how many times a method or block of business logic has been invoked, or the number of times a request was received or sent.

Instrumenting counters programmatically

The following code sample demonstrates how to create and retrieve a counter metric named `counterMetric` using two `GET` requests. In the first `GET` resource, the `/counter1` URI, we create `counterMetric` by invoking `MetricRegistry.counter(Metadata metadata, Tags... tags)`. This will return a new counter metric that we can increment by calling `counter.inc()`, which increments the counter by 1. In the second `GET` resource, the `/counter2` URI, we do something different and call `MetricRegistry.counter(MetricID metricID)`. Here, `MetricID` matches the `MetricID` property that was generated by the metric registry when we first created and registered `counterMetric`. Since it already exists, we are returned the existing `counterMetric` using the metric registry. We then increment it by calling the `inc(long value)` method to increment the counter by a specified amount. In our example, we increment it by 3. In both `GET` resources, we return a string that includes the current count of the counter by invoking `getCount()`.

The full source code for `CounterResource` can be found at `https://bit.ly/2XGDDXZ`:

```
@GET
@Path("/counter1")
public String getCounter1(){

    Metadata counterMetadata = Metadata.builder()
            .withName(COUNTER_METRIC_NAME)
            .withType(MetricType.COUNTER).build();

    Counter counter = metricRegistry
            .counter(counterMetadata, COUNTER_TAG);
    counter.inc(); //increments by one

    return "A counter metric has been created and
        incremented" + "by 1, the total is now " +
            counter.getCount();   }

@GET
@Path("/counter2")
public String getCounter2(){
    MetricID counterMetricID = new
        MetricID(COUNTER_METRIC_NAME,
```

```
            COUNTER_TAG);
    Counter counter =
      metricRegistry.counter(counterMetricID);


    counter.inc(3);


    return "A counter metric was retrieve and
      incremented" + " by 3, the total is now " +
        counter.getCount();
}
```

Now, let's see what happens when we send requests to both GET resources and then view the results through /metrics/application/counterMetric directly:

```
$ curl http://localhost:9080/ch6/counterResource/counter1
A counter metric has been created and incremented by 1, the
total is now 1
```

```
$ curl http://localhost:9080/ch6/counterResource/counter2
A counter metric was retrieve and incremented by 3, the
total  is now 4
$ curl http://localhost:9080/metrics/application/counterMetric
# TYPE application_counterMetric_total counter
application_counterMetric_total{metricType="counter"} 4
```

In the output, we issue GET requests to the /ch6/counterResource/ counter1 and /ch6/counterResource/counter2 endpoints and the counter metric is incremented by 1 and 3, respectively. We then issue a GET request to / metrics/application/counterMetric to view the Prometheus formatted output of our counter metric directly. application_counterMetric_ total{metricType="counter"} is returned, which represents the counter metric with its tag of metricType="counter". It holds a value of 4, as expected.

Note About Prometheus Formatting with Counters

Counter metrics in Prometheus exposition format will have the _total suffix appended to the metric name.

Instrumenting counters with annotations

Using annotations is a much simpler affair. You can annotate the `@Counted` annotation on either a method, constructor, or even a whole class. When the annotated element is invoked, the counter is incremented by 1.

In our example, we'll annotate the `MetricsResource` class with `@Counted`. When a metric annotation is annotated on a class, it will apply to all applicable targets in the class for that annotation. For `@Counted`, this means that all the constructors and methods will be instrumented. This example will also demonstrate the metric names that are generated. Note that since we are using annotations, we do not need to inject `MetricRegistry`.

The full source code for `CounterAnnotatedResource` can be found at `https://bit.ly/3iZiL6D`:

```
@ApplicationScoped
@Path("/counterResource")
@Counted
public class CounterAnnotatedResource {

    @GET
    @Path("/getResource")
    public String getResource() {
        return "Counting the class";
    }
}
```

Let's take the application for a drive. We'll omit showing the `curl` command to the application's REST endpoint and just show the output of querying `/metrics/application`:

```
$ curl http://localhost:9080/metrics/application
# TYPE application_metrics_demo_CounterAnnotatedResource
_getResource_total counter
application_metrics_demo_CounterAnnotatedResource_getResource_
total 1
# TYPE application_metrics_demo_CounterAnnotatedResource
_CounterAnnotatedResource_total counter
application_metrics_demo_CounterAnnotatedResource_
CounterAnnotatedResource_total 1
```

After issuing a single `GET` request to `/ch6/counterResource/getResource`, we should see the aforementioned values when viewing the metric data on the `/metrics/application` endpoint. `application_metrics_demo_ CounterAnnotatedResource_getResource_total` is the counter metric that was created for the `getResource()` method, while `application_metrics_demo_ CounterAnnotatedResource_CounterAnnotatedResource_total` is the counter metric that was created for the constructor of the class. Both values are *1*, as expected.

Concurrent gauge

The concurrent gauge metric is a metric that's used to count the parallel invocation of the instrumented component. Its values can increase or decrease. This metric can be used to count the number of parallel invocations of a method, business logic, requests, and more. Besides counting parallel invocations, the concurrent gauge metric also keeps track of the highest and lowest count that's been recorded within the previously **completed full minute**. A completed full minute denotes the period from 0:00:00.9999999 to 0:00:59.99999999 on the clock. A completed full minute does not mean the last 60 seconds from the current instantaneous time.

Instrumenting concurrent gauges programmatically

In this section, we'll demonstrate how to use a concurrent gauge. They are typically invoked in parallel using a `Runnable` named `sleeper`. This creates – and subsequently retrieves – a concurrent gauge named `concurrentGaugeMetric`. In this example, we will use `MetricRegistry.concurrentGauge(String name)` in our interaction with the metric registry. This is the simplest creation or retrieval method provided by the metric registry as you only need to provide the name. This infers that there are no tags associated with this metric. The sleeper `Runnable` will then increment the concurrent gauge (for example, with `inc()`), sleep for 10 seconds, and then decrement it (for example, with `dec()`). You can only increment or decrement by 1. We'll make parallel invocations using a `for` loop and an `ExecutorService`. However, what's not shown in this code example are the getter methods for the three values; that is, `getCount()`, `getMin()`, and `getMax()`.

The full source code for `ConcurrentGaugeResource` can be found at `https://bit.ly/3ghFyZz`:

```
@GET
@Path("/concurrentGauge")
public String getConcurrentGage() {
    ExecutorService executorService =
```

```
        Executors.newCachedThreadPool();

        Runnable sleeper = () -> {
            ConcurrentGauge concurrentGauge =
                metricRegistry.concurrentGauge
                  (CONCURRENTGAUGE_METRIC_NAME);
            concurrentGauge.inc();
            try {
                Thread.sleep(10000);
            } catch (InterruptedException e) {
                e.printStackTrace();
            }
            concurrentGauge.dec();
        };

        for (int i = 0; i < 10; i++) {
            executorService.submit(sleeper);
        }

        return "Concurrent Gauge created and invoked in
            parallel";
    }
```

For this example, we will send a GET request called /ch6/
concurrentGaugeResource/concurrentGauge. Once the current minute has
completed, we will view the output via /metrics/application:

```
$ curl http://localhost:9080/ch6/concurrentGaugeResource
/concurrentGauge
Concurrent Gauge created and invoked in parallel

$ curl http://localhost:9080/metrics/application
# TYPE application_concurrentGaugeMetric_current gauge
application_concurrentGaugeMetric_current 10
# TYPE application_concurrentGaugeMetric_min gauge
```

```
application_concurrentGaugeMetric_min 0
# TYPE application_concurrentGaugeMetric_max gauge
application_concurrentGaugeMetric_max 0
## after a complete full minute...
$ curl http://localhost:9080/metrics/application
# TYPE application_concurrentGaugeMetric_current gauge
application_concurrentGaugeMetric_current 0
# TYPE application_concurrentGaugeMetric_min gauge
application_concurrentGaugeMetric_min 0
# TYPE application_concurrentGaugeMetric_max gauge
application_concurrentGaugeMetric_max 10
```

In the preceding output, we issued a GET request to /ch6/
concurrentGaugeResource/concurrentGauge. We then followed up with
a GET request, /metrics/application, to view the output. application_
concurrentGaugeMetric_current shows the current value, which is 10, as
expected. application_concurrentGaugeMetric_max and application_
concurrentGaugeMetric_min, which show the maximum and minimum recorded
values of the previous full minute, are 0, as expected. After the current full minute has
completed, we view the results again and we see that the current, max, and min values are
0, 0, and 10, as expected.

> **Note About Metrics with Multiple Values**
>
> The concurrent gauge is our first metric with multiple output values. To display
> all the values with the same metric name, each value of the metric is given its
> own suffix. We will see this pattern in other complex metrics later.

Immediately after our GET request to /ch6/concurrentGaugeResource/
concurrentGaugeParallel, we will see that the current count for the concurrent
gauge is 10. When the 10 seconds have elapsed for each thread and a full minute has
passed, we will see that the current value is 0 and that the maximum value is 10.

Instrumenting concurrent gauges with annotations

To instrument a concurrent gauge with annotations, you must use the
@ConcurrentGauge annotation. This applies to methods, constructors, and classes.
The concurrent gauge annotation will increment when the target is invoked and
decrement when it is finished.

We'll demonstrate the usage of `@ConcurrentGauge` in a similar fashion to the programmatic example. The `sleeper` runnable will invoke the `sleeper()` method, which is annotated with the `@ConcurrentGauge` annotation. In this example, we will specify `absolute=true`, which will then cause the MicroProfile Metrics runtime to use the metric's name. The `/metrics/*` output will be the same as it was for the programmatic example, so it will not be shown here.

The full source code for `ConcurrentGaugeAnnotatedResource` can be found at `https://bit.ly/3xZZhD0`:

```
@GET
@Path("/concurrentGuage")
public String getConcurrentGauge(){
    ExecutorService executorService =
      Executors.newCachedThreadPool();

    Runnable sleeper = () -> sleeper();

    for (int i = 0; i < 10; i++) {
        executorService.submit(sleeper);
    }

    return "Concurrent Gauge created and invoked in
      parallel";
}


@ConcurrentGauge(name = CONCURRENTGAUGE_METRIC_NAME,
   absolute = true)
public void sleeper() {
    try {
        Thread.sleep(10000);
    } catch (InterruptedException e) {
        e.printStackTrace();
    }
}
```

Histogram

The histogram metric, like a histogram graph, processes the data it has been provided with in a statistical distribution. A histogram metric outputs 12 values: count, sum, minimum value, maximum value, mean, standard deviation, and the 50th, 75th, 95th, 98th, 99th, and 99.9^{th} percentiles. Unlike the other metrics, the histogram metric can only be instrumented programmatically. There is no annotation support. You might use a histogram metric to record and calculate the distribution of the sizes of data that your application receives
for processing.

For our demonstration, we'll generate 1,000 random numbers within the range *0-999* and feed them into our histogram. This time, we will use `metricRegistry. histogram(Metadata metadata)` to create our histogram. We won't be showing the `getCount()`, `getSum()`, and `getSnapshot()` getter methods here, which return `Snapshot` objects that contain the getter methods for the remaining statistical values. As this would be too lengthy to list, you can view the `Snapshot` class and its methods here: `https://bit.ly/2QndNFf`.

The full source code for `HistogramResource` can be found at `https://bit. ly/3y4AoWK`:

```
@GET
@Path("/histogram")
public String getHistogram()  {
  Metadata histogramMetadata = Metadata.builder()
  .withName(HISTOGRAM_METRIC_NAME)
  .withUnit(MetricUnits.MILLISECONDS)
  .withDescription("This histogram tracks random
    millesconds")
  .withType(MetricType.HISTOGRAM).build();

  Histogram histogram =
    metricRegistry.histogram(histogramMetadata);

  Random random = new Random();
  for (int i = 0; i < 1000 ; i++) {
      int randomInt = random.nextInt(1000);
      histogram.update(randomInt);
  }
```

```
    int count = (int) histogram.getCount(); //returns
        long value of count
    Snapshot snapshot = histogram.getSnapshot(); //rest
        of the stats

    return "Histogram created/retrieved and is tracking
        random milliseconds";
    }
}
```

Let's see what results we get:

```
$ curl http://localhost:9080/ch6/histogramResource
/histogram
Histogram created/retrieved and is tracking random milliseconds
$ curl http://localhost:9080/metrics/application
# TYPE application_histogramMetric_mean_seconds gauge
application_histogramMetric_mean_seconds 0.5048109999999999
# TYPE application_histogramMetric_max_seconds gauge
application_histogramMetric_max_seconds 0.998
# TYPE application_histogramMetric_min_seconds gauge
application_histogramMetric_min_seconds 0.0
# TYPE application_histogramMetric_stddev_seconds gauge
application_histogramMetric_stddev_seconds 0.2884925116515156
# TYPE application_histogramMetric_seconds summary
# HELP application_histogramMetric_seconds This histogram
tracks random millesconds
application_histogramMetric_seconds_count 1000
application_histogramMetric_seconds_sum 504.81100000000004
application_histogramMetric_seconds{quantile="0.5"} 0.507
application_histogramMetric_seconds{quantile="0.75"} 0.755
application_histogramMetric_seconds{quantile="0.95"}
0.9510000000000001
application_histogramMetric_seconds{quantile="0.98"} 0.974
application_histogramMetric_seconds{quantile="0.99"} 0.981
application_histogramMetric_seconds{quantile="0.999"} 0.995
```

In the preceding output, we issued a GET request to /ch6/histogramResource/ histogram and we followed up with a GET request to /metrics/application to view the results. As expected, the count is 1,000, as reported by the application_ histogramMetric_seconds_count value. The remaining metric values are the calculated values. As there are a large number of values, we will not be explicitly covering all of them. The names provided for the metric values are self-explanatory to indicate what values they represent.

> **Note About Prometheus Formatting with Histograms**
>
> If a unit has been defined, the metric name is appended to the unit as _<unit>. Prometheus only accepts certain **base units**, so the MicroProfile Metrics runtime will scale the value to the appropriate base unit. For example, if milliseconds were specified as the unit, the values will be scaled to a base unit of seconds.
>
> Also, notice that the quantile metric values share the same name but use tags to identify which percentile it is representing.

Meter

The meter metric, like the histogram metric, aggregates input values and performs calculations to produce results. Instead of statistical distributions, the meter calculates rates in units per second. The unit that's specified for the metric will be ignored. This only applies to the Prometheus output. The meter outputs the mean rate and the 1, 5, and 15-minute exponentially weighted moving average rates. Meter can be useful for monitoring the traffic on a specific method or component in your microservice.

Instrumenting meters programmatically

In our example, we'll demonstrate using the meter metric to monitor the rate of requests to two GET resources: /meter and /meter2. With the first GET resource, we will use the last variant of the register/retrieve methods that we have yet to use with MetricRegistry.meter(String metricName, Tags... tags). Once the metric has been created or retrieved, we will invoke the mark() method, which increases the meter's recorded hits by 1. With the second GET resource, we can pass a long parameter value so that we can invoke mark(long value), which increments the number of hits to the meter by the specified value. Notice that we use MetricID in the /meter2 GET resource to retrieve the metric we created and registered in the /meter resource.

The full source code for `MeterResource` can be found at `https://bit.ly/3ASCV8j`:

```
private final Tag METER_TAG = new Tag("metricType",
  "meter");


@GET
@Path("/meter")
public String getMeter(){
 Meter meter = metricRegistry.meter(METER_METRIC_NAME,
   METER_TAG);
    meter.mark();
    return "Meter created/retrieved and marked by 1";
}


@GET
@Path("/meter2")
public String getMeter2(@QueryParam("value")
  @DefaultValue("1") int value){
    MetricID meterMetricID = new
      MetricID(METER_METRIC_NAME, METER_TAG);
    Meter meter = metricRegistry.meter(meterMetricID);
    meter.mark(value);
    return "Meter created/retrieved and marked by " +
      value;
  }
}
```

Not shown are the getter methods for the values; that is, `getCount()`, `getMeanRate()`, `getOneMinuteRate()`, `getFiveMinuteRate()`, and `getFifteenMinuteRate()`. Let's run through hitting both `GET` resources and view the result at `/metrics/application`:

```
$ curl http://localhost:9080/ch6/meterResource/meter
Meter created/retrieved and marked by 1
$ curl http://localhost:9080/ch6/meterResource/meter2?value=3
Meter created/retrieved and marked by 3
$ curl http://localhost:9080/metrics/application
# TYPE application_histogramMetric_total counter
```

```
application_histogramMetric_total{metricType="meter"} 4
# TYPE application_histogramMetric_rate_per_second gauge
application_histogramMetric_rate_per_second{metricType="meter"}
0.4348951236275281
# TYPE application_histogramMetric_one_min_rate_per_second
gauge
application_histogramMetric_one_min_rate_per_
second{metricType="meter"} 0.8
# TYPE application_histogramMetric_five_min_rate_per_second
gauge
application_histogramMetric_five_min_rate_per_
second{metricType="meter"} 0.8
# TYPE application_histogramMetric_fifteen_min_rate_per
_second gauge
application_histogramMetric_fifteen_min_rate_per_
second{metricType="meter"} 0.8
```

In the preceding output, we issued a GET request to /ch6/meterResource/ meter,
which increments the meter by 1, followed by a GET request to /ch6/meterResource/
meter2, supplying it with a parameter value to increment the meter by 3. We then
viewed the resulting output in /metrics/application. application_
histogramMetric_total shows that the count is 4, as expected, and that the
remaining values are the calculated values. Once again, the names associated with the
remaining metric values are self-explanatory and will not be explicitly explained.

Instrumenting meters with annotations

To instrument a meter metric with annotations, you must use the @Metered annotation.
This annotation applies to methods, constructors, and classes. Like other annotated
metrics, only a single value is incremented by using the annotation. We'll demonstrate a
sample that uses the @Metered annotation and omit showing the results.

The full source code for MeterAnnotatedResource can be found at https://bit.
ly/3mhnHpk:

```
@GET
@Path("/meter")
@Metered(name=METER_METRIC_NAME, tags={"metricType=meter"})
public String getMeterWithAnnotations() {
    return "Meter created/retrieved and marked by 1
        with annotations";
}
```

Timer and simple timer

Since both the timer and simple timer metrics are very similar, we will demonstrate how to use both metrics together.

The **timer** metric, as its name implies, records the time spent going through the instrumented component. At its core, it keeps track of the total elapsed time. Additionally, it provides the throughput/rate from the hits recorded, as well as the statistical distribution of the recorded times. These outputted values are the same as they are for the histogram and meter metrics.

The **simple timer** metric, on the other hand, is a timer but with the extra bells and whistles stripped off. It only reports on the count, total elapsed time, and, like the concurrent gauge, the highest and lowest recorded time of the previous complete full minute. If you don't require all the extra values that the timer provides, or intend to calculate them yourself later, the simple timer should be your metric of choice.

Instrumenting timers and simple timers programmatically

In our example, we'll instrument a timer and a simple timer in their own GET resources. In both resources, we will provide an example of how to record time using the Context object. This allows us to explicitly mark the beginning and end of what we want to time by calling the time() method from either the timer or simple timer, to start timing, and then calling the Context object's close() method to stop timing. Note that the Context object is an inner interface of both the Timer and SimpleTimer classes, and that you will need to use the appropriate Context object. Both the timer and simple timer metrics can time the execution of a Runnable or Callable object or lambda expression. The following two code snippets are from the same TimersResource class, and the full source code can be found at https://bit.ly/37YaWYy.

The following code snippet shows the GET resource known as /timer, which demonstrates timing with a Runnable object with the timer metric:

```
@GET
@Path("/timer")
public String getTimer() {

    Timer timer = metricRegistry.timer(TIMER_METRIC_NAME);
    Timer.Context timerContext = timer.time();
    timerContext.close();
    Runnable runnableTimer = () -> {
        try {
```

```
                    Thread.sleep(2000);
             } catch (InterruptedException e) {
                 e.printStackTrace();
             }
        };


        // Time a Runnable
        timer.time(runnableTimer);
        return "Timer created/retrieved and recorded total
            elapsed time of " + timer.getElapsedTime();
    }
```

The following code snippet shows the GET resource called /simpleTimer, which demonstrates timing with a Callable object with the simple timer metric:

```
@GET
@Path("/simpleTimer")
public String getSimpleTimer(){

    SimpleTimer simpleTimer =
      metricRegistry.simpleTimer(SIMPLETIMER_METRIC_NAME);
    SimpleTimer.Context simpleTimerContext =
      simpleTimer.time();
    simpleTimerContext.close();


    // Time a Callable
    Callable<String> callable = () -> {
        Thread.sleep(2000);
        return "Finished Callable";
    };
    simpleTimer.time(callable);


    return "SimpleTimer created/retrieved and recorded
        total elapsed time of " + simpleTimer
          .getElapsedTime();
}
```

Not shown are the getter methods for the metric values. For the timer, you can call getCount(), getElapsedTime(), getSnapshot(), getMeanRate(), getOneMinuteRate(), getFiveMinuteRate(), and getFifteenMinuteRate(). For the simple timer, you can call getCount(), getElapsedTime(), getMinTimeDuration(), and getMaxTimeDuration().

Let's call both GET resources and see the results:

```
$ curl http://localhost:9080/ch6/timersResource/timer
Timer created/retrieved and recorded total elapsed time of 2001
milliseconds
$ curl http://localhost:9080/ch6/timersResource/simpleTimer
SimpleTimer created/retrieved and recorded total elapsed time
of 2000 milliseconds
$ curl http://localhost:9080/metrics/application
# TYPE application_simpleTimerMetric_total counter
application_simpleTimerMetric_total 1
# TYPE application_simpleTimerMetric_elapsedTime_seconds gauge
application_simpleTimerMetric_elapsedTime_seconds
2.0005379000000003
# TYPE application_simpleTimerMetric_maxTimeDuration
_seconds gauge
application_simpleTimerMetric_maxTimeDuration_seconds NaN
# TYPE application_simpleTimerMetric_minTimeDuration
_seconds gauge
application_simpleTimerMetric_minTimeDuration_seconds NaN
```

First, we issue `GET` requests to `/ch6/timersResource/timer` and `/ch6/timersResource/simpleTimer` to invoke both of our timers. We then send a request to `/metrics/application` to view the results. As we have already demonstrated the similar max and min behavior of the concurrent gauge, we will not be demonstrating that behavior for the simple timer here. Additionally, as the timer metric outputs a statistical distribution of the recorded times (which includes the total recorded durations) and the throughput of requests, similar to the histogram and meter metrics, the timer metric's output will be omitted. What remains is the output for the simple timer. Notice that the values for `application_simpleTimerMetric_maxTimeDuration_seconds` and `application_simpleTimerMetric_minTimeDuration_seconds` report NaN. This is because there are no recorded values for the previously completed minute. If you would like to view the full output, we encourage you to try out the samples directly. Take a look at the *Technical requirements* section at the beginning of this chapter for instructions on how to run the samples.

Instrumenting timers and simple timers with annotations

To instrument the timer and simple timer metric, you will need to use `@Timed` and `@SimplyTimed`, respectively. These annotations apply to methods, constructors, and classes. They will both record how long it takes to execute the target annotated element.

We will show a simple example demonstrating how to annotate `@Timed` and `@SimplyTimed` on a JAX-RS endpoint.

The full source code for `TimersAnnotatedResource` can be found at `https://bit.ly/3xVroDb`:

```
@GET
@Path("/timers")
@Timed(name=ANNOTATED_TIMER_METRIC_NAME)
@SimplyTimed(name= ANNOTATED_SIMPLETIMER_METRIC_NAME)
public String getTimerWithAnnotations() {
    //some business logic to time
    return "Timer with annotations";
}
```

Gauges

A gauge metric serves to report on some value that is provided by the application. This can be any value, but it is highly recommended that the value is a number as Prometheus only supports numeric gauges. This is not a limitation of JSON output. Additionally, you can only create a numeric gauge using the metric registry's methods for creating a gauge.

Instrumenting gauges programmatically

As we mentioned earlier, the gauge metric does not follow the same pattern of the registration and retrieval method signatures like the other metrics do. This is due to the nature of what the gauge metric does. When registering or retrieving a gauge, you will need to specify a `Supplier` or `Function` object or lambda expression.

The following are the method signatures for registering or retrieving a gauge metric:

```
<T, R extends Number> Gauge<R> gauge(String name, T object,
Function<T, R> func, Tag... tags);
<T, R extends Number> Gauge<R> gauge(MetricID metricID, T
object, Function<T, R> func);
```

```
<T, R extends Number> Gauge<R> gauge(Metadata metadata, T
object, Function<T, R> func, Tag... tags);
```

```
<T, R extends Number> Gauge<R> gauge(Metadata metadata, T
object, Function<T, R> func, Tag... tags);
```

```
<T extends Number> Gauge<T> gauge(MetricID metricID,
Supplier<T> supplier);
```

```
<T extends Number> Gauge<T> gauge(Metadata metadata,
Supplier<T> supplier, Tag... tags);
```

The only notable method you can call with the gauge metric is `getValue()`. Since you should be familiar with the usage of the `MetricID` class, the `Metadata` class, how to create a metric, and Java functions (which we assume you are familiar with), we will not be providing any example code for instrumenting the gauge metric programmatically.

Instrumenting gauges with annotations

To instrument a gauge metric, you will need to use the `@Gauge` annotation. This annotation can only be applied to a method. With the gauge annotation, you must specify the unit parameter. We will show a simple example where the method, and therefore the gauge, will return the current millisecond since the last epoch.

The full source code for `GaugeResource` can be found at `https://bit.ly/3mfj6Ux`:

```
@ApplicationScoped
@Path("/metricsResource")
public class MyMetricsResource {

    @Gauge(name="time.since.epoch", unit =
      MetricUnits.MILLISECONDS)
    public long getGaugeWithAnnotations() {
        return System.currentTimeMillis();
    }
}
```

We'll assume that a `GET` request invokes this method, so we'll just show the resulting `/metrics/application` output here:

```
$ curl http://localhost:9080/metrics/application
# TYPE application_metrics_demo_gaugeResource_time_since
_epoch_seconds gauge
application_metrics_demo_gaugeResource_time_since_epoch
_seconds 1.6181035765080001E9
```

> **Note About Prometheus Formatting with Gauges**
>
> The unit that's defined for the gauge is appended as `_<unit>` and is scaled to the appropriate base unit.

The @Metric annotation

The `@Metric` annotation is a unique annotation that allows you to inject a metric that corresponds to the field or parameter type that it is being annotated on. The `@Metric` annotation contains the same annotation parameters as the other metric annotations. It will return a metric with the matching metadata, if it exists; otherwise, a new metric of the specified type will be created, registered, and injected. Let's look at an example of using both injection strategies.

The full source code for `MetricsResource` can be found at `https://bit.ly/3iBAz7E`:

```
@Inject
@Metric(name="fieldInjectedCounter")
Counter fieldInjectedCounter;


Counter parameterInjectedCounter;
@Inject
public void setCounterMetric(@Metric(name =
    "parameterInjectedCounter") Counter
      parameterInjectedCounter) {
    this.parameterInjectedCounter =
      parameterInjectedCounter;
}
```

In the aforementioned example, `fieldInjectedCounter` is injected with field injection and `parameterInjectedCounter` is injected with parameter injection.

Visualizing metric data with Prometheus and Grafana

The MicroProfile Metrics runtime can only report on instantaneous metric values. To effectively use this data for monitoring purposes, we need to aggregate that data with a tool such as Prometheus. Then, using a tool such as Grafana, we can create a wide variety of visualizations that present the metric data over a configurable time period. Prometheus can scrape data from multiple sources and Grafana will then pull the data from it by performing queries against Prometheus using the **Prometheus Query Language (PromQL)**. This, of course, is not just limited to retrieving the metric data as-is – we can infer additional statistics by performing calculations on the data that we retrieve. This is made possible by a wide variety of functions provided by PromQL. In this subsection, we'll demonstrate the power of using Prometheus and Grafana to monitor your metric data using the optional base REST metric, known as `REST.request`, from the Broker microservice of the StockTrader application.

> **Understanding the `REST.request` Metric**
>
> The `REST.request` metric is a simple timer that is automatically instrumented to all REST endpoints by the MicroProfile Metrics runtime. The instrumented `REST.request` metrics are differentiated from each other with tags related to the class name and the method signature.

The Broker microservice

The Broker service contains multiple JAX-RS/REST endpoints for creating, retrieving, and deleting Broker objects, as well as retrieving portfolio returns with GET, POST, and DELETE requests. This all occurs in the AccountService class. The full source code can be found at https://bit.ly/3sBGvPE.

First, we'll look at the sample output of a REST.request metric so that we can understand the format of the metric name and its tags, before we demonstrate querying it with Grafana. We'll show the output of a GET endpoint that queries all accounts whose method is getAccounts(). The other base metrics – the max time and min time values and the metric description for REST.request – have been omitted from the output:

```
$ curl http://localhost:9080/metrics/base
# TYPE base_REST_request_total counter
base_REST_request_total{class="com.ibm.hybrid.cloud.sample.
stocktrader.account.AccountService",method="getAccounts"} 45
# TYPE application_simpleTimerMetric_elapsedTime_seconds gauge
base_REST_request_elapsedTime_seconds{class="com.
ibm.hybrid.cloud.sample.stocktrader.account.
AccountService",method="getAccounts"} 1.7304427800000002
```

Visualizing with Grafana

In Grafana, we can create a visualization out of each metric by querying the metric name. For example, we can simply query base_REST_request_total and Grafana will display all instances of that metric, which counts the request invocations to a REST endpoint. Alternatively, if we want to see only the metrics from a single microservice, such as AccountService, we can issue the following query:

```
base_REST_request_total{class=" com.ibm.hybrid.cloud.sample.
    stocktrader.account.AccountService"}
```

However, just the total count of a counter doesn't tell us much. We would be more interested in knowing how many times the metrics have increased in the past 10 minutes instead. Here, we can perform the following query:

```
increase(base_REST_request_total[10m]).
```

Or perhaps we want to know the rate at which requests have increased in the past 10 minutes:

```
rate(base_REST_request_total[10m])
```

When using a simple timer, what we would be most interested in is the timing data. However, the elapsed time by itself is nothing significant, but we can calculate a new value that may prove more useful. Using the elapsed time and count, we can calculate the average duration per request with the following query:

```
rate(base_REST_request_elapsedTime_seconds[10m]) / rate(base_
REST_request_total[10m]).
```

The following is a graphical visualization of the aforementioned query. The details of the snapshot are not important; the snapshot serves to illustrate the layout of what you would expect to see when using Grafana. The query is entered at the top, with the visualization displayed in the middle, and a table or list of the queried metrics at the bottom:

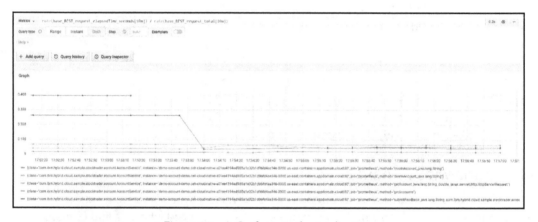

Figure 6.3 – A Grafana graph visualization

These examples only show a sliver of the potential of using Prometheus and Grafana. In the preceding figure, we only used a graph visualization. There are a wide variety of visualizations that exist that suit any specific visualization needs you may have. On top of that, there is a vast array of functions available to use with PromQL to calculate any specific values that you and your team may find useful. It should also be noted that the preceding figure only shows a direct view of a single visualization. Remember that you can build dashboards with multiple visualizations displayed all at once.

We've now come to the end of the MicroProfile Metrics section. With the metrics instrumented in your microservice, you can monitor different parts of your application in detail. In the next section, we'll learn how to observe requests that span multiple microservices with MicroProfile OpenTracing.

Tracing your cloud-native application using MicroProfile OpenTracing

We will conclude our MicroProfile observability journey by looking at the MicroProfile OpenTracing technology. Unlike the other two technologies we've examined in this chapter, MicroProfile OpenTracing is much more lightweight in comparison. We'll cover the importance of this technology while overviewing it and jump straight into learning how to use MicroProfile OpenTracing.

The importance of and an overview of MicroProfile OpenTracing in a cloud-native application

The MicroProfile OpenTracing technology ties in with the concept of **distributed tracing**. In a cloud environment, applications or microservices communicate and interact with one another, which, in turn, can interact with other microservices. This chain of interactions can be quite lengthy, depending on the nature and context of your application deployments. When something unexpectantly fails, it can be a difficult and troublesome task to diagnose where things have gone wrong in such a complex and distributed topology.

This is where distributed tracing comes in. Distributed tracing allows us to track and monitor requests or processes as it navigates from one application to another. Throughout its journey, which is referred to as a **trace**, performance data (for example, time spent), contextual data in the form of tags, and any important logs are retrieved for a **span**. A span defines the individual hierarchal segments that make up a **trace**. Each span can be identified by name.

For example, invoking a method creates a span named *method1*. This method can then invoke another method, which then creates a new **child span**, named *method2*, that is under the scope of the **parent span** from the first method. When the child span is complete (that is, the method finishes invoking), it returns to the first method and when the first method finishes, the trace is completed. There is no limit to how many child spans there can be. The resulting trace records are sent to an external tool or platform that gathers and stores these records, and can provide a way for us to view all the traces and the spans that it comprises.

It is through this that we can analyze and understand the performance and latency of a request, and any additional contextual information from individual spans, as it navigates through multiple microservices. With distributed tracing, we can easily profile the performance and latency of a request and diagnose any errors or failures that occur.

For distributed tracing to be effective in a system, all applications must use the same distributed tracing library. Now, you may be thinking that this is what MicroProfile OpenTracing serves to satisfy. This is not the case. The MicroProfile OpenTracing technology operates on top of the existing **OpenTracing** technology. The OpenTracing technology is a façade that defines a vendor-neutral API for instrumenting distributed tracing in an application. This OpenTracing technology is incorporated into the MicroProfile OpenTracing runtime. To be able to apply to trace instrumentation to your application, you will need to use a compatible **tracer** implementation. You can view the compatible tracers at `https://opentracing.io/docs/supported-tracers/`. However, note that the different MicroProfile OpenTracing runtimes are compatible with different sets of tracer libraries. Consult the documentation of your chosen runtime for more details. It can even be the case that your chosen runtime may support a tracer that isn't on OpenTracing's list of officially supported tracers.

Each application in the system will need to be configured to use the same tracer library. Different tracer libraries may differ in how they communicate the contextual identification data of a trace, which is called the **span context**. The span context contains stateful information that is accompanied by a request as it navigates through the network of microservices. This allows the OpenTracing technology to link spans together into a singular trace when they transcend application boundaries.

MicroProfile OpenTracing amends the OpenTracing technology by defining an additional `@Traced` annotation that complements the use of the OpenTracing technology. However, the main benefit of MicroProfile OpenTracing is that you can automatically instrument traces on inbound and outbound JAX-RS requests. Any JAX-RS application will be traced without the developer having to deal with the MicroProfile OpenTracing API or the OpenTracing API. We will not cover how to use the OpenTracing API in this book, only the amendments that MicroProfile OpenTracing provides. We leave it up to you to explore the OpenTracing API and its documentation at `https://bit.ly/3gEHLis`.

The producer of the implementation library may also provide a platform/server that aggregates the tracing records. We will demonstrate this with the Jaeger Tracing platform at the end of this section.

> **Special Note on OpenTracing**
>
> At the time of writing, the OpenTracing project has combined with OpenCensus to form OpenTelemetry. OpenTelemetry is an all-in-one technology that will satisfy your monitoring needs for tracing, logging, and metrics. Future iterations of the MicroProfile platform may see the incorporation of OpenTelemetry and its subcomponents.

Auto-instrumenting JAX-RS requests

MicroProfile OpenTracing allows you to automatically instrument tracing on JAX-RS requests on both the client and server side. When a request is sent through a JAX-RS client or using MicroProfile Rest Client, a span will be automatically created. If an active span already exists, then it will be a child span of the active span. This span begins when the request is sent by the client.

Similarly, when an incoming JAX-RS request is received, a span will be created. If the request is part of a trace, the MicroProfile OpenTracing runtime will automatically determine that by attempting to extract span context information from the incoming request. If such data exists, then the new span is a child span of a preceding span in this trace. If there are no active spans or extractable span context information, then a new span and, subsequently, a new trace is created. This span begins when the request is received and correlates with the JAX-RS resource method. This default behavior of auto-instrumentation on the JAX-RS resource method can be overridden with the use of the `@Traced` annotation, which will be covered in the *Instrumenting the @Traced annotation and injecting a Tracer* section.

There are some additional rules regarding names and tags that we will cover once we have described how to auto-instrument outbound and inbound JAX-RS requests.

Outbound JAX-RS requests

With outbound JAX-RS requests, the span that is created is given the name of the HTTP method to be invoked. For example, a `GET` request results in a span named `GET`.

Note on Using JAX-RS Clients

If you are using a JAX-RS client to create outbound requests, you will need to pass the ClientBuilder you've created to `ClientTracingRegistrar` for the MicroProfile OpenTracing runtime to create a span for it. You can invoke either the `configure(ClientBuilder clientBuilder)` or `configure(ClientBuilder clientBduilder, ExecutorService executorService)` static methods, which will then return a `ClientBuilder` object that you can use. The implementation of the MicroProfile OpenTracing runtime may have been already configured so that any ClientBuilders used will create a span, thus not needing to invoke the `configure(...)` methods. Consult the documentation of your MicroProfile OpenTracing runtime for details.

Inbound JAX-RS requests

With inbound JAX-RS requests, the span that is created is given the name in the following format:

```
<HTTP method>:<package name>.<class name>.<method name>
```

This is referred to as the **class-method** naming format and is the default format. Alternatively, you can use the **http-path** naming format, which uses the following format:

```
<HTTP method>:<@Path value of endpoint's class>/<@Path value of
endpoint's method>.
```

To enable the http-path format, use the MicroProfile Config configuration element known as `mp.opentracing.server.operation-name-provider` and specify `http-path`.

Span tags

Spans that are created in both inbound and outbound requests use the following tags:

- **Tags.SPAN_KIND**: This is an outgoing JAX-RS request with a value of `"Tags.SPAN_KIND_CLIENT"`. An inbound request has a value of `"Tags.SPAN_KIND_SERVER"`.

- **Tags.HTTP_METHOD**: The value of this is the HTTP method that has been invoked.

- **Tags.HTTP_URL**: This is the value of the HTTP URL that the request has been sent to.

- **Tags.HTTP_STATUS**: This is the status of the HTTP request. It specifies what response was received by the client or what response the server is returning.

- **Tags.COMPONENT**: This value is always `jaxrs`.

- **Tags.ERROR**: This tag is only present if a failure (that is, return code 5xx) occurs during the scope of the span. If an exception object is thrown as well, two logs events will be added to the span. These are called `event=error` and `error.object=<error object instance>`.

Instrumenting the @Traced annotation and injecting a tracer

Provided with MicroProfile OpenTracing is the `@Traced` CDI annotation. This annotation can be applied to methods and classes. When applied to a class, every method in the class is annotated with `@Traced`. The `@Traced` annotation can be used to further fine-tune the spans that make up the trace. It can also be used to override the default auto-instrumentation of JAX-RS resource methods, such as disabling or renaming the span or to further specify spans on other methods in your application.

The `@Traced` annotation contains two parameters:

- **value**: This is a boolean parameter. It is true by default, which implies that the annotated method will be automatically instrumented for tracing. A false value disables automatic tracing for the method. This can be used to disable automatic instrumentation on JAX-RS endpoints.

- **operationName**: This parameter accepts a `String` and defines the name of the span that would be created when the method is invoked.

Note that when both a class and a method inside the class use the `@Traced` annotation, the method annotation and its parameters take priority.

The MicroProfile OpenTracing runtime can also inject an optional `io.opentracing.Tracer` object. Using this OpenTracing object, you can programmatically create and manipulate spans using the OpenTracing API. You can add your own tags, logs, and baggage. We will not cover how to use the OpenTracing API in this book.

The following example shows how to inject the OpenTracing's `Tracer` object, as well as how to use `@Traced` on both a JAX-RS endpoint and a normal business method.

The full source code for `TraceResource` can be found at `https://bit.ly/3AXmiIr`:

```
@Path("/traceResource")
public class TraceResource {

    @Inject
    io.opentracing.Tracer tracer;

    @GET
    @Path("automaticTracing")
    @Traced(value=false)
```

```
public String doNotTraceMe(){
    return "Do NOT trace me!";
}


@Traced(operationName="traceMe")
public void traceMe(){
    System.out.println("Trace me!");
}
}
```

In the aforementioned example, doNotTraceMe() is annotated with
@Traced(value=false), which alerts the OpenTracing runtime to not trace this
JAX-RS endpoint. traceMe() is a normal business method and is annotated with
@Traced(operationName="traceMe") to alert the OpenTracing runtime to trace
this as a span if the code path travels to this method. The span is called "traceMe".

Visualizing traces with Jaeger

For this demonstration, we'll use a simple application consisting of two JAX-RS
resources called OutboundRequestResource and InboundRequestResource.
We'll issue a GET request to OutboundRequestResource at http://
localhost:9080/outbound/tracing, which will then create a ClientBuilder
to send a GET request to InboundRequestResource. This, in turn, will invoke
the epoch() method in a TracedExample class that's been annotated with
@Traced(operationName="epoch"). The resulting trace visualization can be
seen here:

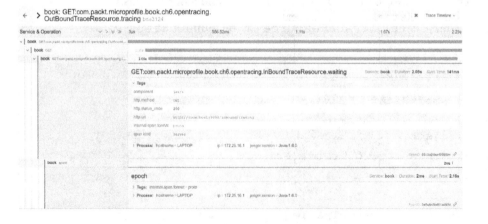

Figure 6.4 – Trace inspection in Jaeger

> **Note**
>
> You can find the full source for `OutBoundTraceResource` at `https://bit.ly/3swFZEb`.
>
> You can find the full source for `InBoundTraceResource` at `https://bit.ly/3xZxrXz`.
>
> You can find the full source for `TracedExample` at `https://bit.ly/3y6pHmM`.

This is a snapshot of what you may expect when inspecting a trace on the Jaeger web client. The preceding figure may be hard to discern, so we will describe it. The top left shows the name of the trace. The trace is named *book: GET:com.packt.microprofile.book.ch6.opentracing.OutBoundTraceResource.tracing*. The trace is given the name of the first span in this trace, which is the GET request that we issued to the /`tracing` endpoint in `OutBoundTraceResource`.

The rest of the interface consists of the sequential listing of the spans that make up the trace. When minimized, it will display the duration of each span and their active durations compared to the other spans as solid horizontal bars. When you click on a span entry, it will expand to show more details, such as its contextual data. In the aforementioned figure, the span that was created from the inbound JAX-RS request from `InBoundTraceResource`, as well as the span that was instrumented from the `@Traced` annotation on the `epoch()` method, have been expanded.

Let's describe the first expanded span, which is the span that was created by the inbound request. It is called *GET:com.packt.microprofile.book.ch6.opentracing.InBoundTraceResource.waiting*. Included in the details are its tags, which we discussed earlier in this section; that is, *component*, *http.method*, *http.status_code*, *http.url*, and *span.kind*. A tag that's appended by Jaeger is in *internal.span.format*. The instrumented span does not contain any tags other than the ones provided by Jaeger.

With the combination of a summary view of a trace and having the ability to view the individual spans that make up the trace, using distributed tracing to profile the paths that a request takes is very useful for analyzing performance and latency. In the aforementioned example, we demonstrated distributed tracing with the Jaeger platform. Another distributed tracing platform that provides an instrumentation library and the facilities to view and analyze the traces is **Zipkin**. Zipkin isn't included on the list of official tracers in the OpenTracing documentation, but you may find that the MicroProfile OpenTracing runtime you chose supports it. Consult the documentation of your runtime for their list of supported libraries and the necessary steps for configuring it.

Summary

In this chapter, we explored the three observability technologies offered by the MicroProfile platform; that is, MicroProfile Health, MicroProfile Metrics, and MicroProfile OpenTracing. From reporting the overall health of your application with health checks to the detailed statistical data that metrics provide, to tracking and profiling requests as they travel through your microservices with distributed tracing, each technology has an invaluable purpose that satisfies the important task of monitoring and observing your cloud-native application. Your application has now harnessed all the features and capabilities that the MicroProfile release platform has to offer. There are additional technologies that come with MicroProfile's standalone releases. We will cover these in the final chapters of this book.

In the next chapter, we will explore the topic of deploying your cloud-native application onto the cloud. We'll see how it interacts with cloud infrastructures such as Docker, Kubernetes, and Istio.

7

MicroProfile Ecosystem with Open Liberty, Docker, and Kubernetes

So far, in the previous chapters of this book, we focused on using the MicroProfile APIs to write a cloud-native application. In this chapter, we will look at how to run a cloud-native application. One of the features of MicroProfile that sets it apart from some other cloud-native application frameworks is that MicroProfile offers multiple implementations of the APIs. This reduces the chance of ending up locked into a particular implementation or finding that the open source community behind the APIs you were utilizing wasn't as vibrant as you thought and the maintainers disappear. In addition, different implementations tend to take different design decisions, which may better suit your needs. At the time of writing, there were four implementations of the most recent release of the MicroProfile APIs: **Open Liberty**, **Payara**, **WebSphere Liberty**, and **WildFly**. In addition, **Helidon**, **JBoss EAP**, **KumuluzEE**, and **Quarkus** implement previous versions.

Once you have chosen an implementation, you need to deploy the application into production. Increasingly, this is achieved using technologies such as **Docker**, **Kubernetes**, and a **Service Mesh**. This will be the focus of this chapter.

In this chapter, we will cover the following topics:

- Deploying cloud-native applications to Open Liberty
- Containerizing cloud-native applications using Docker
- Deploying cloud-native applications to Kubernetes
- MicroProfile and Service Mesh

In this chapter, you will learn how to configure a MicroProfile application to run on Open Liberty, packaging it as a container and deploying it into a Kubernetes runtime like Red Hat OpenShift.

Technical requirements

To build and run the samples mentioned in this chapter, you will need a Mac or PC (Windows or Linux) with the following software:

- **Java Development Kit (JDK)** – Java 8 or later: `http://ibm.biz/GetSemerut`
- Apache Maven: `https://maven.apache.org`
- A Git client: `https://git-scm.com`
- A Docker client: `https://www.docker.com/products`
- The OpenShift client: `https://docs.openshift.com/container-platform/4.6/cli_reference/openshift_cli/getting-started-cli.html`

All of the source code used in this chapter is available on GitHub at `https://github.com/PacktPublishing/Practical-Cloud-Native-Java-Development-with-MicroProfile/tree/main/Chapter07`.

Deploying cloud-native applications to Open Liberty

In this section, we will look at how to deploy a MicroProfile application using **Open Liberty**. We have chosen Open Liberty because we are committers on Open Liberty, but its focus on being current with the latest releases of MicroProfile, performance, and ease of use make it a good option for anyone.

As you might expect from the name, Open Liberty is an open source Java runtime for building and deploying cloud-native applications. It is designed around the idea of components called **features** that can be configured to provide just enough runtime for your application needs. This means if your application doesn't use or need MicroProfile OpenTracing, then you don't need to configure the MicroProfile OpenTracing feature and the runtime will be smaller, faster, and leaner – it'll be better sized for what your application needs. Open Liberty has a feature for programming APIs such as MicroProfile APIs, Java EE, Jakarta EE, and gRPC. It also has features for runtime capabilities such as a feature for integrating with OpenID Connect for authentication.

Open Liberty is configured primarily using a simple XML file format referred to as a `server.xml` file. XML is used for a few reasons:

- The fact that Java has baked-in support for parsing XML is one of the primary reasons.
- XML models hierarchical configuration very well (unlike a properties format)
- Space characters do not affect the semantic interpretation of the file format (unlike YAML).

When parsing the configuration file, Open Liberty takes the approach of ignoring any configuration it doesn't understand. This has several advantages. It means that a `server.xml` file can contain a configuration that isn't valid for the release of Open Liberty being used without causing a startup failure. It also means a simple typo in the configuration won't prevent the server from starting the application.

One of the core responsibilities of the `server.xml` file is to configure which features to load. By using the `server.xml` file to configure which features are to be used and by ensuring behavior changes are only introduced via new features, Open Liberty guarantees that the behavior of the configuration remains unchanged from one release to the next. A simple server configuration that enables all the MicroProfile APIs is as follows:

```
<server>
    <featureManager>
        <feature>microProfile-4.1</feature>
    </featureManager>
</server>
```

Open Liberty configuration can be centralized in a single `server.xml` file, or it can be split up among many configuration files. This both facilitates both sharing of configuration and also separates configuration based on the environment the server configuration is deployed to. An example of this might be the use of an in-memory database in a development environment, but in production, a database such as DB2, Oracle, or MariaDB might be used instead. This is facilitated by two mechanisms. The first is a `server.xml` file that can explicitly include another `server.xml` file. The second is the use of something referred to as **config dropins**. Config dropins consist of two directories, called `defaults` and `overrides`, that are read before and after the main server configuration file. The files in these directories are read in alphabetical order, providing predictability in how configuration is read. Configuration files can also be parameterized using variable replacement syntax. Variables can be defined in the `server.xml` file, as Java system properties, or using environment variables. Variables in `server.xml` can be defined multiple times and the last definition of the variable will be used for variable resolution. A variable might be defined as follows:

```
<server>
    <variable name="microProfile.feature"
        value="microProfile-4.1" />
</server>
```

It can then be referenced elsewhere like this:

```
<server>
    <featureManager>
        <feature>${microProfile.feature}</feature>
    </featureManager>
</server>
```

Variables can also have a default value, which allows configuration to be written that will always work while allowing it to be overridden in production:

```
<server>
    <variable name="http.port" defaultValue="9043" />
</server>
```

Variables have different precedents based on where they are defined from, allowing them to be easily overridden. The precedence order (later precedence overrides previous precedence) is as follows:

1. `server.xml` default values

2. Environment variables

3. The `bootstrap.properties` file

4. Java system properties

5. Variables defined in `server.xml`

6. Variables defined on server startup

This provides multiple simple ways to change the behavior of Open Liberty based on the environment Open Liberty is deployed into.

Open Liberty allows you to package your MicroProfile application as a `WAR` file for deployment into the server. The MicroProfile specifications do not have an opinion on how an application is packaged and deployed, so Open Liberty reuses the `WAR` packaging model from Jakarta EE as the way to package the application. This makes a lot of sense because MicroProfile makes use of several Jakarta EE programming models, and it makes it easier for a MicroProfile application to make use of parts of Jakarta EE that are not in MicroProfile, such as concurrency utilities for Jakarta EE. It also allows you to reuse the existing Maven and Gradle build tools for packaging a MicroProfile application.

There are two ways to deploy a `WAR` file into Open Liberty. The first is by dropping the WAR file into the `dropins` folder, and the second is through the `server.xml` file:

```
<server>
    <webApplication location="myapp.war" />
</server>
```

The primary reason for using the server configuration approach over the `dropins` folder is that it allows you to customize how the application is run, for example, setting the application's `contextRoot`, configuring classloading, or configuring security role bindings.

Open Liberty supports several mechanisms for packaging applications for deployment. The simplest is to package the application as a `WAR` file. This is the least likely in a cloud-native environment though. Open Liberty also supports packaging a server as a `zip` file, an executable `JAR` file, and a Docker container (described in the next section). Open Liberty provides plugins for Maven and Gradle that make it simple to build applications that will run on Open Liberty. One of the features of these plugins is the Open Liberty **dev mode**. Dev mode watches the application code and recompiles it as it changes and deploys it into a running Open Liberty server, providing a fast turnaround time for making changes. It also monitors the Open Liberty configuration so if you add new features or other configuration changes, the server is also updated. To use `dev` mode in Maven, simply add the Open Liberty Maven plugin to the `plugin` section of your `pom.xml` as shown here:

```
<plugin>
    <groupId>io.openliberty.tools</groupId>
    <artifactId>liberty-maven-plugin</artifactId>
    <version>[3.3.4,)</version>
</plugin>
```

This configures the plugin to use the 3.3.4 version of the plugin or a more recent release if one exists.

When you run the `liberty:dev` Maven goal, the plugin will compile the application, downloading any dependencies required to run the application, deploy it into Liberty, and run the server with Java debugger support. This allows you to make changes to the application in any code editor, whether it is a simple editor such as **vi** or a full-fledged IDE such as **IntelliJ IDEA** or **Eclipse IDE**.

Liberty's design makes it very simple to build applications that will run in a container environment such as Docker. There is even a `dev` mode for containers that can be run using `liberty:devc` for this. The next section will discuss how to create a container as the deployment artifact.

Containerizing cloud-native applications using Docker

In this section, we will look at how to containerize a MicroProfile application. There are two key parts to containerizing anything: the first is the creation of an image, and the second is running that image. While Docker was not the first product to do containerization, it did popularize it in a way that developers and operators could understand. Cloud Foundry was a common early alternative that had similar concepts but hid them as internal implementation details rather than making them first-class concepts. With Docker, these two concepts were broken into two parts, exposed by the `docker build` command used to create the image, and the `docker run` command used to run the image. These concepts were further expanded to become standardized, meaning there are now multiple alternatives to `docker build` and `docker run`.

The container image

A **container image** is the container deployment artifact. A container image contains everything required to run the application. This means that a container image can be moved from one environment to another with confidence that it will run in the same way. The motto is to think, create once, run everywhere; however, there are some limitations to this. A container is tied to a CPU architecture, so a container designed for x86 CPUs wouldn't run on ARM or Power ones without a translation layer for the CPU instructions (such as Rosetta 2, which translates Mac x86 instructions to Mac ARM ones to support x86 Mac applications on Macs with an M series ARM processor).

A **Dockerfile** is a set of instructions for how to create a container image. A Dockerfile starts by declaring a named image that it is based on and then identifies a series of steps to add additional content into the container image. A common practice might be for it to be based on an image containing an **Operating System (OS)**, a Java image, or an image that pre-packages the application runtime such as Open Liberty.

While it is convenient to think of a container image as a single large file containing everything in the image, this is not how a container image works. A container image is made up of a series of layers that are identified by an SHA hash. This provides three key advantages:

- It reduces the storage space required to store images. If you have 30 images based on a common base image, you only store that common base image once, not 30 times. While storage space is relatively cheap, if you have a large number of applications, file duplication between the containers would soon add up to large numbers.

- It reduces bandwidth requirements. When you transfer container images to and from a **container registry**, you do not need to upload or download the layers you already have. It is likely you will have many container images, but one common OS image, and a common JVM image.

- It reduces build time. If the input to a layer hasn't changed, there is no need to rebuild it. The input to a layer is any change you made in that line, plus the output of the prior line.

Each layer has a pointer to the layer it was built on top of. When you create a container image, it consists of all the layers from the base image and one new layer for every single line in the Dockerfile. A simple Dockerfile for packaging a simple MicroProfile application might look like this:

```
FROM open-liberty:full-java11-openj9
ADD src/main/config/liberty/server.xml /config
ADD target/myapp.war /config/dropins
```

This creates a container image based on Ubuntu 20.04 with Java SE 11 using the OpenJ9 JRE implementation with all Open Liberty features available to it. It then copies `server.xml` from the default location in a Maven project and the application to the `dropins` folder. This will create an image with all the layers associated with the `open-liberty:full-java11-openj9` image, and two layers associated with this image.

Best practice: using multiple layers

The advantage of this approach is when you push or pull an image, only layers that are not already present are transferred. In the simple MicroProfile example stated previously, when you build and push the image, only the layers associated with the application and server configuration will be transferred. Think of it this way: if you have a base image that is 500 MB in size, and the layers of your image are a total of 5 MB, your image would be a total of 505 MB, but when you push that back to the container registry, only 5 MB would need to be sent since the base image is already there.

This leads to some interesting design questions when designing Docker images. The purpose of a Docker image is clearly to get it running somewhere, and preferably to get that to happen as quickly as possible. This makes it faster to deploy a new image production, to scale it up, or in the event of a problem, to replace the container with a new one. A simple way to build Docker images is to package your application in a single JAR file, add it to the Dockerfile, and then run it:

```
FROM adoptopenjdk:11-openj9
ADD target/myapp.jar /myapp.jar
CMD ["java", "-jar", "/myapp.jar"]
```

This is a popular way to create Docker images and works well if the application is small, but many applications built this way are not small. Consider the case where that jar contains Open Liberty, the application code, and some open source dependencies. That means that every time the application is modified, a new layer containing all that code has to be re-created and deployed. If, on the other hand, the application was split up, then a change to the application would require a much smaller upload:

```
FROM open-liberty:full-java11-openj9
ADD target/OS-dependencies /config/library
ADD target/myapp.war /config/apps/myapp.war
```

In this example, a change to the application code would only rebuild the last layer, meaning the upload will be smaller and distributed faster. A change to the open source dependencies would of course result in that layer being rebuilt, but those tend to change less frequently than the application. If there are many applications that share a common set of libraries (whether open source or not), it might make sense to create a named base image that all applications can use. This would be especially useful if the container images are commonly run on the same host.

A significant thing to understand about the layers is once created, they are immutable. That means if you delete a file created in an earlier layer, it doesn't remove the files from the image; it just marks them as deleted so they cannot be accessed. This means that when transferring the container image around, you will copy the bytes for the file, but it won't ever be accessible. If the file is contributed to by a base image, this will be unavoidable, but if you control the image, then it is something to avoid.

Dockerfile instructions

As previously stated, a Dockerfile is a series of instructions detailing how to create a Docker image. There are several instructions for creating an image. The first instruction in all the examples so far is the FROM instruction.

FROM

The FROM instruction defines the container image that is the base of the image you are creating. All Dockerfiles are required to start with FROM. A Dockerfile can have multiple FROM lines: these are commonly used to create a multi-stage build. An example of this might be if you need some kind of extra tools to build your image that you don't want to be present when you run it. An example of this might be wget or curl for downloading files and unzip for expanding a zip file. A simple multi-stage build might look like this:

```
FROM ubuntu:21.04 as BUILD
RUN apt-get update
RUN apt-get install -y unzip wget
RUN wget https://example.com/my.zip -O my.zip
RUN unzip my.zip /extract
FROM ubuntu:21.04
COPY /extract /extract --from=BUILD
```

In this example, the first stage installs wget and unzip, downloads a file, and unzips it. The second stage starts from the base image and then copies the extracted files into the new image layer. If a single-stage Dockerfile were created, this would have resulted in an image with three additional layers containing the binaries for unzip and get, the zip file, and extract. The multi-stage build only contains extract. To do this with a single-stage Docker build is less readable and would look like this:

```
FROM ubuntu:21.04
RUN apt-get update && \
    apt-get install -y unzip wget && \
    wget https://example.com/my.zip -O my.zip && \
    unzip my.zip /extract && \
    rm my.zip && \
    apt-get uninstall -y unzip wget && \
    rm -rf /var/lib/apt/lists/*
```

This Dockerfile uses a single RUN command to run multiple commands to create only a single layer and it has to undo each step before the end. The last line is required to tidy up files created by apt. The multi-stage Dockerfile is much simpler. Another common use for multi-stage builds is to use the first stage to build the application, and then the second stage for running:

```
FROM maven as BUILD
COPY myBuild /build
WORKDIR build
RUN mvn package
FROM open-liberty:full-java11-openj9
COPY /target/myapp.war /config/apps/ --from=BUILD
```

COPY and ADD

The COPY and ADD instructions perform a similar function. ADD has a superset of the function of COPY so it is generally advised to only use ADD if you need the extended function. The first argument for both instructions specifies the source file (or directory) and by default is interpreted to be copying from the machine running the build. The command is always relative to the directory the build is run from and you cannot use .. to navigate to the parent directory. The use of the from argument, as shown in the previous section, redirects the copy to be from another container image. The second argument is the location in the container the file should be copied to.

The ADD command provides some additional features over and above the COPY command. The first is it allows you to specify a URL to download the file from as the first argument. The second feature is it will unzip a tar.gz file into a directory. To go back to the first multi-stage build example, if the output was a tar.gz file, it would mean it could be simplified to just be the following:

```
FROM ubuntu:21.04 as BUILD
ADD https://example.com/my.tar.gz /extract
```

RUN

The RUN instruction simply executes one or more commands using the shell from the OS layer. This allows you to do pretty much anything you want or need to provide the command available in the base OS image. For example, it is uncommon for unzip or wget to be in the base Linux OS images, so those commands will fail unless action is taken to install them. Each RUN instruction creates a new layer, so if you create a file in one RUN command and delete it in another, due to the immutability of the layers, the file will exist but not be visible anymore. For this reason, it is often important to use the && operator to string multiple commands together in a single layer. An example of this was shown previously, but is repeated here:

```
FROM ubuntu:21.04
RUN apt-get update && \
    apt-get install -y unzip wget && \
    wget https://example.com/my.zip -O my.zip && \
    unzip my.zip /extract && \
    rm my.zip && \
    apt-get uninstall -y unzip wget && \
    rm -rf /var/lib/apt/lists/*
```

ARG and ENV

ARG defines a build argument that can be specified at build time. The ARG values are set when running docker build using the build-arg argument. ARG can have a default value, in case it isn't provided at build time. These build arguments are not persisted after the build finishes, so they are not available at runtime and are not persisted in the image.

ENV defines an environment variable that is available both at build and runtime.

Both of these are referenced in the same way, so the key difference is the visibility of the value.

ENTRYPOINT and CMD

When running a container, you need something to happen, such as starting the Open Liberty server. What happens can be defined by the Dockerfile using the instructions ENTRYPOINT and CMD. The difference between the two instructions is how they interact with the docker run command. When running a Docker container, any arguments after the Docker image name are passed into the container. CMD provides a default value in case no command-line arguments are provided. ENTRYPOINT defines a command that will be run and any command-line arguments provided to docker run are passed in after ENTRYPOINT. Both CMD and ENTRYPOINT have the same syntax. The Open Liberty container specifies both of these, so images based on them do not tend to specify them.

WORKDIR

The WORKDIR instruction is used to change the current directory for future RUN, CMD, COPY, and ENTRYPOINT instructions.

USER

When building an image, the default user account used for executing commands is the root one. For some operations, this is reasonable and fair. If doing an OS update, you typically need to execute as root. However, when running the containers using, the root account is a clear security issue. The Dockerfile has a USER instruction that sets the user account used for RUN instructions as well as the process that executes in the container when it is run. This makes it simple to set the account to a non-root account. The Open Liberty images in previous examples set USER to 1001, which means that any of the previous examples based on it will not run using the root account, but the one based on the Java image would. One problem with the previous Dockerfile examples is that the ADD and COPY instructions write to the files so they are owned by the root user, which can cause issues at runtime. This can be resolved by updating the ADD or COPY instructions to change the ownership as they are written:

```
FROM open-liberty:full-java11-openj9
ADD --chown=1001:0 src/main/config/liberty/server.xml/config
ADD --chown=1001:0 target/myapp.war /config/dropins
```

Alternatively, the RUN instruction can be used to execute the chown command-line tool. This will create a new layer but might be required if the ADD or COPY instruction moves multiple files and only some should have their ownership changed.

Although Dockerfiles are the most used way to create a container image, there are alternative ways to build container images. A few examples follow.

Source-to-Image

Source-to-Image (**S2I**) is a technology that converts an application source into a container image. Instead of creating a **Dockerfile**, an **S2I** builder ingests the source code, runs the build, and encodes it in a container image. This allows the developer to focus on the application code and not the creation of the container. By encoding the best practices for building a container in an **S2I** builder, it can be reused across applications, making it more likely that a set of applications all have well-designed container images. There are **S2I** builders for many languages and frameworks, including Open Liberty. **S2I** is an open source technology created by Red Hat to help developers adopt OpenShift, although it can be, and is, used to create containers that can run anywhere.

Cloud Native Buildpacks

Buildpacks were originally created by Heroku to simplify deploying applications into their **Platform as a Service (PaaS)**. It was picked up and used by Cloud Foundry. Buildpacks predate container technology, meaning they don't create **Open Container Initiative (OCI)** compatible container images. Recently, though, an effort has been underway to shift Buildpacks into the container world with **Cloud Native Buildpacks**. These work similarly to **S2I** in that they encode the creation of the container image in code rather than a Dockerfile, in a way that can be used between and across applications. Unlike **S2I** builders, Buildpacks do not start from the application source, but the application artifact, for example, a WAR file.

Having created a container image, the next step is to run it. While a developer might use Docker to run the image on their desktop when running in production, the most common way to run container images is with Kubernetes, which we will discuss in the next section.

Deploying cloud-native applications to Kubernetes

Kubernetes started as a project in Google to allow them to manage software at scale. It has since moved to become an open source project managed by the **Cloud Native Computing Foundation** (CNCF) and has contributors from all over the industry. Every major (and most minor) public cloud provider uses Kubernetes to manage the deployment of containers. There are also private cloud products such as Red Hat OpenShift that provide a distribution of Kubernetes for deployment either on-premises or on a public cloud but dedicated to a single company.

A Kubernetes deployment is known as a **cluster**. To run containers and provide a highly available, scalable environment a cluster consists of a control plane and a set of key resources that provide it with the ability to run or manage containers, scale them, and keep the containers running in the event of any failures. When running a container in Kubernetes, the container is placed in a Pod, which is then run on a node based on decisions made by the control plane.

A **Pod** provides a shared context for running a set of containers. All the containers in a Pod run on the same node. Although you can run multiple containers in a Pod, normally a Pod will contain a single application container, and any other containers running in the Pod will be sidecars providing some administrative or support function to the application container.

In a traditional automated operation environment, the automation will describe how to set the environment up. When using Kubernetes instead of describing how to set up the environment, the description describes the desired end state, and it is up to the control plane to decide how to make this happen. The configuration for this is provided as one (or, more often, a set of) YAML document(s). The net effect of this is when deploying to Kubernetes, you do not describe the deployment by defining pods on a node and putting a container into it. Instead, you define a **Deployment** that will express the container you want to deploy and how many replicas of the container should be created. A simple deployment of a single instance of Open Liberty can be done with this YAML:

```
apiVersion: apps/v1
kind: Deployment
metadata:
  labels:
    app: demo
  name: demo
spec:
  replicas: 1
  selector:
    matchLabels:
      app: demo
  template:
    metadata:
      labels:
        app: demo
    spec:
      containers:
      - image: openliberty/open-liberty:full-java11-openj9-ubi
        name: open-liberty
```

This YAML can then be deployed using the `kubectl apply` command. This results in a single Pod running Open Liberty being deployed. While the container is running and could respond to HTTP requests, there is no route for network traffic to get to the container. The key to enabling network traffic to reach a deployment is the Kubernetes **Service**. The Service defines the port the process in the container is listening on and the port it should be accessed via the Kubernetes networking stack. A Service for this can be defined using this YAML:

```yaml
apiVersion: v1
kind: Service
metadata:
  labels:
    app: demo
  name: demo
spec:
  ports:
  - name: 9080-9080
    port: 9080
    protocol: TCP
    targetPort: 9080
  selector:
    app: demo
  type: ClusterIP
```

A Service allows other containers running Kubernetes to access it, but it doesn't allow services outside the cluster to access it. There are several options for how to expose the container externally, for example, port forwarding, an ingress controller, or OpenShift has the concept of **routes**. A route essentially just exposes a service externally to the cluster. You can specify the host and path, or you can let Kubernetes default it. To expose this Open Liberty server externally, you can define a route using this YAML:

```yaml
kind: Route
apiVersion: route.openshift.io/v1
metadata:
  name: demo
  labels:
```

```
      app: demo
spec:
  to:
    kind: Service
    name: demo
    weight: 100
  port:
    targetPort: 9080-9080
```

These three YAML files have deployed a container and exposed it externally so it can be accessed and used. The three YAML files can be placed in a single file using - - - as a separator, but there is an alternative option for managing deployment than using YAML to configure everything, and that option is to use an Operator.

An **Operator** is a way of packaging, deploying, and managing a set of resources related to an application. They were originally intended to help manage stateful applications where just throwing away and starting a new Pod might result in data loss; however, they can also be used to simplify the deployment of applications. Operators watch for the definition of a **Custom Resource** that it understands and configures the relevant Kubernetes resources to run that application. An Operator can do things such as managing the deployment and updating of an application when new images become available. Open Liberty provides an Operator that can manage the deployment of applications built on Open Liberty. As an example, all the previous YAML files can be simply replaced with this YAML:

```
apiVersion: openliberty.io/v1beta1
kind: OpenLibertyApplication
metadata:
  name: my-liberty-app
spec:
  applicationImage: openliberty/open-liberty:full-java11-
    openj9-ubi
  service:
    type: ClusterIP
    port: 9080
  expose: true
```

MicroProfile Health in Kubernetes

The MicroProfile Health specification allows you to configure support for liveness and readiness checks. These probes allow the Kubernetes control plane to understand the health of the container and what action to take. An unsuccessful liveness probe will trigger the Pod to be recycled as it indicates that a problem has occurred that cannot be resolved. A readiness probe, on the other hand, will simply cause Kubernetes to stop routing traffic to the Pod. In both cases, you need to have multiple instances to ensure that during any outage of one container, the clients will remain unaware. To configure these liveness and readiness probes, you ensure that the Open Liberty server is configured to run MicroProfile Health:

```
<server>
    <featureManager>
        <feature>mpHealth-3.0</feature>
    </featureManager>
</server>
```

Then, when defining the application, configure the liveness and readiness probes:

```
apiVersion: openliberty.io/v1beta1
kind: OpenLibertyApplication
metadata:
  name: my-liberty-app
spec:
  expose: true
  applicationImage: openliberty/open-liberty:full-java11-
    openj9-ubi
  readinessProbe:
    httpGet:
      path: /health/ready
      port: 9080
    initialDelaySeconds: 30
  livenessProbe:
    httpGet:
      path: /health/live
      port: 9080
    initialDelaySeconds: 90
  replicas: 1
```

This configures the liveness and readiness probes to make an HTTP get request to the MicroProfile health endpoints for liveness and readiness. It also configures a wait period after the container starts before making the first check. This gives the container a chance to run any startup routines before it starts polling to determine the status.

MicroProfile Config in Kubernetes

MicroProfile Config provides a way to receive configuration in your application that can be provided in the environment. In Kubernetes, this kind of configuration is typically stored in a **ConfigMap** or a **Secret**. As discussed previously, in *Chapter 5, Enhancing Cloud-Native Applications*, a ConfigMap is essentially a set of key/value pairs stored in Kubernetes that can be bound into a Pod so it is available to the container. To receive configuration in your application from Kubernetes, ensure that the Open Liberty server is configured to run MicroProfile Config:

```
<server>
  <featureManager>
    <feature>mpConfig-2.0</feature>
  </featureManager>
</server>
```

There are many ways to create a ConfigMap, and *Chapter 5, Enhancing Cloud-Native Applications*, demonstrated one mechanism. Another way to define a ConfigMap is to apply a ConfigMap with the following YAML:

```
kind: ConfigMap
apiVersion: v1
metadata:
  name: demo
data:
  example.property.1: hello
  example.property.2: world
```

Now, when deploying your application, you can either bind a single environment variable from this ConfigMap, or all of them. To bind the value of example.property.1 from the ConfigMap as a variable called PROP_ONE to an Open Liberty application, you would use the following YAML:

```
apiVersion: openliberty.io/v1beta1
kind: OpenLibertyApplication
```

```yaml
metadata:
  name: demo-app
spec:
  expose: true
  applicationImage: openliberty/open-liberty:full-java11-
    openj9-ubi
  env:
    - name: PROP_ONE
      valueFrom:
        configMapKeyRef:
          key: example.property.1
          name: demo
  replicas: 1
```

A ConfigMap could (as in the aforementioned example) contain a lot of properties that the container may need to access, instead of binding a single entry, or entries one by one, you can bind all the entries. The following YAML would define an application with all the values of the ConfigMap bound:

```yaml
apiVersion: openliberty.io/v1beta1
kind: OpenLibertyApplication
metadata:
  name: demo-app
spec:
  expose: true
  applicationImage: openliberty/open-liberty:full-java11-
    openj9-ubi
  envFrom:
    - configMapRef:
        name: demo
  replicas: 1
```

One of the more recent features of MicroProfile Config is the concept of configuration profiles. The idea is that you can provide the configuration for running the application in development, test, and production environments and have MicroProfile Config only load the configuration for the desired profile. To configure this, you also need to define the config profile. The MicroProfile Config specification says that a property in a profile name starts with `%<profile name>`; however, `%` isn't valid in an environment variable name so it is replaced with `_`. Example YAML for this is the following:

```yaml
apiVersion: openliberty.io/v1beta1
kind: OpenLibertyApplication
metadata:
  name: demo-app
spec:
  expose: true
  applicationImage: openliberty/open-liberty:full-java11-
    openj9-ubi
  env:
    - name: mp.config.profile
      value: dev
  envFrom:
    - configMapRef:
        name: dev
      prefix: '_dev.'
    - configMapRef:
        name: test
      prefix: '_test.'
    - configMapRef:
        name: prod
      prefix: '_test.'
  replicas: 1
```

ConfigMaps in Kubernetes are good for storing data that isn't sensitive, but when it comes to storing API keys, credentials, and so on, Kubernetes has an alternative concept known as Secrets. Secrets can represent multiple different kinds of Secrets, but here we are just going to consider simple key/value pairs. The Kubernetes platform provides better protection for Secrets than ConfigMaps, although many people prefer to use third-party products for Secret management. It is still good to understand how Secrets work because third-party products tend to follow the same conventions to access sensitive data from within the container.

Secrets are encoded using base64 encoding, which isn't fantastic protection. Open Liberty allows passwords it loads to be AES encrypted, and provides an API for decrypting protected strings, so your base64-encoded secret could be a base64-encoded AES encrypted string. However, since you would still need to provide the decryption key to Open Liberty and this is not a security hardening book, we will not go into further details here. Referencing a single key pair from a secret from deployment is done almost identically to referencing from a ConfigMap, but using `secretKeyRef` rather than `configMapKeyRef`; for example, with this YAML:

```yaml
apiVersion: openliberty.io/v1beta1
kind: OpenLibertyApplication
metadata:
  name: demo-app
spec:
  expose: true
  applicationImage: openliberty/open-liberty:full-java11-
    openj9-ubi
  env:
    - name: PROP_ONE
      valueFrom:
        secretKeyRef:
          key: my_secret
          name: secret.config
  replicas: 1
```

If you deploy the secret YAML and bind to it as in the aforementioned example, your container will have an environment variable called PROP_ONE whose value is super secret.

Just like with a ConfigMap, you can bind all the key/value pairs in a secret to the container, and just like with the prior example, it is done in a very similar way to ConfigMaps:

```
apiVersion: openliberty.io/v1beta1
kind: OpenLibertyApplication
metadata:
  name: demo-app
spec:
  expose: true
  applicationImage: openliberty/open-liberty:full-java11-
    openj9-ubi
  envFrom:
    - secretRef:
        name: secret.config
  replicas: 1
```

Secrets can also be bound as files in the container file system and this can be preferable for security-sensitive data. When you do this, the secret will be defined in the file system and the value of the secret will be the content of the file. MicroProfile Config cannot consume secrets bound this way, but it provides a way to add additional ConfigSources, allowing you to easily load the configuration. The YAML for binding a secret to the file system is to essentially mount it as a volume. The following example YAML will result in every key/value in the secret `secret.config` being mounted as a file in the file system of the container under the directory `/my/secret`:

```
apiVersion: openliberty.io/v1beta1
kind: OpenLibertyApplication
metadata:
  name: demo-app
spec:
  expose: true
  applicationImage: openliberty/open-liberty:full-java11-
    openj9-ubi
  volumeMounts:
    - mountPath: /my/secrets
      name: secret
  volumes:
    - secret:
        secretName: secret.config
```

```
    name: secret
 replicas: 1
```

To enable the injection of the bound Secrets, you need a **ConfigSource** that will read these properties. A ConfigSource is registered using the **ServiceLoader** pattern, so placing the classname in META-INF/services/org.eclipse.microprofile.config. spi.ConfigSource on the application classpath will automatically cause it to be loaded. A short example ConfigSource that will do this is the following:

```java
public class FileSystemConfigSource implements ConfigSource {
    private File dir = new File("/my/secrets");

    public Set<String> getPropertyNames() {
        return Arrays.asList(dir.listFiles())
                    .stream()
                    .map(f -> f.getName())
                    .collect(Collectors.toSet());
    }


    public String getValue(String s) {
        File f = new File(dir, s);
        try {
            if (f.exists())
                Path p = f.toPath();
                byte[] secret = Files.readAllBytes(f);
                return new String(secret,
                                StandardCharsets.UTF_8);
        } catch (IOException ioe) {
        }
        return null;
    }
}
```

```
    public String getName() {
        return "kube.secret";
    }

    public int getOrdinal() {
        return 5;
    }
}
```

This config source will load the content of a file with the property name read from a well-defined directory. If the file cannot be read, it will act as if the property is not defined. Kubernetes will update the file content when the secret is updated, which means that updates can be visible to the application automatically since this code will reread the file each time the property is read.

In the next section, we will discuss some considerations when using a Service Mesh with MicroProfile.

MicroProfile and Service Mesh

When deploying into a Kubernetes cluster, some people choose to make use of a Service Mesh. The goal of a Service Mesh is to move certain considerations of microservices out of the application code and to place it around the application. A Service Mesh can remove some application concerns such as service selection, observability, fault tolerance, and, to a certain degree, security. One common Service Mesh technology is **Istio**. The way Istio works is by inserting a sidecar into the Pod for the containers and all inbound and network traffic is routed via that sidecar. This allows the sidecar to perform activities applying access control policies, routing requests to downstream services, and applying fault tolerance policies such as retrying requests or timing them out. Some of these capabilities overlap with some of the MicroProfile capabilities, for example, Istio can handle attaching and propagating OpenTracing data with requests. If you use **Istio**, you clearly do not need to make use of MicroProfile OpenTracing, although using both would complement each other rather than cause conflict.

One area where the use of a Service Mesh and MicroProfile can conflict in negative ways is fault tolerance. For example, if you configure 5 retries in MicroProfile and 5 retries in Istio and they all fail, you will end up with a total of 25 retries. As a result, it is common when using a Service Mesh to disable the MicroProfile fault tolerance capabilities. This can be done with the environment variable of `MP_Fault_Tolerance_NonFallback_Enabled` set to `false`. This will disable all the MicroProfile fault tolerance support except for the fallback capability. This is because the logic to perform on a failure is intrinsically an application consideration and not something that can be extracted into the Service Mesh. This can simply be disabled using the following YAML:

```
apiVersion: openliberty.io/v1beta1
kind: OpenLibertyApplication
metadata:
  name: demo-app
spec:
  expose: true
  applicationImage: openliberty/open-liberty:full-java11-
    openj9-ubi
  env:
    - name: MP_Fault_Tolerance_NonFallback_Enabled
      value: 'false'
  replicas: 1
```

This configures the application to have a hardcoded environment variable that disables the non-fallback MicroProfile Fault Tolerance behaviors. This could also be done with a ConfigMap.

Summary

In this chapter, we have reviewed the MicroProfile implementation that is used in the rest of the book, some best practices for building a container for a MicroProfile application, and how to deploy that application into Kubernetes. While the chapter isn't an exhaustive review of the capabilities available in Kubernetes, it does focus on the particular considerations for deploying MicroProfile applications to Kubernetes, and why they interact with Kubernetes services. This chapter should have provided you with a good starting point for creating and deploying MicroProfile applications using Open Liberty, containers, and Kubernetes.

The next chapter will describe an example application that makes use of MicroProfile for a set of microservices deployed in a container to a Kubernetes cluster.

Section 3: End-to-End Project Using MicroProfile

In this section, the rubber meets the road – you will learn how to build and test the application in its intended cloud deployment environment. You will also learn how to successfully deploy and manage a multi-service application.

This section comprises the following chapters:

- *Chapter 8, Building and Testing Your Cloud-Native Application*
- *Chapter 9, Deployment and Day 2 Operations*

8

Building and Testing Your Cloud-Native Application

In the previous chapters, we've looked at various MicroProfile technologies in isolation. Now, let's come back to our example application, the **IBM Stock Trader**, first introduced in *Chapter 3, Introducing the IBM Stock Trader Cloud-Native Application*, to see those in use across various microservices. In this chapter, we'll focus on how to build those microservices, how to construct the container image for each and push them to an image registry, how to unit test them, and the usage of various MicroProfile features.

In this chapter, we're going to cover the following main topics:

- Compiling the Stock Trader microservices
- Building the Stock Trader container images
- Testing the Stock Trader microservices
- Stock Trader usage of MicroProfile

By the end of this chapter, you will be familiar with how to build the various pieces of such a cloud-native application, how to try out each of them, and how to demonstrate their usage.

Technical requirements

To build and test the microservices as described in this section, you will need to have the following tools installed:

- **Java Development Kit (JDK)** – Java 8 or later: `http://ibm.biz/GetSemeru`
- Apache Maven: `https://maven.apache.org`
- A Git client: `https://git-scm.com`
- A Docker client: `https://www.docker.com/products`

Compiling the Stock Trader microservices

In this section, we will look at how to create a local copy of the source code for each microservice, and how to compile it and package it up into an archive that can be deployed onto an application server.

GitHub

A public GitHub organization called *IBMStockTrader*, at `https://github.com/IBMStockTrader`, contains repositories for each of the dozen or so microservices comprising the application.

Let's focus on the `trader` repository, and clone its contents:

```
jalcorn@Johns-MBP-8 StockTrader % git clone
  https://github.com/IBMStockTrader/trader
Cloning into 'trader'...
```

```
remote: Enumerating objects: 2840, done.
remote: Counting objects: 100% (247/247), done.
remote: Compressing objects: 100% (132/132), done.
remote: Total 2840 (delta 58), reused 0 (delta 0), pack-
   reused 2593
Receiving objects: 100% (2840/2840), 28.25 MiB | 322.00
   KiB/s, done.
Resolving deltas: 100% (1049/1049), done.
jalcorn@Johns-MBP-8 StockTrader % cd trader
jalcorn@Johns-MBP-8 trader % ls
BUILD.md                    Jenkinsfile                 lab
CONTRIBUTING.md             Jenkinsfiledemo             manifest.yml
Dockerfile                  LICENSE                     manifests
Dockerfile-build            README.md                   pipeline-template.yaml
Dockerfile-lang             build_parameters.sh         pom.xml
Dockerfile-tools            chart                       src
Dockerfile.basicregistry cli-config.yml
jalcorn@Johns-MBP-8 trader %
```

The most important files here are `Dockerfile` and the `pom.xml` (both of which
we'll discuss shortly), and the `src` directory, which contains all of the source code. This
includes the Java code (under `src/main/java` – each of the Stock Trader microservices
has its own sub-package under `com.ibm.hybrid.cloud.sample.stocktrader`),
the web artifacts (under `src/main/webapp`), and the Open Liberty configuration
(under `src/main/liberty/config` – we'll look at this further in the *Building the
Stock Trader container images* section). All of the microservices in the application follow
this same structure. Let's take a look at the contents of the `src` directory:

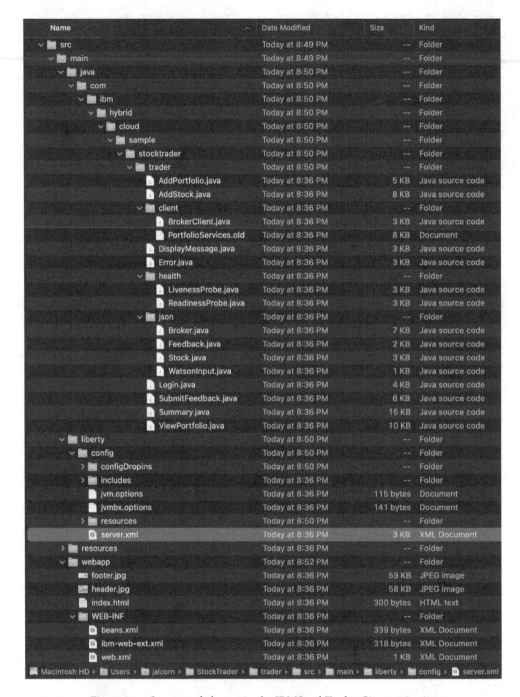

Figure 8.1 – Source code layout in the IBMStockTrader Git repositories

Now that we've seen the source code structure in each Git repository, let's look at how to use *Maven* to build it and package the results up for deployment to the Docker container for the Open Liberty application server.

Maven

The pom.xml file tells Maven what to build and how. Here are the steps:

1. First, you need to include the following stanza in the pom.xml file so that usage of org.eclipse.microprofile.* packages will compile:

    ```
    <dependency>
        <groupId>org.eclipse.microprofile</groupId>
        <artifactId>microprofile</artifactId>
        <version>4.0.1</version>
        <type>pom</type>
        <scope>provided</scope>
    </dependency>
    ```

    This is the *umbrella* dependency that puts all of the MicroProfile 4 features on the compile-time classpath. You can also just choose particular MicroProfile features if you prefer; for example, to put just *MicroProfile Health* on the compile-time classpath, you'd specify org.eclipse.microprofile.health.

    Note the <scope>provided</scope> line – this tells Maven that, though it should add such JAR files to the compile-time classpath, it should *NOT* bundle such JAR files inside the WAR file being built. The application server (Open Liberty, in our case) hosting the WAR file *provides* such JAR files, and having an additional copy inside the application can cause class loader issues, so we tell it provided to avoid that.

2. Next, let's use Maven to build our Trader microservice. Most modern **Integrated Development Environments** (**IDEs**) have built-in Maven support so that you can run a build via a click in a **Graphical User Interface** (**GUI**). But here, we'll look at how to use Maven from a Terminal window.

    If you don't have Maven installed, on a Mac you can use the command brew install maven to install it. Note that Maven also depends on Java, and you will need the JAVA_HOME environment variable to point to your Java installation. Let's use mvn compile to compile our code:

    ```
    jalcorn@Johns-MBP-8 trader % mvn compile
    [INFO] Scanning for projects...
    ```

```
[INFO]
[INFO] --------< com.stocktrader:trader >-------------
[INFO] Building StockTrader - trader 1.0-SNAPSHOT
[INFO] ---------------[ war ]----------------------
[INFO] --- maven-resources-plugin:2.6:resources
  (default-resources) @ trader ---
[INFO] Using 'UTF-8' encoding to copy filtered
  resources.
[INFO] Copying 1 resource
[INFO]
[INFO] --- maven-compiler-plugin:3.1:compile (default-
  compile) @ trader ---
[INFO] Changes detected - recompiling the module!
[INFO] Compiling 15 source files to /Users/jalcorn
  StockTrader/trader/target/classes
[INFO] ---------------------------------------------
[INFO] BUILD SUCCESS
[INFO] ---------------------------------------------
[INFO] Total time:  1.913 s
[INFO] Finished at: 2021-05-09T12:26:19-05:00
[INFO] ---------------------------------------------
jalcorn@Johns-MBP-8 trader %
```

As you can see, it takes less than a couple of seconds to compile all of the code. Of course, if any compilation errors occurred, they will be shown when this is run.

3. Next, let's package up the WAR file, via mvn package. Some of the several pages of output are snipped out to save space, but the important part is shown here:

```
jalcorn@Johns-MBP-8 trader % mvn package
[INFO] Scanning for projects...
[INFO]
[INFO] ---------< com.stocktrader:trader >-------------
[INFO] Building StockTrader - trader 1.0-SNAPSHOT
[INFO] --------------[ war ]----------------------
[INFO] --- maven-war-plugin:2.6:war (default-war) @
  trader ---
[INFO] Packaging webapp
[INFO] Assembling webapp [trader] in
```

```
    [/Users/jalcorn/StockTrader/trader/target/TraderUI]
[INFO] Processing war project
[INFO] Copying webapp resources
    [/Users/jalcorn/StockTrader/trader/src/main/webapp]
[INFO] Webapp assembled in [180 msecs]
[INFO] Building war: /Users/jalcorn/StockTrader/trader
    /target/TraderUI.war
[INFO] ------------------------------------------------
[INFO] BUILD SUCCESS
[INFO] ------------------------------------------------
[INFO] Total time:  28.813 s
[INFO] Finished at: 2021-05-09T12:26:03-05:00
[INFO] ------------------------------------------------
jalcorn@Johns-MBP-8 trader %
```

Note that the command mvn package, which takes about half a minute due to
starting and stopping the Open Liberty server, actually does run the compile as well,
so you would only use the command mvn compile directly when wanting a very
fast way to check for compile errors.

4. Lastly, we can run some basic integration tests via the command mvn verify.

This will execute any test classes you might have under src/test/java (highly
recommended, to catch problems early), such as our HealthEndpoint IT.java
and HomePageIT.java under src/test/java/com/ibm/hybrid/cloud/
sample/stocktrader/trader/test:

```
jalcorn@Johns-MBP-8 trader % mvn verify
[INFO] Scanning for projects...
[INFO]
[INFO] ----------< com.stocktrader:trader >----------
[INFO] Building StockTrader - trader 1.0-SNAPSHOT
[INFO]
[INFO] --- maven-failsafe-plugin:3.0.0-M5:integration-
    test (default) @ trader ---
[INFO]
[INFO] ------------------------------------------------
[INFO]  T E S T S
[INFO] ------------------------------------------------
[INFO] Running com.ibm.hybrid.cloud.sample.stocktrader
```

```
       .trader.test.HealthEndpointIT
Testing endpoint http://localhost:9080/health/ready
Testing endpoint http://localhost:9080/health/live
[INFO] Tests run: 2, Failures: 0, Errors: 0, Skipped:
0, Time elapsed: 1.149 s - in com.ibm.hybrid
.cloud.sample.stocktrader.trader.test.HealthEndpointIT
[INFO] Running com.ibm.hybrid.cloud.sample.stocktrader
   .trader.test.HomePageIT
Testing endpoint http://localhost:9080/trader/login
Response code : 404, retrying ... (0 of 5)
[INFO] Tests run: 1, Failures: 0, Errors: 0, Skipped:
0, Time elapsed: 3.02 s - in com.ibm.hybrid.cloud
.sample.stocktrader.trader.test.HomePageIT
[INFO]
[INFO] Results:
[INFO]
[INFO] Tests run: 3, Failures: 0, Errors: 0, Skipped: 0
[INFO]
[INFO] -------------------------------------------------
[INFO] BUILD SUCCESS
[INFO] -------------------------------------------------
[INFO] Total time:  15.277 s
[INFO] Finished at: 2021-05-09T12:52:12-05:00
[INFO] -------------------------------------------------
jalcorn@Johns-MBP-8 trader %
```

Again, some output (related to things like starting the server) was snipped out for brevity, but the important parts are shown. Note that it's normal to see some 404 errors, as tests sometimes start trying to hit URLs before the server is fully started; that's why it retries up to 5 times before giving up.

Now that we've seen how to compile, package, and test our code, let's look at how to containerize it and test the container.

Building the Stock Trader container images

As discussed in previous sections, we use *Open Liberty* as the application server hosting most of the Stock Trader microservices. And we use *Docker* to produce the container images that ultimately get run in a Kubernetes cluster such as the *OpenShift Container Platform* cluster.

The following subsections will describe how we configure the server, and how we package it up into a container image.

Open Liberty

There are a variety of MicroProfile compliant Java application servers on the market. As a reminder from *Chapter 3*, *Introducing the IBM Stock Trader Cloud-Native Application*, most of the Stock Trader microservices (Trader, Broker, Broker-Query, Portfolio, Account, Trade History, Messaging, Notification-Slack, Collector, and Looper) are based on the open source Open Liberty application server. For variety, there are three other microservices based on different servers:

- Stock Quote, which runs on Red Hat's **Quarkus**.

- Notification-Twitter, which runs on **traditional WebSphere Application Server (tWAS)**.

- Tradr is the only non-Java microservice, which is written in Node.js.

But here, we'll focus on the ones that run on Open Liberty.

The most important file for configuring an Open Liberty server is the `server.xml` file. This defines the features that should be enabled in the server, and the configuration for each of those features. You can enable all of the MicroProfile 4.1 features by listing the `microProfile-4.1` feature in your `server.xml` as follows:

```
<featureManager>
    <feature>microProfile-4.1</feature>
</featureManager>
```

Otherwise just like with the Maven dependencies, if you prefer to enable fewer features, such as if you only want *MicroProfile Health* and *MicroProfile Metrics*, you can instead list them separately as shown here:

```
<featureManager>
    <feature>mpHealth-3.1</feature>
```

```
        <feature>mpMetrics-3.1</feature>
    </featureManager>
```

In addition to the features you enable, some of them support stanzas for configuration. Many of the Java Enterprise Edition resources are configured here, such as the following:

- JDBC DataSources for talking to relational databases such as IBM DB2.

- JMS ActivationSpecs for talking to messaging systems such as IBM MQ.

- CloudantDatabase for talking to a NoSQL datastore such as IBM Cloudant.

For the MicroProfile features in particular, here is how the Stock Trader microservices configure the *MicroProfile JWT* and *MicroProfile Metrics* features:

```
<mpJwt id="stockTraderJWT" audiences="${JWT_AUDIENCE}"
    issuer="${JWT_ISSUER}" keyName="jwtSigner"
        ignoreApplicationAuthMethod="false" expiry="12h"
            sslRef="defaultSSLConfig"/>
<mpMetrics authentication="false"/>
```

These features have been discussed in the previous chapters, so we won't repeat that here. One thing to note though is that we are referencing environment variables such as ${JWT_ISSUER}, rather than hardcoding such values; this way, we don't have to rebuild the container image if we want to modify the values – instead, we would just update the value in a Kubernetes *ConfigMap* or *Secret*, and our operator would configure the .yaml file for the *Deployment* to obtain and pass the appropriate values as environment variables.

Beyond the server.xml file, other Open Liberty-specific files in the src/main/liberty/config directory include jvm.options (used to pass JVM system properties, and so on), and your key store and/or trust store files (such as key.p12 and trust.p12 in the src/main/liberty/config/resources/security directory). The files are laid out here in the same directory structure as is required in the Open Liberty server so that we can just copy the entire directory into the appropriate location in the Docker container for Open Liberty, as we'll see in the next section.

Docker

Once you have all of the input files ready that need to become part of the Docker container image, you use a `Dockerfile` to say what files you want copied where. You can also run commands other than `COPY`, such as setting file permissions or installing additional tools in the container:

1. First, let's take a look at the `Dockerfile` for the Trader microservice:

```
# If building locally, you have to complete a maven build
first, before running the Docker build
FROM openliberty/open-liberty:kernel-slim-java11-openj9-
ubi

USER root


COPY --chown=1001:0 src/main/liberty/config /config


# This script will add the requested XML snippets to
enable Liberty features and grow image to be fit-for-
purpose using featureUtility.
# Only available in 'kernel-slim'. The 'full' tag already
includes all features for convenience.
RUN features.sh


COPY --chown=1001:0 target/TraderUI.war /config/apps/
TraderUI.war


USER 1001
RUN configure.sh
```

The first (non-comment) line says we want to start from the Open Liberty container image. Since the tag we are using does not specify a specific (monthly) release of Open Liberty (such as 21.0.0.7, which is the release in the seventh month of 2021), it is a good idea to do an explicit `docker pull` of the image before running a build, to ensure you have the latest (as Docker would think you already have an image with such a tag, even though the one you have locally might be many months old). For example, do the following:

```
jalcorn@Johns-MBP-8 trader % docker pull openliberty/
open-liberty:kernel-slim-java11-openj9-ubi
kernel-slim-java11-openj9-ubi: Pulling from openliberty/
open-liberty
```

```
Digest: sha256:e072abc78effdbff787b6af34aeaab
29315a6f9f2b376896a0bf09706a5438d6
```

```
Status: Image is up to date for openliberty/open-
liberty:kernel-slim-java11-openj9-ubi
```

```
docker.io/openliberty/open-liberty:kernel-slim-java11-
openj9-ubi
```

```
jalcorn@Johns-MBP-8 trader %
```

Note that this is requesting an image based on the **Universal Base Image** (**UBI**), which is a special build of **Red Hat Enterprise Linux** (**RHEL**) 8.4 that is optimized for Docker. It also says you want an image that includes Java 11 (there are other tags, such as for Java 8 or Java 15). And lastly, it says you want to start from the `kernel-slim` image, which means no features beyond the kernel are packaged in the image, in the interest of size.

The next important line says we want to copy the `src/main/liberty/config` directory into the `/config` directory in the container image. This `/config` directory is actually a soft link to `/opt/ol/wlp/usr/servers/defaultServer` in Open Liberty (or to `/opt/ibm/wlp/usr/servers/defaultServer` on commercial WebSphere Liberty, which you'd get via `FROM ibmcom/websphere-liberty:kernel-java11-openj9-ubi`). We copy the whole directory (and its subdirectories), rather than a separate `COPY` per file, to reduce the number of layers in the resulting Docker image.

2. Next, we run a script called `features.sh`, which downloads all of the features we specify in `server.xml` we copied into the Docker image in the previous step. If instead of using the `kernel-slim` image we had instead used the `full` image, this step would not be needed. Note we want to run this before we copy our WAR file (that Maven produced) into the container so that we don't need to rerun this time-consuming step each time we make a small change to our application.

3. Next, we copy our WAR file (or the Messaging microservice copies in an `ear` file instead, as it has our one EJB – an MDB) into the container. Note `--chown 1001:0`, which tells it what user and group should own the file – without this, the server, which does *NOT* run as root, would not have authority to access the files.

4. Finally, we run the `configure.sh` script, which does some further tweaking of file permissions, and which builds the shared class cache to improve performance.

5. Let's now run our build, which will execute each line of the `Dockerfile`:

```
jalcorn@Johns-MBP-8 trader % docker build -t trader .
[+] Building 45.7s (10/10) FINISHED
 => [internal] load build definition from Dockerfile 0.0s
```

```
=> => transferring dockerfile: 37B 0.0s
=> [internal] load .dockerignore 0.0s
=> => transferring context: 2B 0.0s
=> [internal] load metadata for docker.io/openliberty
/open-liberty:k   0.0s
=> [1/5] FROM docker.io/openliberty/open-liberty:kernel-
slim-java11-  0.0s
=> [internal] load build context 0.3s
=> => transferring context: 11.41MB 0.2s
=> CACHED [2/5] COPY --chown=1001:0 src/main/liberty/
config /config   0.0s
=> CACHED [3/5] RUN features.sh 0.0s
=> [4/5] COPY --chown=1001:0 target/TraderUI.war /
config/apps/Trader  0.1s
=> [5/5] RUN configure.sh 44.8s
=> exporting to image 0.4s
=> => exporting layers 0.4s
=> => writing image sha256:d0a03e6e7fd2873a8361aa9c9c
  ad22dd614686778  0.0s
=> => naming to docker.io/library/trader 0.0s
jalcorn@Johns-MBP-8 trader %
```

6. We now have a Docker image produced, which we can push to an image registry, so that it's available for your operator to access and use in a Kubernetes environment such as the **OpenShift Container Platform** (**OCP**). For example, here we push it to Docker Hub:

```
jalcorn@Johns-MBP-8 trader % docker tag trader:latest
ibmstocktrader/trader:latest
jalcorn@Johns-MBP-8 trader % docker push ibmstocktrader/
trader:latest
The push refers to repository [docker.io/ibmstocktrader/
trader]
c139b5a83739: Pushing   13.9MB/62.74MB
dae5b07894dc: Pushing   2.888MB/11.4MB
0b797df05047: Pushing   5.893MB/69.17MB
7daae910987c: Pushed
3efa9ea44ae4: Layer already exists
7d02e9817200: Layer already exists
```

```
267522994240: Layer already exists
0db07c8859ff: Layer already exists
2b4eefc8e725: Layer already exists
8a9f64ec0b16: Layer already exists
9b61e11e8907: Layer already exists
09b9a9d4c9f4: Layer already exists
83713a30b4bb: Layer already exists
1e8cd6732429: Layer already exists
476579af086a: Layer already exists
jalcorn@Johns-MBP-8 trader %
```

Now that we've built the *Trader* microservice, repeat the aforementioned steps for the *Stock Quote* microservice, which we'll also use later in this chapter. As a quick recap, run the following commands:

- `git clone https://github.com/IBMStockTrader/stock-quote`
- `cd stock-quote`
- `mvn package`
- `docker build -t stock-quote .`

In the next section, we will look at how to test the container images we just built.

Testing the Stock Trader microservices

Now that we've learned how to build our microservices, the next important step, before deploying them to an OpenShift environment, is to first perform some unit tests on them to make sure they are working as desired.

Testing the frontend microservice

We can perform such unit tests by using locally installed Docker on our laptops. Let's run the Docker container we just built for Trader, and try it out:

```
jalcorn@Johns-MBP-8 portfolio % docker run -p 9443:9443
-e JWT_AUDIENCE=test -e JWT_ISSUER=test -e TEST_MODE=true
trader:latest
```

```
Launching defaultServer (Open Liberty 21.0.0.4/wlp-1.0.51.
cl210420210407-0944) on Eclipse OpenJ9 VM, version 11.0.11+9
(en_US)
[AUDIT] CWWKE0001I: The server defaultServer has been launched.
<snip>
[INFO] SRVE0169I: Loading Web Module: Trader UI.
[INFO] SRVE0250I: Web Module Trader UI has been bound to
default_host.
[AUDIT] CWWKT0016I: Web application available (default_host):
http://5708495d563b:9080/trader/
[AUDIT] CWWKZ0001I: Application TraderUI started in 5.701
seconds.
[AUDIT] CWWKF0012I: The server installed the following
features: [appSecurity-2.0, appSecurity-3.0, cdi-2.0,
distributedMap-1.0, el-3.0, federatedRegistry-1.0, jaxrs-
2.1, jaxrsClient-2.1, jndi-1.0, json-1.0, jsonb-1.0, jsonp-
1.1, jsp-2.3, jwt-1.0, jwtSso-1.0, ldapRegistry-3.0,
microProfile-4.0, monitor-1.0, mpConfig-2.0,
mpFaultTolerance-3.0, mpHealth-3.0, mpJwt-1.2, mpMetrics-3.0,
mpOpenAPI-2.0, mpOpenTracing-2.0, mpRestClient-2.0, oauth-2.0,
openidConnectClient-1.0, opentracing-2.0, servlet-4.0, ssl-1.0,
transportSecurity-1.0].
[INFO] CWWKF0008I: Feature update completed in 8.604 seconds.
[AUDIT] CWWKF0011I: The defaultServer server is ready to run
a smarter planet. The defaultServer server started in 9.631
seconds.
```

This docker run command starts the container, tells it to expose its port 9443 (the
default HTTPS port for Open Liberty), and passes a few environment variables.

> **Note**
>
> The environment variable TEST_MODE is used to facilitate testing the Trader
> microservice, which usually needs connectivity to a Broker microservice. It has
> an option to bypass that and work with hardcoded data.

Now that our container is running, let's hit `https://localhost:9443/trader` in a browser. After logging in (as `stock/trader`), we can see the hardcoded `TEST_MODE` data:

Figure 8.2 – Testing the Trader UI microservice via docker run

Congratulations, you have successfully tested the *Trader* microservice in a container!

Testing a backend microservice

Testing a frontend microservice in a browser is pretty straightforward since the web browser takes care of login cookies for you, but when it comes to testing one of the backend microservices, it is a bit more difficult, due to the use of the **JSON Web Token** (**JWT**) for **Single Sign-On** (**SSO**) purposes. The *Stock Quote* microservice is an example of such a backend microservice that uses **MicroProfile JWT** to ensure that no caller is allowed in without first having passed a login challenge, which returns a JWT upon success.

Start the Docker container for the Stock Quote microservice we built earlier via `docker run -p 9080:9080 -e JWT_AUDIENCE=test -e JWT_ISSUER=test stock-quote:latest`. Like before, this exposes a port so that we can communicate with it; in this case, it is port `9080`, used for standard (unencrypted) HTTP access.

However, just directly invoking the REST API exposed by the Stock Quote microservice, by running a command such as `curl http://localhost:9080/stock-quote/TEST`, will result in a `401` error being returned due to the missing SSO credentials.

> **Note**
>
> `TEST` is another special value that returns hardcoded data, bypassing the call to the internet to get an actual stock quote.

We can address this problem by using our frontend Trader microservice to do a login and then looking in the Web Inspector built into the browser to find out the value of the JWT cookie. This will be a little different in each browser; in my case, I'm using Safari on my Mac, and I select **Develop | Show Web Inspector** from the menu bar. Then I just find the **summary** request (this is the servlet showing all of the portfolios) and copy the value of its **JWT** cookie to the clipboard:

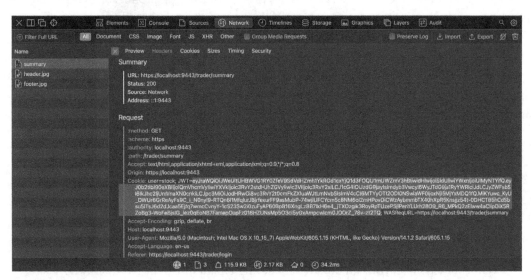

Figure 8.3 – Getting the JWT value from the Web Inspector

Then just paste that big string into an `Authorization` header in `curl`, as shown here:

```
jalcorn@Johns-MBP-8 StockTrader % curl -H "Authorization:
eyJraWQiOiJWeUltUHBWVG1RYOZfeV9SdVdHZmhlYkRGdlcxYjQld3FO
QU1mUWZmV3hBIiwidHlwIjoiSldUIiwiYWxnIjoiUlMyNTYifQ.eyJ0b2tlbl
90eXBlIjoiQmVhcmVyIiwiYXVkIjoic3RvY2stdHJhZGVyIiwic3ViIjoic3R
vY2siLCJ1cG4iOiJzdG9jayIsImdyb3VwcyI6WyJTdG9ja1RyYWRlciJdLCJy
ZWFsbSI6IkJhc2ljUmVnaXN0cnkiLCJpc3MiOiJodHRwOi8vc3RvY2stdHJhZG
VyLmlibS5jb20iLCJleHAiOjE2MjIxNTA0MDUsImlhdCI6MTYyMjE0MzIwNX0.
k2z65b36MJU4fhpqq7S66pYV8rwZalT3aQK-hoOnINeVarg6k3AHIP6lN_ZHsT
KX5W4b8q81o5gC0KSdEFN6VSi3qdC7a02aotICbuuZh459F7IuPOC5rWbwrUa
kznNxh2I7s8Nurhcb2_UDq1WM0POyZYMpuDokys-CeH5w3QyLZ7tx_IS6czU9
yh17bX4pp3eNH0JLCZybB_i-rBHh8cwzKLk3q73CvPhHJ2jw_zw79viaSUs
WOeIkF21S-iB2v4PYw7nTz54pp02pu_eHi8W-hRCebNOO7xsG_JNZUPEg1oN
b9O8b0d_7V8qyKD5m_YpSh45y_CZ9j82i_Ho_9A " http://localhost:90
80/stock-quote/TEST
{"date":"2021-05-10","price":123.45,"symbol":
"TEST","time":0}% jalcorn@Johns-MBP-8 StockTrader %
```

As you can see, we got back a stock price of `123.45` from this quick unit test of our backend Stock Quote microservice. Note that JWTs automatically expire, so after a while, you'll have to do this again to get a fresh one if your `curl` calls start getting rejected. Of course, there are also GUI REST test clients that can simplify this common issue of how to pass credentials to a backend service.

Now that we've seen the approach for how to build and test the containers for each of our microservices, let's dive a bit deeper into the usage of MicroProfile 4.1 features in the Stock Trader application.

Using MicroProfile features in Stock Trader

Let's start with a view of which Stock Trader microservices use which MicroProfile features. Note that there are two ways a microservice can benefit from a given MicroProfile feature – implicitly or explicitly:

- In the implicit case, just listing the feature in your `server.xml` file gives you value; for example, you can obtain default implementations for readiness and liveness probes just by enabling the `mpHealth-3.1` feature.

- In the explicit case, you directly code to the APIs offered by the feature, such as implementing your own custom logic for whether your microservice is healthy by coding to classes in the `org.eclipse.microprofile.health` package from within your own Java classes.

In the following table, we can see which microservices use which feature, with the *not* sign meaning not at all, the *dash* meaning implicit usage, and the *checkmark* meaning explicit usage:

	Config	Metrics	Health	OpenAPI	OpenTracing	JWT	Fault Tolerance	REST Client
Trader	✓	✓	✓	–	–	✓	⊘	✓
Broker	✓	–	–	–	–	✓	⊘	✓
Portfolio	✓	✓	✓	–	✓	✓	⊘	✓
Stock Quote	⊘	–	–	–	–	⊘	✓	✓
Account	✓	✓	–	–	✓	✓	⊘	✓
Trade History	✓	–	✓	✓	–	⊘	⊘	✓
Messaging	⊘	⊘	⊘	⊘	⊘	⊘	⊘	✓
Notification Slack	⊘	–	–	–	–	⊘	⊘	✓
Collector	✓	✓	–	–	–	✓	⊘	⊘
Looper	✓	–	–	–	–	⊘	⊘	✓

Table 8.1 – MicroProfile usage in each Stock Trader microservice

Note that the tWAS-based Notification-Twitter and the Node.js-based Tradr aren't listed (since they don't run on a MicroProfile-compliant server) and that the Messaging microservice is just an MDB with no HTTP endpoint, so most MicroProfile features don't apply to it. Also, with Stock Trader, we tend to use the (Istio-based) *OpenShift Service Mesh* to define our Fault Tolerance policies via .yaml files, rather than directly coding to the mpFaultTolerance feature.

Implicit usage of MicroProfile features

MicroProfile delivers significant benefits to applications that are being modernized to a MicroProfile-compliant application server, even if the applications aren't updated to code to the APIs of the various MicroProfile features. This can be useful, such as in situations where you are modernizing from the traditional WebSphere Application Server to Open Liberty, but don't want to have to make a lot of code updates. In the following sub-sections, we'll examine which MicroProfile features can provide such implicit benefits.

MicroProfile Health

As mentioned previously, you can get automatic implementations of the Kubernetes startup, readiness, and liveness probes, just by enabling the mpHealth-3.1 feature in your server.xml file. Note that startup probes are relatively new in Kubernetes, added in version 1.16, which corresponds to OpenShift version 4.3. And support for them was added rather recently in MicroProfile, starting in version 4.1, which is the first version containing MicroProfile Health version 3.1.

A startup probe is useful if your application takes a long time to start (such as if it loads and caches a lot of data from a database).

A readiness probe is important so that work won't get routed to a newly started pod until it is actually ready to process such requests.

The default readiness implementation will return false until the server and all of its applications are fully started, and from then on will return true, until a signal is received that the server is stopping (such as when a *HorizontalPodAutoscaler* scales down the number of pods for a deployment). This is also the default startup probe implementation – so really, you only get additional value from a startup probe, above and beyond what you get from the default readiness probe implementation if you provide your own explicit implementation.

The default liveness implementation will return true as long as the server can process inbound HTTP requests. This will usually be the case unless all of the threads in the web container are hung/in use, or something really bad like an OutOfMemoryError has occurred. Kubernetes will automatically kill any pod that fails its liveness probe a specified consecutive number of times and start a fresh one to replace it.

Here are the results of directly calling the startup, readiness, and liveness probes on our container:

```
jalcorn@Johns-MBP-8 StockTrader % curl http://localhost:9080/
health/started
{"checks":[],"status":"UP"}
% jalcorn@Johns-MBP-8 StockTrader % curl http://localhost:9080/
health/ready
{"checks":[],"status":"UP"}%
jalcorn@Johns-MBP-8 StockTrader % curl http://localhost:9080/
health/live
{"checks":[],"status":"UP"}%
jalcorn@Johns-MBP-8 StockTrader %
```

MicroProfile metrics

There are three kinds of metrics: base, vendor, and application. The first two kinds will be available automatically to anyone that periodically scrapes the /metrics endpoint (such as *Prometheus*), just by enabling the mpMetrics-3.0 feature in the server.xml file. The third kind is only available when the application is coded to the annotations or explicit API calls from the org.eclipse.microprofile.metrics package.

Base metrics are defined by the MicroProfile Metrics specification, and generally include JVM-level metrics related to heap size, garbage collection, and thread counts, in addition to various counters and timings. Vendor metrics vary by each application server, and include things such as JDBC and JMS connection pool usage and other things that the app server manages for you. Let's take a look at a few of the available base and vendor metrics (the full set would take many pages to display) from our running Stock Quote container:

```
jalcorn@Johns-MBP-8 StockTrader % curl http://localhost:9080/
metrics
# TYPE base_classloader_loadedClasses_count gauge
# HELP base_classloader_loadedClasses_count Displays the number
of classes that are currently loaded in the Java virtual
machine.
base_classloader_loadedClasses_count 12491
# TYPE base_thread_count gauge
# HELP base_thread_count Displays the current number of live
threads including both daemon and non-daemon threads.
base_thread_count 53
# TYPE base_memory_usedHeap_bytes gauge
# HELP base_memory_usedHeap_bytes Displays the amount of used
heap memory in bytes.
base_memory_usedHeap_bytes 6.675884E7
# TYPE vendor_servlet_request_total counter
# HELP vendor_servlet_request_total The number of visits to
this servlet since the start of the server.
vendor_servlet_request_total{servlet="StockQuote_com_ibm_
hybrid_cloud_sample_stocktrader_stockquote_StockQuote"} 1
# TYPE vendor_threadpool_size gauge
# HELP vendor_threadpool_size The size of the thread pool.
vendor_threadpool_size{pool="Default_Executor"} 8
```

```
# TYPE vendor_servlet_responseTime_total_seconds gauge
```

```
# HELP vendor_servlet_responseTime_total_seconds The total
response time of this servlet since the start of the server.
```

```
vendor_servlet_responseTime_total_seconds{servlet="StockQuote_
com_ibm_hybrid_cloud_sample_stocktrader_stockquote_StockQuote"}
0.9500412
```

```
jalcorn@Johns-MBP-8 StockTrader %
```

MicroProfile OpenTracing

Another of the observability-related features is MicroProfile OpenTracing. This will automatically generate trace spans for any JAX-RS operation, simply by enabling the mpOpenTracing-2.0 feature. These trace spans are sent to any registered tracer, such as for Jaeger. If you have the Jaeger tracer registered, you should see the following in your container's output, indicating that trace spans are being sent on each JAX-RS operation:

```
[INFO] Initialized tracer=JaegerTracer(version=Java-1.5.0,
serviceName=StockQuote, reporter=CompositeReporter(reporters=
[RemoteReporter(sender=UdpSender(host=localhost, port=6831),
closeEnqueueTimeout=1000), LoggingReporter(logger=org.slf4j.
impl.JDK14LoggerAdapter(io.jaegertracing.internal.reporters.
LoggingReporter))]), sampler=RemoteControlledSampler
(maxOperations=2000, manager=HttpSamplingManager(hostPort=
localhost:5778), sampler=ProbabilisticSampler(tags={sampler.
type=probabilistic, sampler.param=0.001})), tags={hostname=5f0
6cf0b9a96, jaeger.version=Java-1.5.0, ip=172.17.0.2},
zipkinSharedRpcSpan=false, expandExceptionLogs=false,
useTraceId128Bit=false)
```

```
[INFO] CWMOT1001I: A JaegerTracer instance was created for the
StockQuote application.  Tracing information is sent to
localhost:6831.
```

The other important feature of MicroProfile Open Tracing is that a *span* can chain to as many calls as needed, so rather than just seeing one span showing that A called B and another span showing that B called C, a span could encompass showing the call path from A to B to C, including when they occurred, how long each part took, and much more. Being able to see, for example, a span that includes Trader calling Broker calling Portfolio calling Stock Quote is valuable to those wanting to see how all of these various microservices fit together at runtime, and whether they are performing as expected.

MicroProfile OpenAPI

The MicroProfile OpenAPI feature is quite cool since it will generate documentation about your JAX-RS class, simply by enabling the `mpOpenAPI-2.0` feature in your `server.xml` file. If someone wants to know what operations your microservice makes available, all they have to do is `curl http://localhost:9080/openapi` to get a `.yaml` file that explains each of the available operations, their input parameters, and the data structure they return.

One nice bonus item you get with Open Liberty is the ability to have it generate a human-friendly web page rendering of this information (sometimes this is referred to as the Swagger UI). Just hit `http://localhost:9080/openapi/ui` in a browser to see an HTML rendering. Let's take a look at the HTML rendering for our Broker microservice:

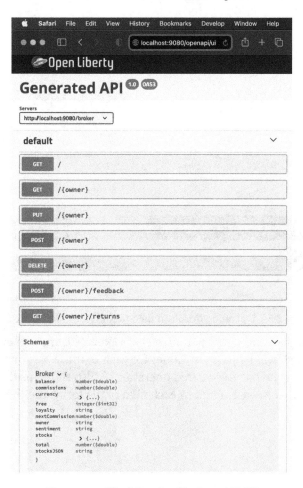

Figure 8.4 – The MicroProfile OpenAPI UI

Here we can see there's a **GET** operation that takes no path parameters (that returns a summary of all portfolios), as well as **GET**, **PUT**, **POST**, and **DELETE** operations for a particular portfolio, and a couple of other operations (one sends feedback to the *Watson Tone Analyzer*, and the other gets the return on investment for a particular portfolio). We also can see the structure of the `Broker` JSON object that these operations return.

We can also drill into one of the operations and see details about it – let's pick the **PUT** operation that's used to update a portfolio with a trade of stock:

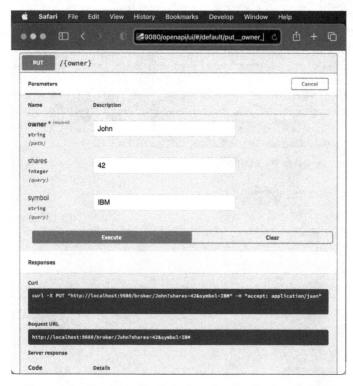

Figure 8.5 – Operation details in the MicroProfile OpenAPI UI

Now we can see what path and query parameters are expected, and can even click the **Try it out** button, which will let us fill in values for each of those parameters, and then click **Execute** to actually invoke the desired operation. It also shows us the corresponding `curl` command for what we've entered in each field of the form, and the results of invoking the operation.

MicroProfile JWT

The final MicroProfile feature that offers implicit value is MicroProfile JWT. Simply by enabling the mpJWT-1.2 feature in your server.xml file (and a few other stanzas in the server.xml file, a stanza in the WAR file's web.xml, and a signing key in your keystore/truststore), you can cause the app server to reject any calls that don't have the required JWT in either the Authorization HTTP header or in a cookie.

This is a very powerful feature, in that you get nice single sign-on enforcement, without having to edit your Java code at all. If someone tries to invoke your microservice without attaching an appropriate JWT, it will get rejected with a 403 error:

```
jalcorn@Johns-MBP-8 StockTrader %
curl -I http://localhost:9080/broker
HTTP/1.1 403 Forbidden
X-Powered-By: Servlet/4.0
Content-Type: text/html;charset=ISO-8859-1
$WSEP:
Content-Language: en-US
Connection: Close
Date: Tue, 11 May 2021 05:27:45 GMT


jalcorn@Johns-MBP-8 StockTrader %
```

When this occurs, you will see the following message get logged by your container:

```
[ERROR] CWWKS5522E: The MicroProfile JWT feature cannot perform
authentication because a MicroProfile JWT cannot be found in
the request.
```

Getting such powerful security enforcement, without any Java coding on your part, is a very nice feature provided by MicroProfile!

Summary

You should now have a feel for how to build and unit test any of the microservices in the Stock Trader application. You should also now be comfortable with how to containerize such microservices, and then run such containers and invoke such microservices.

Note that, often, rather than running such build steps as we've covered in this chapter manually from Command Prompt, you will have a DevOps pipeline that runs such steps for you, such as automatically kicking off via a webhook when you commit a change to your Git repository. For example, see this blog entry on such a CI/CD pipeline for the Trader microservice, which also performs various security and compliance checks: `https://medium.com/cloud-engagement-hub/are-your-ci-cd-processes-compliant-cee6db1cf82a`. But it's good to understand how to do stuff manually, rather than it just seeming like some magical, mysterious thing occurs to get to where your container image is built and available in your image registry.

We've also covered how Stock Trader benefits from many of the MicroProfile features, even though it is not explicitly coded to such features. The fact that modernizing to a MicroProfile-compliant app server offers such benefits "for free," without your developers having to spend time modifying their code, is a strong motivator for engaging in such an application modernization effort.

In the next chapter, we will look at how to deploy this application to an OpenShift cluster, via its operator, and will look at how we can use it to perform some *Day 2* operations.

9
Deployment and Day 2 Operations

So far, we've seen many code snippets and screenshots of our example application, the **IBM Stock Trader**. Now, let's learn how to deploy it to your own **OpenShift Container Platform** cluster or any **Kubernetes** platform of your choice. As important as getting it running is, it is also very important to learn how to maintain it and tune it to meet your needs.

Unlike many *Hello World* samples that you might see on the internet, that either have no operator at all (just having you manually apply `.yaml` files to install), or they perhaps have a very simple operator per microservice, the **IBM Stock Trader** example has a **composite operator** that not only installs all of the microservices but also configures the connectivity to all prerequisite services, including all the credentials used for authentication.

This composite operator also provides an advanced form **User Interface** (**UI**) in the OpenShift console, used both at initial deployment time to pick which of the optional pieces you want and how to configure them, and also used on *day 2* and beyond to fine-tune various values as desired. And for those who prefer a command-line or automated experience (or who use plain **Kubernetes** without access to the sophisticated OpenShift console), the operator works well in that situation as well, as you prepare and apply the `.yaml` file for the custom resource defined by the operator.

In this chapter, we're going to cover the following main topics:

- Understanding the role of operators
- Installing the operator via the OpenShift console
- Deploying the application via the operator form UI
- Deploying the application via the command line
- Day 2 operations

By the end of this chapter, you will be familiar with using the operator to deploy the application, either from the UI or the CLI, and how to use it to maintain the application going forward.

Technical requirements

To use the operator as described in this section, you will need to have the following tools installed:

- A Git client – `https://git-scm.com`
- A Kubernetes client (`kubectl`) – `https://kubernetes.io/docs/tasks/tools/#kubectl`

In addition, you will need to have a Kubernetes cluster available. For the CLI parts of this chapter, you can use any Kubernetes distribution you prefer. But to try out the UI parts of this chapter, the Kubernetes distribution will need to be OpenShift Container Platform (OCP), since the screenshots are all from the OpenShift console. Ask your administrator how to give `kubectl` access to your cluster, and for the URL of the console if using OCP.

Understanding the role of operators

Before diving into the specifics of the IBM Stock Trader operator, let's step back for a bit and consider what operators do and why they are a good thing. To do so, it's important to recall from *Chapter 7, MicroProfile Ecosystem with Open Liberty, Docker, and Kubernetes*, that Kubernetes defines a model where there are several built-in object types, such as Deployments, Services, Ingresses, ConfigMaps, and Secrets. In the true object-oriented philosophy, such objects not only have data but have behavior; it is the operators' job to participate in and guide the full **Create, Retrieve, Update, and Delete (CRUD)** life cycle of the objects they manage.

One key point is that Kubernetes not only has its built-in objects, but also has an extensibility model where vendors can add to that *vocabulary*, defining additional types of objects and how they should act in the Kubernetes environment. Kubernetes calls this a **CustomResourceDefinition (CRD)**. A CRD is essentially a schema of what fields describe the configuration for a particular instance of the **CustomResource (CR)**. I often think of it as a *CR* is to its *CRD* as *XML* is to its *XSD*.

Before the rise of operators, an earlier technology known as **Helm** was used to install an application in Kubernetes. It did what it was meant to – it applied the yaml file to each Kubernetes built-in object needed by an application, with some ability to parameterize the fields in each yaml file. The Stock Trader application itself had a Helm chart (at `https://github.com/IBMStockTrader/stocktrader-helm`), before the arrival of OpenShift version 4, which was a pretty big redesign of the OpenShift architecture with operators at the heart of it all.

Though Helm worked, it was a limited technology, in that it did nothing to help with running the applications once they were installed. An operator, on the other hand, is always listening for, and ready to react to, any change to a CR of the CRD type it operates upon. Operators also can offer *day 2* operations, as we'll see later in this chapter.

> **Note**
>
> There are different ways to write an operator, one of which is to wrap a Helm chart. The operator for the Stock Trader application is one such Helm-based operator. Take a look at (or clone) the `https://github.com/IBMStockTrader/stocktrader-operator` repo to browse its source code, to open issues, or to submit **pull requests (PRs)** to improve the operator.

Another way of thinking about it is that operators expand the kinds of objects that Kubernetes knows how to manage; for example, one managing a CRD of the `PacktBook` type would enable commands such as `kubectl get PacktBooks` or `kubectl describe PacktBook microprofile`, in the same way, you would act upon built-in Kubernetes objects such as `Deployments` or `Services`.

Now let's learn how to use the operator for our Stock Trader application. We'll start with the OpenShift console UI approach, and then will look at how to use it from a CLI as well.

Installing the operator via the OpenShift console

As a quick reminder from *Chapter 3, Introducing the IBM Stock Trader Cloud-Native Application*, the **IBM Stock Trader** application is comprised of about a dozen microservices (many of which are optional), and about the same number of prerequisite resources, such as databases and messaging systems. The composite operator guides you through providing all of the settings for each of those microservices and for configuring their connectivity to those various backend resources, as we can see here:

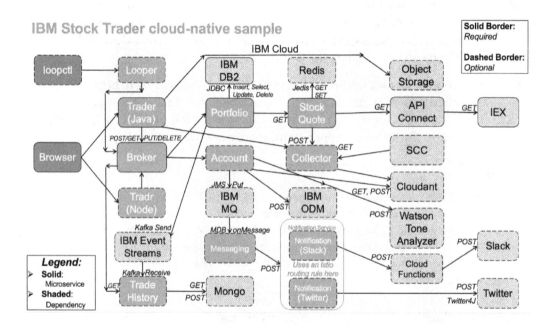

Figure 9.1 – Architectural diagram

As we can see, there are a lot of parts that need to be configured for everything to work. The operator guides us through providing such configuration information for each piece (though it does *NOT* actually install the backend resources – it just asks for the endpoint and credential details to connect to pre-existing resources, which could be running in your cluster, or accessed from elsewhere, such as a **DB2-as-a-Service** (**DB2aaS**) out in the cloud). In the next two sections, we'll learn about OperatorHub and how to install the operator in our cluster.

OperatorHub

The **OpenShift** 4.x console includes a catalog of operators called **OperatorHub**. There are several built-in catalog sources, and administrators can plug in additional sources to make more operators appear in the catalog that they have purchased from vendors (such as the catalog sources for the various IBM Cloud Paks) or that their own developers have created. Let's take a look at the **OperatorHub** portion of the OpenShift console by clicking on **Operators | OperatorHub** in the left navigation menu:

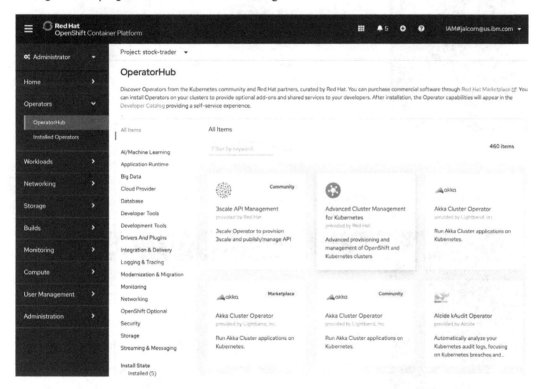

Figure 9.2 – OperatorHub

Here we can see we have 460 operators available, 5 of which are currently installed in our cluster. Let's learn how to install our own catalog source so that we can cause our own operator(s) to show up here:

1. We'll start by clicking on **Administration | Cluster Settings** in the left navigation menu.

2. Then we choose the **Global Configuration** tab and click on **OperatorHub** in the alphabetical list as shown next (you can type something like Hub, in the filter field, and the list will filter to just entries containing that string):

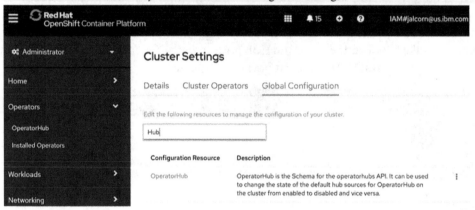

Figure 9.3 – Cluster Settings

3. Then, on the resulting page, click on the **Sources** tab.

    You'll see that four sources are pre-configured (all from Red Hat), and the number of operators contributed by each:

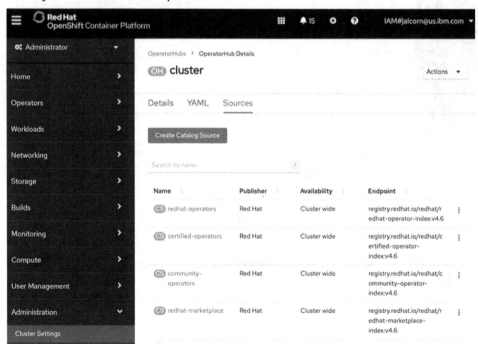

Figure 9.4 – Catalog Sources

If your administrator has set up your cluster to show operators beyond the default ones, you may see more than the initial four.

4. Then just click on the **Create Catalog Source** button to provide the details for our new source containing the operator for the **IBM Stock Trader** application:

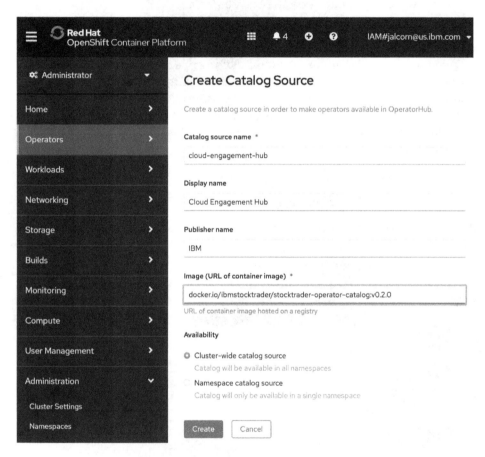

Figure 9.5 – Details for the IBM Stock Trader catalog source

> **Note**
>
> We chose to make it a **Cluster-wide catalog source** so that it is available regardless of what namespace you are using in your cluster. If you prefer (or only have authority in a particular namespace), you could instead choose **Namespace catalog source**. Note that if you are in a really locked-down environment using an ID with limited security privileges, you might need to ask an administrator to perform this action for you.

5. You can type whatever values you want in the first three fields (I chose my team's name, `Cloud Engagement Hub`).

6. The final field, specifying where to find the Docker image for the catalog source, is the most important and needs to be set to `docker.io/ibmstocktrader/ stocktrader-operator-catalog:v0.2.0`.

> **Note**
>
> Of course, you could clone the `IBMStockTrader/stocktrader-operator` GitHub repository and build your own image (per the instructions at `https://github.com/IBMStockTrader/ stocktrader-operator/blob/master/bundle/README.md`) and push it to your own image registry and specify that here, but to keep things simple, we're using the pre-built version we keep hosted in **Docker Hub** for convenience.

7. Once you click the **Create** button, it will return you to the list of catalog sources.

    At first, there will just be a dash for the number of operators from that new source, until OpenShift is able to download the specified Docker container image and parse its contents. Once it does, it will update to show the correct number of operators, which is just one in our case, as shown here:

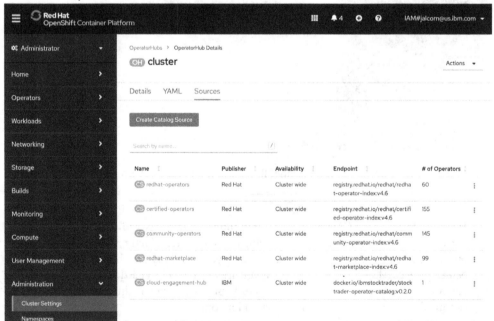

Figure 9.6 – Details for the IBM Stock Trader catalog source

8. Now if you return to the **OperatorHub** page for your cluster (via **Operators |**
    OperatorHub in the left navigation menu), our new operator will appear.

    Note that, rather than scrolling down dozens of times to find it, you can type
    something like stock, in the filter field, and then it will only show the ones
    containing that string:

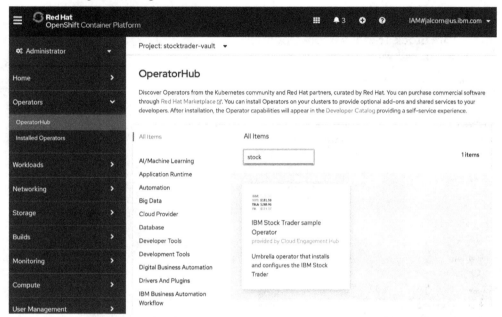

Figure 9.7 – The IBM Stock Trader operator in our cluster's OperatorHub

Congratulations! You have now made the operator for the IBM Stock Trader application
available in the OperatorHub catalog. In the next section, we'll look at how to install
the operator.

Installing the operator

Now that we've made our operator available in our cluster's catalog, let's make use of it:

1. Just click on the tile for the operator. Doing so will show further details about the operator that we just made available in the previous section:

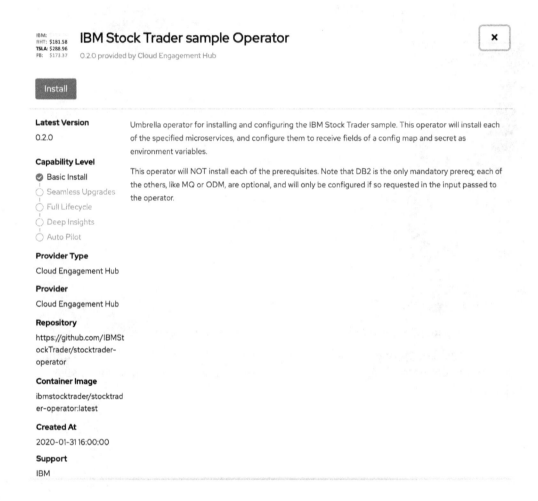

IBM:
RHT: $181.58
TSLA: $288.96
FB: $173.37

IBM Stock Trader sample Operator

0.2.0 provided by Cloud Engagement Hub

[×]

Install

Latest Version

0.2.0

Capability Level

✅ Basic Install
○ Seamless Upgrades
○ Full Lifecycle
○ Deep Insights
○ Auto Pilot

Provider Type

Cloud Engagement Hub

Provider

Cloud Engagement Hub

Repository

https://github.com/IBMSt
ockTrader/stocktrader-
operator

Container Image

ibmstocktrader/stocktrad
er-operator:latest

Created At

2020-01-31 16:00:00

Support

IBM

Umbrella operator for installing and configuring the IBM Stock Trader sample. This operator will install each of the specified microservices, and configure them to receive fields of a config map and secret as environment variables.

This operator will NOT install each of the prerequisites. Note that DB2 is the only mandatory prereq; each of the others, like MQ or ODM, are optional, and will only be configured if so requested in the input passed to the operator.

Figure 9.8 – The IBM Stock Trader operator info page

As you can see, this shows some basic information about the operator, including its readme file. Nothing needs to be done in this dialog – just click on the **Install** button.

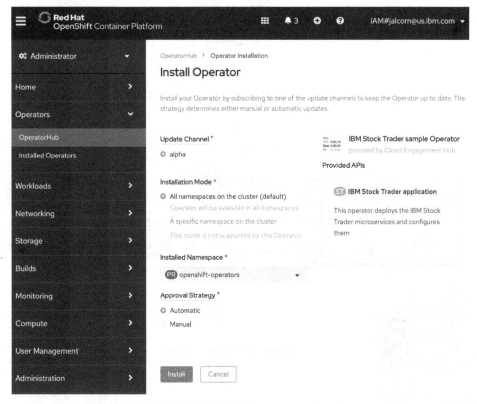

Figure 9.9 – The IBM Stock Trader operator subscription page

Here we see information about how the operator will behave in our cluster; for example, we can see that, like all OperatorHub-integrated operators that you install to work on all namespaces in your cluster, the actual namespace where the operator will run is called **openshift-operators**. Note that the act of *installing* an operator is technically about making a *subscription* to that operator (more on that in the *Deploying the application via the CLI* section, next).

2. Once you click the **Install** button, you'll briefly see a dialog saying it is being installed (until its pod starts and passes its readiness check), and then it will tell you whether it has been successfully installed.

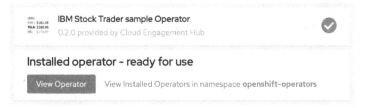

Figure 9.10 – The IBM Stock Trader operator is installed

Congratulations! You have now installed the operator for the **IBM Stock Trader** application. In the next section, we'll look at how to use that operator to deploy the application.

Deploying the application via the operator form UI

To deploy the application, we will follow these steps:

1. Click on the **View Operator** button shown in *Figure 9.10*. You will be taken to a page showing you information about the operator, which of course looks very similar to what we saw when we first clicked on the operator in **OperatorHub**.

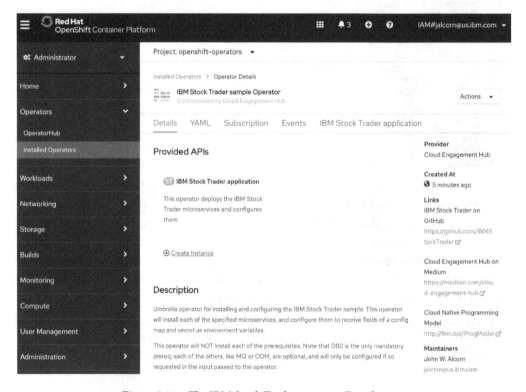

Figure 9.11 – The IBM Stock Trader operator Details page

2. We can use the **Create Instance** link shown in *Figure 9.11* to launch into the dialog for installing an instance of our **IBM Stock Trader** application:

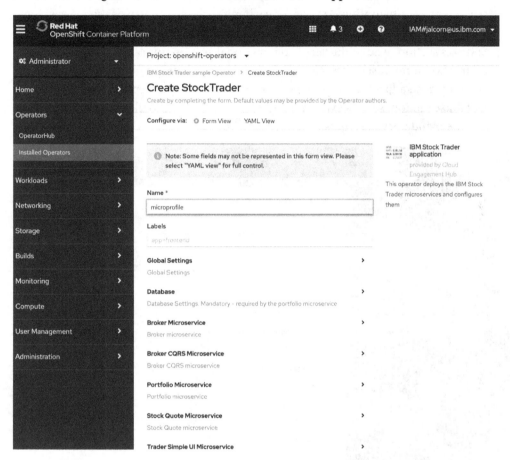

Figure 9.12 – The IBM Stock Trader operator form UI

3. Next, we will provide a **Name** for this instance.

Note that you can use this operator to install as many instances as you want; for example, one instance might use a local *DB2* database, and another might use a *DB2aaS* in the cloud. Each instance will use the **Name** you specify here as the prefix on all resources created; for example, if we type `microprofile` as the instance name to use here, then the portfolio deployment that gets created will be named `microprofile-portfolio`.

Since this is a composite operator – that is, one that installs the entire application, not one for just a particular microservice – it uses expandable/collapsible sections to separate the configuration settings for each microservice. It also has such a section for each service it depends upon, such as a **Database** section and an **IBM MQ Settings** section. And at the very top is a **Global** section, for settings that apply to all of the chosen microservices. Note that most settings have good, reasonable defaults and only need adjusting in special scenarios. The one big exception to that is the **Database** section, so let's expand it and see what we need to fill in there, as this is the one mandatory prerequisite service that we can't run without:

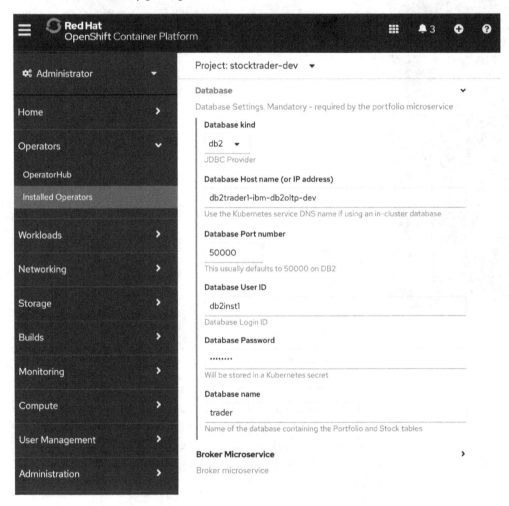

Figure 9.13 – The Database section of the IBM Stock Trader operator form UI

4. As you can see, standard *endpoint* type information must be provided, such as the **Database Host name (or IP address)** of the database server and the **Database Port Number** used to connect to it, as well as credential information needed to authenticate to it. Very similar information is requested for each of the later sections, such as for **Cloudant**, **ODM**, or **MQ**.

Let's expand one of the optional microservices, such as the **Account microservice**:

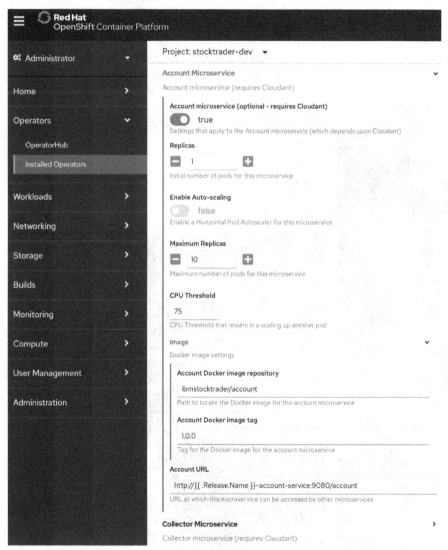

Figure 9.14 – The Account microservice section of the IBM Stock Trader operator form UI

Note the little true/false switch at the top, where you specify whether you want to enable this optional microservice. The rest of the settings in that section will only apply if you choose to enable this microservice. Note also the section for specifying where the Docker container image is found for this microservice; by default, it will be prefilled with the location in *Docker Hub* where we host pre-built versions of each microservice for convenience, though you can type your own value here if you have built the microservice yourself (as described in the previous chapter) and pushed it to your own image registry.

Note that the first time or two you install the application, having the form UI guide you through everything is very helpful, but over time this can get a bit old, filling in each value for each microservice and each prerequisite service they depend upon. Therefore, there is also the option to simply provide the answers to all of these questions in a .yaml file, which you can just drag and drop into the second tab of this form (**YAML View**):

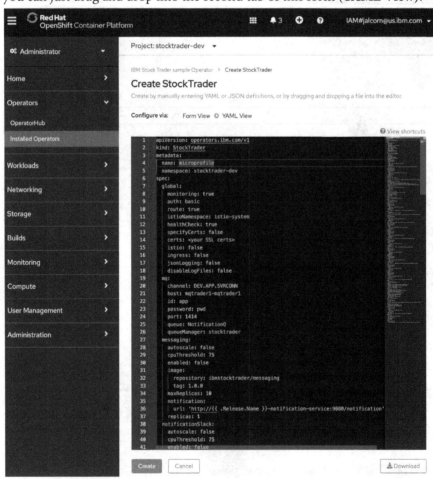

Figure 9.15 – The YAML View tab of the IBM Stock Trader operator form UI

Whichever way you provide the input, the same end result will occur, once you click the **Create** button at the bottom of the page. You should see your new instance appear in the list of instances of the **IBM Stock Trader** application, with the **Name** you provided:

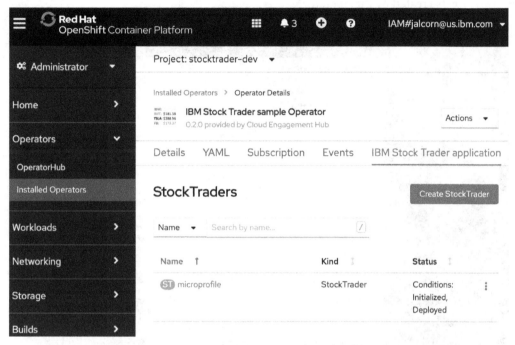

Figure 9.16 – The **StockTraders** section of the IBM Stock Trader operator UI

If we click on that name, we will see info about our newly deployed instance. There are several tabs; the **Resources** tab is especially useful, to see which of the Kubernetes resources discussed in *Chapter 7, MicroProfile Ecosystem with Open Liberty, Docker, and Kubernetes*, gets created by the operator:

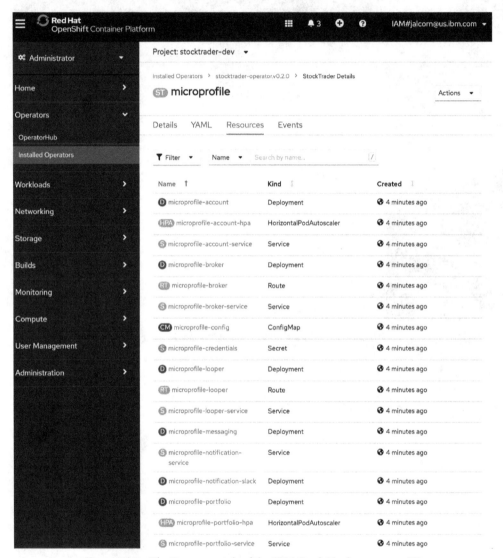

Figure 9.17 – The Resources tab of the IBM Stock Trader operator UI

How much appears here depends on which microservices you chose to enable. Since it can be a long list, there is a **Filter** button near the top left, which can be used to filter the list down to just certain types of Kubernetes objects:

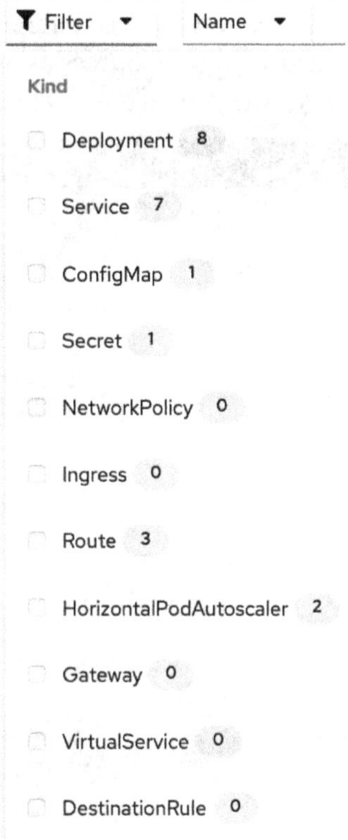

Figure 9.18 – The Filter dialog of the IBM Stock Trader operator form UI

Here we can see that in this instance, we have 8 Deployments (microservices), 7 Services (one of the microservices is an MDB with no HTTP endpoint, so it has no Service), 1 ConfigMap, 1 Secret, 3 Routes, and 2 HorizontalPodAutoscalers. If we had enabled other options, such as the **Istio** true/false setting in the **Global** section of our form/yaml, then we'd have seen additional items such as **Gateway**, **VirtualService**, **DestinationRule**, and **NetworkPolicy** as non-zero. We can also view resources as usual in the OpenShift console by clicking on **Workloads | Pods** to see all of the running pods:

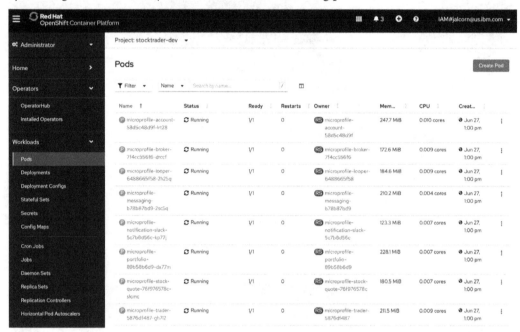

Figure 9.19 – The pods for each microservice comprising the IBM Stock Trader application

We've now seen how to install the IBM Stock Trader application via the OpenShift console. In the next section, we'll look at how we would use the operator via the `kubectl` **Command-Line Interface** (**CLI**) instead.

Deploying the application via the CLI

Sometimes you need to do things via an approach other than using a graphical user interface. Maybe you just prefer using a CLI. Or, perhaps you want to automate such work as steps in a **Continuous Integration / Continuous Deployment** (**CI / CD**) pipeline. Or, maybe you are using a Kubernetes distribution other than **Red Hat OpenShift Container Platform** (**OCP**), such as from one of the hyperscalers, such as **Amazon Web Services** (**AWS**) or **Microsoft Azure**. To deploy the application without the benefit of the OpenShift console, follow these steps:

1. The first thing you'll need to do is to make sure that the **Operator Lifecycle Manager** (**OLM**) feature is installed in your Kubernetes cluster. This can be done via the **operator-sdk** (which you can install on your Mac via `brew install operator-sdk`) by following the instructions at `https://olm.operatorframework.io/docs/getting-started/`.

> **Note**
>
> `operator-sdk` is used to produce an operator such as the one for the IBM Stock Trader application. The exact command that generated the starting point for this operator was `operator-sdk init --plugins helm --group operators --kind StockTrader --domain ibm.com --version v1 --helm-chart ../stocktrader-helm/stocktrader-1.5.0.tgz`.

2. The next step is to create the catalog source for the **IBM Stock Trader** application. Create a `.yaml` file with the following contents:

```
apiVersion: operators.coreos.com/v1alpha1
kind: CatalogSource
metadata:
  name: cloud-engagement-hub
spec:
  publisher: IBM
  displayName: Cloud Engagement Hub
  image: 'docker.io/ibmstocktrader/stocktrader-
    operator-catalog:v0.2.0'
```

The only value that really matters is the `image` field – you can specify anything you want for the other fields. Name the file whatever you want, such as `catalog-source.yaml`. Make sure you are logged in to your cluster from your terminal window and then run the command `kubectl apply -f catalog-source.yaml`. After a minute or so, the catalog source will be available, just like when done via the OpenShift console.

3. Next, you will install the operator via the catalog source. Create another `.yaml` file with the following contents:

```
apiVersion: operators.coreos.com/v1alpha1
kind: Subscription
metadata:
  name: stocktrader-operator
```

```
  namespace: openshift-operators
spec:
  channel: alpha
  installPlanApproval: Automatic
  name: stocktrader-operator
  source: cloud-engagement-hub
  sourceNamespace: openshift-marketplace
  startingCSV: stocktrader-operator.v0.2.0
```

Name it whatever you want, such as `subscription.yaml`. Then, run `kubectl apply -f subscription.yaml`. Once this is complete, the operator will be installed and available.

4. The final step is to apply the yaml for the instance you want to create of the IBM Stock Trader application. As discussed in the *Understanding the role of operators* section, an operator defines a CRD – in this case, for an object of the `StockTrader` type – and here we are creating a CR of that type.

The Stock Trader CR yaml has the same structure as what we saw in the OpenShift console; each expandable section maps to an indentation level in the .yaml file. For example, there's a section for every microservice, and for each prerequisite service they depend upon. Here's a snippet of an example `CR yaml`, most of which is cut out to avoid having many pages of yaml content:

```
apiVersion: operators.ibm.com/v1
kind: StockTrader
metadata:
  name: microprofile
spec:
  global:
    auth: basic
    healthCheck: true
    ingress: false
    istio: false
    istioNamespace: mesh
    route: true
    traceSpec: "*=info"
```

```
    jsonLogging: false
    disableLogFiles: false
    monitoring: true
    specifyCerts: false
  database:
    type: db2
    db: BLUDB
    host: dashdb-txn-sbox-yp-dal09-
      08.services.dal.bluemix.net
    id: my-id-goes-here
    password: my-password-goes-here
    port: 50000
  account:
    enabled: true
    replicas: 1
    autoscale: false
    maxReplicas: 10
    cpuThreshold: 75
    image:
      repository: ibmstocktrader/account
      tag: 1.0.0
    url: http://{{ .Release.Name }}-account-
      service:9080/account
```

Any field not specified in the yaml you pass will use its default value, so you really only need to fill in fields that you want to set to a non-default value. For a full example of a `Stock Trader CR yaml file`, you can either copy/paste what appears when you switch to the **YAML View** tab of the operator page (as we saw in *Figure 9.15*) or go look in GitHub at `https://github.com/IBMStockTrader/stocktrader-operator/blob/master/config/samples/operators_v1_stocktrader.yaml`.

5. Once you have your CR yaml file filled out, save it with whatever filename you prefer, such as `stock-trader.yaml`, and then deploying an instance of the IBM Stock Trader application is as simple as running `kubectl apply -f stock-trader.yaml`. This will take a couple of minutes to complete.

Once it does, you can see which pods are running for the microservices you selected by running a simple `kubectl get pods` command:

```
[jalcorn@Johns-MBP-8 StockTrader % kubectl get pods -n stocktrader
NAME                              READY   STATUS    RESTARTS   AGE
ceh-broker-7448d98558-g86nq       1/1     Running   0          5h52m
ceh-portfolio-79764cf956-59v42    1/1     Running   0          5h52m
ceh-stock-quote-7bb8dcccc5-jtn82  1/1     Running   0          5h52m
ceh-trader-6f4c94474b-hnt26       1/1     Running   0          5h52m
jalcorn@Johns-MBP-8 StockTrader %
```

Figure 9.20 – Console output

Congratulations! You have confirmed that you have deployed the IBM Stock Trader application, after creating and applying just three yaml files! Now that you've learned how to deploy the application, let's learn what we can do next via the operator.

Understanding day 2 operations

People in the Kubernetes community often say that deployment is *day 1* and that the kinds of things you do to maintain the application afterward are *day 2* operations. Some examples of *day 2* operations include the following:

- Scaling a given microservice up or down
- Upgrading to a newer version of a microservice
- Setting a trace string to perform problem determination

Let's look at each one of these in detail.

Scaling a microservice

One of the benefits of a microservices architecture is that you can independently scale each microservice. Rather than having to scale up all parts of a monolithic application at once, you can scale just the part that is experiencing the throughput or response time issues.

One thing to be aware of when using resources generated by an operator is that the operator itself *owns* those resources, and won't let you change them directly. For example, if you wanted to edit the Portfolio deployment to scale the number of pods, attempting to do so might momentarily appear to work, but in reality, the operator is constantly watching and will revert any resource that gets edited outside of its purview. There is a process called **reconciliation** that advanced operators can use to decide whether and how to merge the requested changes, but a simple Helm-based operator, like the one for Stock Trader, will just reject any attempt to directly edit one of the Kubernetes resources that it generated.

The proper way to make such a change is to edit the CR yaml for the instance of the Stock Trader deployment instead. You can do so either via the OpenShift console or from the CLI. If using the CLI, you can pick which text editor gets used, by setting the KUBE_ EDITOR environment variable to whatever text-based editor you want. For example, if you develop on a Mac and prefer its nano editor to the old-fashioned vi editor, just issue the command export KUBE_EDITOR=nano.

So, if you want to scale up your Portfolio deployment from one pod to two, you can simply run kubectl edit StockTrader microprofile, and that will load its current yaml into the specified editor, where you would go down to the portfolio section and change the value of its replicas field to 2, save the file and exit, and that will cause the generated Portfolio deployment to be updated to have two pods:

```
portfolio:
  replicas: 2
  autoscale: false
  maxReplicas: 10
  cpuThreshold: 75
  image:
    repository: ibmstocktrader/portfolio
    tag: 1.0.0
  url: http://{{ .Release.Name }}-portfolio-
    service:9080/portfolio
```

> **Note**
>
> Instead of hardcoding the number of replicas, you can also enable **Horizontal Pod Autoscaling (HPA)**, which will let Kubernetes dynamically decide how many replicas (pods) are needed, based on a specified CPU threshold and a specified maximum number of replicas. Use autoscale: true to enable HPA, and Kubernetes will scale up the number of pods if the threshold is met, and will scale back down when activity subsides.

Upgrading a microservice

Another change you might want to make to a deployed Stock Trader instance is to upgrade to a newer version of a given microservice. For example, if one of the developers built and pushed a new version of the Account microservice to your Docker image registry, you would use the operator to point at the new version. Again, you wouldn't directly edit the Account deployment, but would instead edit the `Stock Trader CR yaml file`, and then the operator would make the changes to the Account deployment on your behalf.

If you had been using the `1.0.0` tag for the image for the Account microservice, and you wanted to move up to the `1.0.1` version, you would use the aforementioned approach as you did for scaling, but this time, when you get the CR yaml into your `nano` editor, you would go down to the **account** section and edit the **tag** field to be `1.0.1`. When you save CR yaml and exit the editor, the operator will update the Account deployment to use the new `tag image`. This will cause a new Account pod to be started using the `1.0.1` tag, and once it passes its readiness check, the original `1.0.0` level pod will be terminated (Kubernetes calls this a **rolling upgrade** since it avoids any downtime during which no version of the application would be available):

```
account:
  enabled: true
  replicas: 1
  autoscale: false
  maxReplicas: 10
  cpuThreshold: 75
  image:
    repository: ibmstocktrader/account
    tag: 1.0.1
  url: http://{{ .Release.Name }}-account-
    service:9080/account
```

By always acting upon the `StockTrader CR yaml` file as a whole, rather than having to worry about the generated yaml for each microservice, the operator keeps you focused at the level of the business application, while still giving you the flexibility to version the various pieces independently.

Performing problem determination

Another thing you often will need to do with an application is to try to figure out what is going on when something isn't working as expected. This process is called **Problem Determination** (**PD**), or is sometimes referred to as **Root Cause Analysis** (**RCA**) when doing a post-mortem to figure out what led to the failure. Again, the operator can assist you here, such as by letting you turn on additional tracing in the Open Liberty container hosting each microservice.

As before, you edit the CR yaml to effect such a change. There is a `traceSpec` field in the `global` section of the CR yaml that you'd edit to provide the desired trace specification. For example, if you wanted to turn on the fine-level trace for the Broker microservice, you would set the `traceSpec` field to the fully qualified class name of the Broker microservice, which is `com.ibm.hybrid.cloud.sample.stocktrader.broker.BrokerService`, to a value of `fine`. Note that you probably still want to keep `info` level trace on everything else, so you would use a colon to separate the two parts of the trace specification.

Another thing you may want to do to assist with PD is to turn on JSON logging. This causes the logs to be output in a format that can be consumed by tools such as *ElasticSearch* so that you can easily filter through the logs coming from the various microservice pods in a single federated logging dashboard such as *Kibana*.

> **Note**
>
> The combination of *ElasticSearch*, *LogStash*, and *Kibana* is often referred to as the **ELK Stack**; sometimes, *FluentD* is used instead of *LogStash*, so then the combination is referred to as **EFK**; for details on using the OperatorHub operators to set up **ELK/EFK** in your own cluster, see `https://docs.openshift.com/container-platform/4.6/logging/cluster-logging-deploying.html`. Note that there are other more enterprise-quality log analysis tools too, such as *LogDNA* or *Instana*.

Let's take a look at a *Kibana* dashboard:

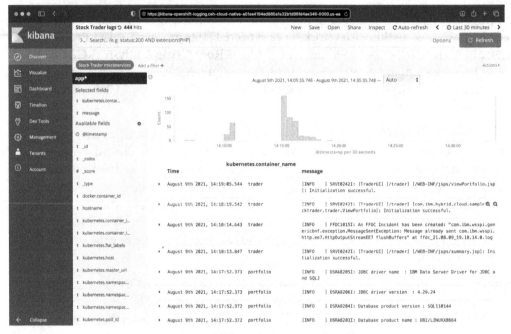

Figure 9.21 – A federated observability dashboard filtered for the IBM Stock Trader microservices

In *Figure 9.21*, we see log messages from the various microservices comprising the IBM Stock Trader application, interleaved based on the timestamp of when each JSON log message was sent. Being able to see all of the logging coming from all of the microservices in a cloud-native appliction in one dashboard, rather than having to go and view each microservice's output separately, greatly enhances the problem determination experience.

An additional benefit of JSON logging is that it gives you control over what sources send their logs to the log analysis tool for your Kubernetes cluster. In addition to choices such as HTTPS access logs or audit records, one of the choices is to send trace records there, as we just discussed with the *traceSpec* setting (otherwise, you'd have to `kubectl cp` the `trace.log` file off of the pod to investigate the trace log or mount your own *Persistent Volume* (*PV*) into the `/logs` location of the container and the trace log would go there):

```
global:
  auth: basic
  healthCheck: true
  ingress: false
  istio: false
  istioNamespace: mesh
```

```
route: true
traceSpec: "com.ibm.hybrid.cloud.sample.stocktrader
  .broker.BrokerService=fine:*=info"
jsonLogging: true
disableLogFiles: false
monitoring: true
specifyCerts: false
```

There are many other *day 2* operations you can perform with the operator. But this should get the point across that the operator is the one in control of all configurations for your application, so it is used to effect any changes when needed.

Summary

We've now explored some of the benefits of having an operator help you out with both deployment and day 2 operations of a composite application to your Kubernetes cluster. While it is possible to deploy a given microservice without the use of an operator, having one guiding you is like having a co-pilot suggesting good default values where appropriate so that you get your application deployed with optimal configuration settings. And having one in the post-deployment stage, helping you with *day 2* operations such as scaling, upgrading, and problem determination, ensures you have the best experience maintaining your application once it is in production use.

We've now covered all of the core MicroProfile features and have shown them in use in a real-world microservices-based application running in a Kubernetes platform such as OCP. Going forward, the remaining chapters will cover some of the auxiliary MicroProfile features (such as reactive messaging) and will look ahead to the future of MicroProfile beyond the current 4.x state.

Section 4: MicroProfile Standalone Specifications and the Future

In this section, you will learn about some of MicroProfile's *standalone* technologies, such as context propagation, reactive messaging APIs, a Java-based GraphQL specification, and **Long-Running Actions (LRAs)**. Lastly, you will learn about what to expect from MicroProfile in the future and how you can be part of the community.

This section comprises the following chapters:

- *Chapter 10, Reactive Cloud-Native Applications*
- *Chapter 11, MicroProfile GraphQL*
- *Chapter 12, MicroProfile LRA and the Future of MicroProfile*

10
Reactive Cloud-Native Applications

Up until now, we have mainly talked about traditional cloud-native applications that adopt **imperative programming** with clearly defined input and output. Imperative programming is the oldest programming paradigm. Applications using this paradigm are built using a clearly defined sequence of instructions making it easier to understand. Its architecture requires that the connection services are predefined.

However, sometimes, a cloud-native application does not know which services it should call. Its purpose might be just sending or receiving messages or events and staying responsive and reactive. Thus, imperative programming no longer applies to these kinds of applications. Under such circumstances, you will need to rely on **reactive programing** and use an event-driven architecture to achieve reactive, responsive, and message-driven applications. We will discuss reactive cloud-native applications in this chapter.

First, you will learn the difference between imperative and reactive applications. Then we will talk about how to create reactive cloud-native applications using **MicroProfile Reactive Messaging 2.0**.

We will cover the following topics:

- Differentiating between imperative and reactive applications
- Using **MicroProfile Context Propagation** to improve asynchronous programming
- Developing reactive cloud-native applications using **MicroProfile Reactive Messaging**

To fully understand this chapter, you should have Java knowledge on multithreading, the `CompletableFuture` class, and `CompletionStage` interface from Java 8.

By the end of this chapter, you should be able to understand what reactive cloud-native applications are, how you can create reactive cloud-native applications that avoid block I/O problems, and be able to utilize messaging libraries such as Apache Kafka.

Differentiating between imperative and reactive applications

When developing imperative applications, the application developers define how to perform a task. You may design a synchronous application to start with. However, to deal with heavy loads and improve performance, you might think about switching from synchronous programming to asynchronous programming to speed up by performing multiple tasks in parallel. When using synchronous programming, on hitting block I/O, a thread has to wait, and no other tasks can be performed on that thread. However, in the case of asynchronous programming, multiple threads can be dispatched to perform other tasks if one thread is blocked.

Asynchronous programming dispatches multiple threads but it does not fix the blocking I/O issues. If there are blockages, eventually the application will consume all threads. Consequently, the application will run out of resources. One of the characteristics of imperative programming is that one application needs to know which services to interact with. Under some circumstances, it might not know nor care about the downstream services. Therefore, imperative programming is not applicable in this kind of situation. Here, reactive programming comes to the rescue.

Reactive programming is a paradigm concerned with data streams and the propagation of changes. This paradigm is used to build a cloud-native application that is message-driven, resilient, and responsive.

A reactive application adopts the design principle from the **Reactive Manifesto**. The Reactive Manifesto (`https://www.reactivemanifesto.org/`) outlines the following four characteristics:

- **Responsive**: The application responds in a timely manner under all conditions.
- **Elastic**: The system stays responsive under various amounts of load, and can scale up or down based on demand.
- **Resilient**: The system is resilient in all situations.
- **Message Driven**: The system relies on asynchronous messaging as a communication channel among the components.

Reactive applications use asynchronous programming to achieve temporal decoupling. As we mentioned previously, asynchronous programming involves dispatching more threads. Each thread normally requires some **Security**, **Contexts and Dependency Injections** (**CDI**), or **Transaction** context associated with it so that it can continue the process from the previous thread. However, if you use the `java.util.concurrent.ForkJoinPool` class for creating new threads, no context will be associated with the new thread that is dispatched. Therefore, to continue an unfinished task from one thread on a different new thread, you will need to push some context from the previous thread to the new threads for continued task execution. MicroProfile Context Propagation can be used to achieve this, which we will discuss next.

Using MicroProfile Context Propagation to manage context

MicroProfile Context Propagation (`https://download.eclipse.org/microprofile/microprofile-context-propagation-1.2/`) defines a mechanism for propagating context from the current thread to a new thread. The types of context include the following:

- **Application**: This normally includes the thread context class loader as well as `java:comp`, `java:module`, and `java:app`.
- **CDI**: The scope of the CDI context, such as `SessionScoped` and `ConversationScoped`, is still active in the new unit of work, such as a new `CompeletionStage`.
- **Security**: This includes the credentials that are associated with the current thread.
- **Transaction**: This is the active transaction scope that is associated with the current thread. This context is not normally expected to be propagated, but cleared instead.

Apart from the aforementioned context, an application can introduce custom context if needed.

To propagate the aforementioned context, this specification introduces two interfaces:

- ManagedExecutor: This interface provides an asynchronous execution mechanism for defining thread context propagation.

- ThreadContext: This interface enables finer control over the capture and propagation of thread context. You can associate this interface with a particular function.

In the following subsections, we will briefly discuss how to use the two aforementioned interfaces to propagate the context that was associated with the current thread across various types of units of work such as CompletionStage, CompletableFuture, Function, and Runnable.

Using ManagedExecutor to propagate context

ManagedExecutor differs from other known executors, such as ForkJoinPool, which do not have the facilities to propagate contexts. To use ManagedExecutor to propagate contexts, you will need to create an instance of ManagedExecutor, which can be achieved via the builder pattern:

```
ManagedExecutor executor = ManagedExecutor.builder()
        .cleared(ThreadContext.TRANSACTION)
        .propagated(ThreadContext.ALL_REMAINING)
        .maxAsync(10)
        .build();
```

The aforementioned code snippet is used to create an executor object of ManagedExecutor that cleared Transaction context and propagated all the other remaining contexts. This executor supports a maximum of 10 concurrent executions. You can then invoke some method of the executor to create an object of CompletableFuture for asynchronous programming as follows:

```
CompletableFuture<Long> stage1 =
    executor.newIncompleteFuture();
stage1.thenApply(function1).thenApply(function2);
stage1.completeAsync(supplier);
```

The preceding code snippet demonstrates using the executor object to create an incomplete CompletableFuture stage1, which then executes function1. After function1 completes, function2 will then be executed. Finally, the future stage1 will be completed with the given supplier function.

Apart from ManagedExecutor, another way to propagate context is to use the ThreadContext interface. Let's discuss it in more detail in the next section.

Using ThreadContext to propagate context

ThreadContext offers a fine-grained control for capturing and restoring context. To use ThreadContext, you need to create an instance of ThreadContext, which can be constructed via the builder pattern as follows:

```
ThreadContextthreadContext = ThreadContext.builder()
  .propagated(ThreadContext.APPLICATION, ThreadContext
    .SECURITY).unchanged().cleared(ThreadContext
      .ALL_REMAINING).build();
```

The aforementioned code snippet creates an instance of ThreadContext that propagates the application and security context from the current thread and clears other contexts. Afterward, you can create a CompletionStage instance by calling the threadContext.withContextCapture() method:

```
CompletionStage stage =
  threadContext.withContextCapture(someMethod);
stage.thenApply(function1).thenAccept(aConsumer);
```

In the aforementioned code snippet, both the function1 and aConsumer functions will inherit the application and security context from the current thread.

Alternatively, you can create a contextual function from a threadContext object and then provide this contextual function to CompletableFuture, as shown here:

```
Function<String, String> aFunction =
  threadContext.contextualFunction(function1);
CompletableFuture.thenApply(aFunction)
    .thenAccept(aConsumer);
```

In the preceding code snippet, when `aFunction` is executed, the thread that runs this `aFunction` will inherit the application and security context from its parent thread, which means the thread will be able to perform similar functions as the thread that creates the `aFunction` object, while the `aConsumer` function will not inherit the application and security context from its parent thread. In order to use Context Propagation, you need to make the APIs available to your application.

Making the MicroProfile Context Propagation API available

MicroProfile Context Propagation API JARs can be made available for Maven and Gradle projects. If you create a Maven project, you can directly add the following to your pom.xml file:

```
<dependency>
    <groupId>org.eclipse.microprofile.context-
        propagation</groupId>
    <artifactId>microprofile-context-propagation-
        api</artifactId>
    <version>1.2</version>
</dependency>
```

Alternative, if you create a Gradle project, you need to add the following dependency:

```
dependencies {
  providedCompile org.eclipse.microprofile.context-
      propagation: microprofile-context-propagation-api:1.2
}
```

We have briefly discussed how to capture and restore contexts as part of asynchronous programming. As mentioned previously, asynchronous programming does not solve the blocking I/O issue but works around it by dispatching new threads if a thread is blocked. To solve the blocking I/O issue, you will need to consider building a reactive application. In the next section, we discuss using MicroProfile Reactive Messaging to help you build a reactive application.

Using MicroProfile Reactive Messaging to build a reactive application

MicroProfile Reactive Messaging 2.0 (`https://download.eclipse.org/microprofile/microprofile-reactive-messaging-2.0/`) provides a mechanism for building event-driven cloud-native applications. It enables decoupling between the services via messaging. MicroProfile Reactive Messaging provides the `@Outgoing` annotation for publishing messages and `@Incoming` for consuming messages. The following figure illustrates how messages travel from the publisher (**Method A**) to the consumer (**Method B**). The message can be sent to a messaging store, such as Apache Kafka, MQ, and so on, and will then be delivered to a consumer such as **Method B**:

Figure 10.1 – Messaging flow

In Reactive Messaging, CDI beans are used to produce, process, and consume messages. These messages can be sent and received via remote brokers or various message transport layers such as Apache Kafka, MQ, and so on. Let's discuss a few key elements of MicroProfile Reactive Messaging: messages, message acknowledgment, channels, message consumption, message production, message processing, and `Emitter`.

Message

A **message** is a piece of information wrapped in an envelope. Additionally, this piece of information can include an acknowledgment logic, which can be either positive or negative. The following are a few ways to produce a message:

- `Message.of(P p)`: This method wraps the given payload p without any acknowledgment logic.

- `Message.of(P p, Supplier<CompletionStage<Void>> ack)`: This method wraps the given payload p and provides the `ack` acknowledgment logic.

- `Message.of(P p, Supplier<CompletionStage<Void>> ack, Function<Throwable, CompletionSTage<<Void>> nack)`: This method wraps the given payload p, provides the `ack` acknowledgment logic and the `nack` negative acknowledgment logic.

Alternatively, if you have a `Message` object, you can create a new `Message` object from it by getting its payload and then optionally supplying a new positive or negative acknowledgment, as shown here:

```
Message<T> newMessage =
    aMessage.withPayload(payload).withAck(...).withNack(...)
```

The aforementioned code snippet creates `newMessage` from `aMessage` and provides new payload, positive acknowledgment, and negative acknowledgment logic.

You might be wondering how to perform message acknowledgment and negative acknowledgment. We will discuss them in more detail in the next section.

Message acknowledgment

All messages must be acknowledged either positively or negatively, and can be acknowledged either explicitly or implicitly using the MicroProfile Reactive Messaging implementation.

There are two different types of acknowledgment: **positive acknowledgment** and **negative acknowledgment**. Positive acknowledgment means messages were processed successfully whereas negative acknowledgment means messages were unsuccessfully processed.

Acknowledgment can be explicitly specified by the `@Acknowlegment` annotation. This annotation is used in conjunction with the `@Incoming` annotation. You can specify one of the following three acknowledgment policies:

- **@Acknowlegment(MANUAL)**: You need to explicitly call `Message#ack()` to acknowledge the message being received.

- **@Acknowledgment(PRE_PROCESSING)**: A Reactive Messaging implementation that acknowledges the message before the annotated method is executed.

- **@Acknowledgment(POST_PROCESSING)**: A Reactive Messaging implementation that acknowledges the message once the method completes if the method does not emit data or the emitted data is acknowledged.

The following is an example of a manual acknowledgment. The `consume()` method acknowledges the message consumption manually via calling the `msg.ack()` method on the `msg` object:

```
@Incoming("channel-c")
@Acknowledgment(Acknowledgment.Strategy.MANUAL)
```

```
public CompletionStage<Void> consume(Message<I> msg) {
  System.out.println("Received the message: " +
    msg.getPayload());
  return msg.ack();
}
```

If the @Acknowledgment annotation is absent, what acknowledgment policy do you think should then be used? The answer to this is, it depends on the method signature where the @Incoming annotation is applied. The default acknowledgment is as follows:

- If the method parameter or return type contains the type of message, the default acknowledgment is MANUAL.

- Otherwise, if the method is only annotated with @Incoming, the default acknowledgment is POST_PROCESSING.

- Finally, if the method is annotated with both @Incoming and @Outgoing, the default acknowledgment is PRE_PROCESSING.

Now that we have covered the necessary concepts of messages and their acknowledgment policies. You might be wondering where the message will be sent to or consumed from, meaning its destination or source respectively. These are called channels, which we will discuss in the next section.

Channel

A **channel** is a string representing the source or destination of messages. MicroProfile Reactive Messaging has two types of channels:

- **Internal channels**: These channels are local to the application and allow for multi-step processing between the message source and message destination.

- **External channels**: These channels connect to remote brokers or various message transport layers such as Apache Kafka, an AMQP broker, or other messaging technologies.

Messages flow from an upstream channel and then to a downstream channel till they reach the consumer to have the messages consumed. Next, we discuss how these messages are consumed.

Message consumption using @Incoming

A message can be consumed by a method with the `@Incoming` annotation on a CDI bean. The following example consumes messages from the `channel-a` channel:

```
@Incoming("channel-a")
CompletionStage<Void> method(Message<I> msg) {
    return message.ack();
}
```

This method is called whenever a message is sent to the `channel-a` channel. This method acknowledges the received messages. The supported method signatures for consuming data are as follows:

- `Subscriber<Message<I>> consume(); Subscriber<I> consume();`
- `SubscriberBuilder<Message<I>, Void> consume();` `SubscriberBuilder<I, Void> consume();`
- `void consum(I payload);`
- `CompletionStage<Void> consume(Message<I> msg);` `CompletionStage<?> consume(I payload);`

In the preceeding list, `I` is the incoming payload type.

Another way to receive messages is to inject either `org.reactivestreams.Publisher` or `org.eclipse.microprofile.reactive.streams.operators.PublisherBuilder` and use the `@Channel` annotation, as shown here:

```
@Inject
@Channel("channel-d")
private Publisher<String> publisher;
```

The preceding code snippet means a `publisher` instance will be connected to the `channel-d` channel. Then a consumer can directly receive messages from the publisher.

We have discussed the messaging flows and message consumption. Next, we look at how a message is generated.

Message production using @Outgoing

A method on a CDI bean with the `@Outgoing` annotation is a message producer. The following code snippet demonstrates message production:

```
@Outgoing("channel-b")
public Message<Integer> publish() {
    return Message.of(123);
}
```

In the aforementioned code snippet, the `publish()` method is called for every consumer request and it publishes the `123` message to the `channel-b` channel. Only one publisher can use `@Outgoing` with a specified channel name per application, which means only one publisher can publish messages to a particular channel. Otherwise, an error will occur during application deployment. After messages are published to a channel, consumers can consume messages from the specified channel. The supported method signatures for producing data are as follows:

- `Publisher<Message<O>> produce(); Publisher <O> produce();`
- `PublisherBuilder<Message<O>> produce (); Publisher Builder<O> produce();`
- `Message<O> produce(); O produce();`
- `CompletionStage<Message<O>> produce(); CompletionStage<O> produce();`

In the preceeding list, `O` is the outgoing payload class type.

A method can act as a message consumer and a message producer. This kind of method is called a **message processor**.

Message processing using both @Incoming and @Outgoing

A message processor is a message producer as well as a consumer, which means it has both `@Incoming` and `@Outgoing` annotations. Let's look at this method here:

```
@Incoming("channel-a")
@Outgoing("channel-b")
public Message<Integer> process(Message<Integer> message) {
    return message.withPayload(message.getPayload() + 100);
}
```

The `process()` method receives messages, which are integers, from the `channel-a` channel and then adds `100`. Afterward, it publishes the new integer to the `channel-b` channel. The supported method signatures for processing data are as follows:

- `Processor<Message<I>, Message<O>> process(); Processor<I, O> process();`

- `ProcessorBuilder<Message<I>, Message<O>> process(); ProcessorBuilder<I, O> process();`

- `PublisherBuilder<Message<O>> process(Message<I> msg); PublisherBuilder<O> process(I payload);`

- `PublisherBuilder<Message<O>> process(PublisherBuilder<Message<I>> publisherBuilder); PublisherBuilder<O> process(PublisherBuilder<I> publisherBuilder);`

- `Publisher<Message<O>> method(Publisher<Message<I>> publisher); Publisher<O> method(Publisher<I> publisher);`

- `Message<O> process(Message<I> msg); O process(I payload);`

- `CompletionStage<Message<O>> process(Message<I> msg); CompletionStage<O> process(I payload);`

In the preceeding list, `I` is the incoming payload class type and `O` is the outgoing payload class type.

So far, message consumption and production are methods on CDI beans. These CDI beans can be `Dependent` or `ApplicationScoped`. We have already covered CDI in *Chapter 4, Developing Cloud-Native Applications*.

We have covered message publication and message consumption via methods on CDI beans, which will be automatically triggered by the Reactive Messaging implementation when your application is up and running. You might be wondering what to do if you want to publish some messages whenever an endpoint is triggered. We will discuss how to do that in the next section.

Using Emitter to publish messages

In order to publish messages from a JAX-RS resource, you can inject an `Emitter` object and then call the `send()` method. Let's look at the following example:

```
@Inject @Channel("channel-c")
private Emitter<String> emitter;
```

```
public void publishMessage() {
    emitter.send("m");
    emitter.send("n");
    emitter.complete();
}
```

In the aforementioned code snippet, first you can inject an `Emitter` with the target channel. Then, you can send messages by calling the `emitter.send()` method. This example directly sends a message payload. You can send a message by wrapping up the payload, as detailed here:

```
@Inject @Channel("channel-e")
private Emitter<String> emitter;
public void publishMessage() {
    emitter.send(Message.of("m");
    emitter.send(Message.of("n");
    emitter.send(Message.of("q")
}
```

Often, the speed of message publication may not be the same as that of message consumption. **Back pressure** can often occur when message publication is faster than message consumption. How do you handle back pressure? Normally, you can slow down the message producer; buffer the unconsumed messages; or drop the unconsumed messages. MicroProfile Reactive Messaging introduced the `@OnOverflow` annotation to handle back pressure when using `Emitter` to publish messages. Here is an example demonstrating how to use a buffering strategy to handle back pressure:

```
@Inject @Channel("channel-d")
@OnOverflow(value=OnOverflow.Strategy.BUFFER,
  bufferSize=100)
private Emitter<String> emitter;
public void publishMessage() {
    emitter.send("message1");
    emitter.send("message2");
    emitter.complete();
}
```

In the preceding code snippet, an `Emitter` object `emitter` was connected to `channel-d` with the back pressure strategy of using a buffer with the capacity of `100` elements. The `emitter` object sent two messages and completed them. The `@OnOverflow` annotation supports the following configuration, as shown in the following table:

Value attribute of OnOverflow	Description
`OnOverflow.Strategy.BUFFER`	The buffer size will be specified by the value of bufferSize if it is present. Otherwise, it will be the value of the `mp.messaging.emitter.default-buffer-size` property. Otherwise, 128 elements will be used.
`OnOverflow.Strategy.UNBOUNDED_BUFFER`	The buffer size is unlimited.
`OnOverflow.Stragegy.THROW_EXCEPTION`	An exception will be thrown from the sender if consumers can't keep up.
`OnOverflow.Strategy.DROP`	The most recent messages will be dropped if the consumers can't keep up.
`OnOverflow.Strategy.FAIL`	A failure will be propagated to the sender and this will cause the sender to stop emitting messages.
`OnOverflow.Strategy.LATEST`	Only the recent messages are kept and the earlier unconsumed messages will be dropped.
`OnOverflow.Strategy.NONE`	Ignores the back pressure signals and the sender will continue producing messages.

Table 10.1 – Back pressure strategies

We have learned how message production and consumption use the `@Outgoing` and `@Incoming` annotations. MicroProfile Reactive Messaging connects outgoing and incoming channels to external technologies such as Apache Kafka, Web Socket, AMQP, JMS, and MQTT. The connection is achieved via a reactive messaging connector. We are going to discuss the connector in detail in the next section.

Using a connector to bridge to an external messaging technology

A connector can act as a publisher, consumer, or processor. It is a CDI bean, which implements the two MicroProfile Reactive Messaging interfaces `IncomingConnectorFactory` and `OutgoingConnectorFactory` to receive messages and dispatch messages respectively. Reactive Messaging implementations provide out-of-the-box connectors for supported message technologies, such as Kafka, MQTT, MQ, and so on. However, you can create a connector yourself if the connector you need was not provided by the implementor. Here is an example of a connector that connects to Apache Kafka:

```
@ApplicationScoped
@Connector("my.kafka")
public class KafkaConnector implements
    IncomingConnectorFactory, OutgoingConnectorFactory {
    // ...
}
```

Once a connector is defined, further configurations shown next are required to match the channels from your cloud-native application to the external messaging technologies bridged by the connector. In the following configurations, the `channel-name` must match the value in the `@Incoming` or `@Outgoing` annotations while `attribute` can be any kind of string:

- `mp.messaging.incoming.[channel-name].[attribute]`: The property is used to map the channel with the annotation of `@Incoming` to the external destination provided by the corresponding messaging technology.

- `mp.messaging.outgoing.[channel-name].[attribute]`: This property is to map the channel with the annotation of `@Outgoing` to the external destination provided by the corresponding messaging technology.

- `mp.messaging.connector.[connector-name].[attribute]`: This property is to specify the connector details.

If your cloud-native application connects to Apache Kafka, you might supply the following configuration for the following consumer method:

```
@Incoming("order")
CompletionStage<Void> method(Message<I> msg) {
    return message.ack();
}
```

In the following configuration, the mp.messaging.incoming.order.connector property specifies the connector name as liberty-kafka and then specifies further configuration for that connector with the mp.messaging.connector.liberty-kafkabootstrap.servers property. Then it specifies the channel order by mapping the topic-order Kafka topic via the mp.messaging.incoming.order.topic property:

```
mp.messaging.incoming.order.connector=liberty-kafka
mp.messaging.connector.liberty-kafka.bootstrap.
    servers=localhost:9092
mp.messaging.incoming.order.topic=topic-order
```

We have covered MicroProfile Reactive Messaging. Let's put it all together. If you need to create a consumer that consumes messages from an event streaming system such as Apache Kafka, you just need to create a CDI bean and write a method with the @Incoming annotation to connect a particular channel. Similarly, if you need to produce messages, you will need to create a CDI bean and write a method with the @Outging annotation to connect with a producer channel. Finally, you configure the channel as shown in the preceding configuration to state the channel is connected to the Apache Kafka connector. Open Liberty provides the liberty-kafka Kafka connector. This Open Liberty guide (https://openliberty.io/guides/microprofile-reactive-messaging.html) demonstrates how to create Java microservices.

To use the APIs from MicroProfile Reactive Messaging, you need to specify the Maven or Gradle dependencies as covered next.

Making the MicroProfile Reactive Messaging API available

MicroProfile Reactive Messaging API JARs can be made available for Maven and Gradle projects. If you create a Maven project, you can directly add the following to your pom.xml file:

```
<dependency>
  <groupId>
    org.eclipse.microprofile.reactive.messaging
  </groupId>
  <artifactId>
    microprofile-reactive-messaging-api
  </artifactId>
  <version>2.0</version>
</dependency>
```

Alternative, if you create a Gradle project, you need to add the following dependency:

```
dependencies {
  providedCompile org.eclipse.microprofile.reactive
    .messaging: microprofile-reactive-messaging-api:2.0
}
```

You have now learned how to create a reactive cloud-native application for when you need to interact with messaging technologies and require a message-driven architecture.

Summary

In this chapter, we have learned the differences between imperative and reactive applications. We discussed briefly how to use MicroProfile Context Propagation to propagate contexts for asynchronous programming and then covered MicroProfile Reactive Messaging concepts to discuss how to use Reactive Messaging to create a reactive cloud-native application. Through this chapter, you will now be able to connect the built application with your chosen messaging technologies such as Apache Kafka. You also now understand that whenever you need to create a message-driven application, you should consider using MicroProfile Reactive Messaging.

In the next chapter, we will cover MicroProfile GraphQL to learn how to use GraphQL in your cloud-native applications to improve performance if you need to frequently execute queries.

11
MicroProfile GraphQL

GraphQL is a distributed query language that addresses some of the shortcomings of **REpresentational State Transfer** (**REST**). In particular, GraphQL addresses the notions of **over-fetching** (receiving more data than the client intended) and **under-fetching** (requiring the client to make multiple requests to get the data it requires). GraphQL applications make use of a schema file that presents clients with the queries and mutations at its disposal, as well as the entities it can access and manipulate.

The ease of use and robustness of GraphQL explains why its popularity is growing, especially in cloud-native applications. **MicroProfile GraphQL** (**MP GraphQL**) makes it easy to create GraphQL-based applications.

In this chapter, we're going to cover the following main topics:

- Understanding GraphQL basics and when to use it
- Building services with MP GraphQL
- Consuming GraphQL services with client **application programming interfaces** (**APIs**)

By the end of this chapter, you will have learned what GraphQL is and when it is appropriate to use it, and you will be able to build your own GraphQL application ready to deploy in open source, cloud-ready servers such as Open Liberty.

Technical requirements

To build and run the samples mentioned in this chapter, you will need a Mac or PC (Windows or Linux) with the following software:

- **Java Development Kit** (JDK) version 8 or higher (`http://ibm.biz/GetSemeru`)
- Apache Maven (`https://maven.apache.org/`)
- A Git client (`https://git-scm.com/`)

All of the source code used in this chapter is available on GitHub at `https://github.com/PacktPublishing/Practical-Cloud-Native-Java-Development-with-MicroProfile/tree/main/Chapter11`.

Once you have cloned the GitHub repository, you can start the Open Liberty server where these code samples will execute by entering the `Chapter11` directory and executing the following command from the command line:

```
mvn clean package liberty:run
```

You can then stop the server in the same command window by pressing *Ctrl + C*.

Now we've got the prerequisites taken care of, let's start by learning the basics of GraphQL.

Understanding GraphQL basics and when to use it

As with REST, GraphQL is a means of accessing and modifying remote data over web-based transports. It uses a publicly visible schema, allowing clients to know exactly which entities it can query, which fields can be modified, and so on. This is similar to how OpenAPI describes RESTful APIs. The schema acts as a contract between the client and the service. GraphQL strictly enforces the schema, preventing clients from accessing or modifying entities or fields that are not defined within it. This strictness provides a lot of freedom for developers of both clients and services, which we'll cover later in this section.

GraphQL supports the following operations:

- **Queries**: Queries are read operations and are analogous to GET requests in REST.

- **Mutations**: Mutations are used for modifying data—that is, creating, updating, and/ or deleting it.

- **Subscriptions**: Subscriptions are used so that clients can receive notifications of specific events, such as when a particular entity has been created or a field has dropped below a certain threshold, or even unrelated events.

Unlike REST, where different parts of the API are spread out across multiple **HyperText Transfer Protocol (HTTP)** endpoints, GraphQL applications typically use a single HTTP endpoint, and the operations are embedded in the HTTP request's body.

GraphQL operations and schemas use their own syntax, but the response is in **JavaScript Object Notation (JSON)** format. This allows GraphQL services and clients to be written in any language. While we plan to cover creating services in Java, it is also currently possible to write service and client applications in JavaScript, Python, Go, Haskell, Perl, Ruby, Scala, and many others.

The schema defines the types of entities accessible for the service, as well as the operations that can be performed. Built-in or primitive GraphQL types are called **scalars**. Any service is free to define its own scalar types, but the GraphQL specification states that all services must use at least these five standard scalars:

- `int`—A 32-bit signed integer

- `float`—Signed double-precision floating-point number

- `string`—A sequence of characters using **Unicode Transformation Format-8 (UTF-8)** encoding

- `boolean`—`true` or `false`

- `ID`—A string that is intended to be a unique **identifier (ID)** for an entity; it is not intended to be human-readable

GraphQL objects can be made up of scalars or other objects. Each operation must explicitly specify all fields that it wishes to view in the response. For complex types (types that include other types or scalars), this might mean specifying fields several layers deep.

Requiring clients to specify all fields in a query ensures backward compatibility when you add new fields to existing objects. A client cannot be caught off guard if a new field appears on an object since their existing query didn't specify it!

Another advantage of requiring clients to specify all fields that they are interested in is that it avoids **over-fetching**. Over-fetching occurs when more data is sent over the network than is necessary. One common example of over-fetching in REST is weather data. If you issue a RESTful request to check the current conditions for a particular location from various weather sites, you will see an enormous amount of information, but most of that data is unused when you just wanted to know what the outside temperature is and whether or not it's raining.

By sending queries as the payload of an HTTP request, GraphQL also avoids **under-fetching**. As you've probably guessed, under-fetching occurs when the data returned is insufficient. Using the weather example, suppose you also wanted to know the temperature at your friends' homes in other cities. You'd have to issue similar RESTful requests to the weather site for each location. But in GraphQL, you can issue multiple queries in a single HTTP request, enabling you to get exactly the data you need with a single round trip to the server and making it fast and efficient!

Queries and mutations have their own syntax, though it is similar to JSON and other query languages. Generally, these operations start with `query` or `mutation` and then a label for the operation, then, inside curly braces, you would specify the query or mutation to invoke with any parameters inside parentheses. You would then add the fields you are interested in inside curly braces. We'll see some example queries and mutations later in this chapter.

GraphQL also allows **partial results** to be sent when an exception occurs. Suppose the weather data for precipitation is unavailable due to some unforeseen system failure. A GraphQL service could still send temperature data to the clients, along with some error data for the missing precipitation fields, whereas a RESTful service would likely return a `503` (service unavailable) error. Some data is still better than none, right?

Since the schema is exposed to clients, various tools can introspect the schema, allowing users to construct queries and mutations and test them in real time. One such tool, which we'll discuss later, is called **GraphiQL** (`https://github.com/graphql/graphiql`).

While REST is still the more widely used communication architecture in the cloud, GraphQL is quickly gaining in popularity as it addresses many of the gaps in REST. So, which approach is right for you? The answer, as with most things, is *it depends*. GraphQL primarily only works with JSON as the response type; if you want to use other data types, you might want to consider REST or an alternative approach. If your data is hierarchical in nature, it might lend itself better to REST.

Another consideration is security-based in relation to **Uniform Resource Indicator** (URI) paths: GraphQL uses a single URI for all operations, while REST uses different paths for different entities. With REST, it would be possible to use a firewall to grant access to certain entities for all clients (for example, `/public/*`) while restricting access to other entities (for example, `/private/*`). This isn't possible in GraphQL without splitting the service into separate public and private services, which might not be ideal.

Similarly, HTTP caching is more complicated with GraphQL. Since REST uses URI paths, both clients and servers can cache entity results based on the path used. It is possible to cache based on paths in GraphQL, but this would require clients to pass their queries as HTTP `GET` query parameters. This could be cumbersome for the client, as well as being a potential security risk as proxy servers would be able to see query parameters, and you may still have issues with caching, depending on the spacing and formatting of the query. Fortunately, most implementations of GraphQL use query caching on the server side to reduce unnecessary duplication of work.

So, when would you use GraphQL? GraphQL tends to cost a little more on the server (in order to filter results to get the client exactly what it wants), but that trade-off means that client-side processing is significantly reduced. So, if you have a lot of clients or want to optimize your client performance, GraphQL is a good approach.

GraphQL tends to reduce network traffic since it avoids under-fetching and over-fetching. In environments where network bandwidth is expensive, GraphQL is ideal.

It should also be noted that nothing prevents you from writing both GraphQL and RESTful APIs for the same service. This might add more maintenance, but it allows your clients to choose.

Now we understand what GraphQL is and when we should use it, let's explore how we can build GraphQL applications using MicroProfile.

Building services with MP GraphQL

In this section, we will learn how to develop a GraphQL application using the MP GraphQL APIs and runtime framework. We'll cover building queries and mutations, and how to invoke them using an interactive web tool called **GraphiQL**. We'll also cover entities and enumerated types. Finally, we'll cover a technique to reduce unnecessary server-side computations and deliver partial results.

Most GraphQL APIs for Java require you to write a schema first and then build the Java code around it. This approach tends to cause some level of dual maintenance, and it can slow down development as you evolve your application. MP GraphQL uses a **code-first** approach, meaning that you write the code using patterns similar to **Jakarta RESTful Web Services (JAX-RS)**, and the framework generates the schema at runtime. This makes development and maintenance faster and easier. Let's start by building a basic `Hello World` query service.

Developing queries

As with JAX-RS, MP GraphQL is based on annotations. The first annotation to consider is `@GraphQLApi`. This annotation is a **Contexts and Dependency Injection (CDI)** bean-defining annotation, which means that when you apply this annotation to a class, it becomes a CDI bean. This enables the CDI framework to manage its life cycle and inject dependencies. This annotation is required on classes that contain query or mutation methods.

The next annotation we'll consider is `@Query`. When this annotation is applied to methods, it tells the MP GraphQL runtime to create a top-level query in the schema. Let's see a simple example, as follows:

```
@GraphQLApi
public class SimpleApi {

    @Query
    public String hello() {
        return "Hello World";
    }
}
```

The `@GraphQLApi` annotation tells the runtime to manage the life cycle of this bean, and the `@Query` annotation tells the runtime to generate a query in the schema with no parameters that returns a `String` scalar. If we run this example in an MP GraphQL server such as Open Liberty, we can then see the schema file by browsing to `http://localhost:9080/ch11/graphql/schema.graphql`. Then, we'll see something like this:

```
"Query root"
type Query {
  hello: String
}
```

Using **GraphiQL**, which comes built in to Open Liberty, we can execute this query from a web-based client. Simply browse to `http://localhost:9080/ch11/graphql-ui` and then enter this query string:

```
query hello {
    hello
}
```

Then, click the triangular *play* button to see the results. You should see something like this:

Figure 11.1 – Simple query in GraphiQL

Notice that the result is a JSON object with a field labeled `data`. The results of the query are always under the `data` field. If an error were to occur, there would be a separate `errors` field instead of, or in addition to, the `data` field. This field would include details of the error(s).

This is a nice start, and you can probably guess that you could have multiple query methods in this class that could return different data, but queries are much more powerful when they have parameters. In previous chapters, we've been working with the **Stock Trader** application. Let's GraphQL-ize that application in our following examples.

If we want the client to be able to specify parameters to a query, we simply add Java method parameters to the `@Query`-annotated methods. Let's take a look at what we might do for the `Portfolio` service, as follows:

```
@GraphQLApi
public class PortfolioGraphQLApi {

    @Inject
    private PortfolioDatabase portfolioDB;

    @Query
```

```
    @Description("Returns the portfolio of the given
      owner.")
    public Portfolio portfolio(@Name("owner") String owner)
        throws UnknownPortfolioException {
        return Optional.ofNullable(portfolioDB.getPortfolio
          (owner)).orElseThrow(() -> new
            UnknownPortfolioException(owner));
    }
    //...
}
```

There are a few new things to consider here. First, we inject `PortfolioDatabase` instance. This is nothing more than a wrapper around a `HashMap`, but it could just as well access a real relational or NoSQL database to retrieve stock portfolio data. CDI injects this for us. *Muchas gracias!*

Next, the `portfolio` query method also has a `@Description` annotation applied to it. This allows us to specify a human-readable description that will appear in the generated schema, which is useful for describing the intent of the query and its parameters.

Speaking of parameters, the method takes a `String` parameter called `owner`. The `@Name` annotation tells the runtime which name to use when generating the schema.

> **Best practice**
>
> Use @Name annotations on parameters for portability. Some MP GraphQL implementations may not be able to determine the parameter name from the code and will end up writing the schema with parameter names such as `arg0`, `arg1`, and so on. The @Name annotation guarantees that the runtime will generate the specified parameter name in the schema.

Another thing worth noting in the aforementioned code is that instead of returning a `string` or other primitive, we are returning a `Portfolio` object. This is a custom object in our application. By doing so, the runtime will introspect the `Portfolio` Java object and will generate it as an entity in the schema. It will also generate any other object that it references. Let's take a look at the schema generated from this code, as follows:

```
type Portfolio {
  accountID: ID
  loyalty: Loyalty
  owner: String
```

```
    stocks: [Stock]
    total: Float!
}

"Query root"
type Query {
    "Returns the portfolio of the given owner."
    portfolio(owner: String): Portfolio
}

type Stock {
type Stock {
    commission: Float!
    dateOfLastUpdate: String
    pricePerShare: Float!
    shares: Int!
    symbol: String!
    total: Float!
}
}

enum Loyalty {
    BRONZE
    GOLD
    SILVER
}
```

First, we see the Portfolio type (entity) and its various fields and their types. So, the accountID field is a string; the total field is a float, with the exclamation mark indicating that the value for this field must be non-null; the stocks field is an array of Stock objects, with the square brackets indicating an **array**.

We also see the text description for our query. The query section indicates that the portfolio query takes a single String parameter called owner and returns a Portfolio object.

The Stock type is pulled in because it is referenced by the Portfolio type. Likewise, the Loyalty **enumerated type** (**enum**) is referenced by the Portfolio type. Enums in GraphQL are generated from Java enums and behave similarly.

Let's take one last look at the code that generated this schema, and we'll see that the `portfolio` method throws an `UnknownPortfolioException` exception. This exception is handled by the framework. When the exception is thrown, the framework will return an error response to the client. Let's see what happens when we query for two portfolios—one that exists and one that doesn't, as follows:

Figure 11.2 – Multiple queries: one successful, one failing with an expected exception

Figure 11.2 shows us that we can send multiple queries in the same request. It also shows us that we can receive partial results. In this case, the query to find portfolio details for `Emily J` was successful, but the query to find portfolio details for `Andy M` failed because his portfolio is not yet in the database.

Now we have a basic understanding of how to create query methods, let's take a look at how we can create mutations.

Developing mutations

When we think of **create, read, update, and delete (CRUD)** operations, queries are the *read* part, while mutations are everything else. That said, queries and mutations are just labels—a GraphQL query could certainly create, update, or delete entities, and a mutation could simply return a view of an entity, but that is not the intended practice.

> **Best practice**
>
> Query methods should never manipulate entity data. Use queries for returning the current state of entities and mutations for changing that data.

To create a mutation method, you would just apply the @Mutation annotation to your Java method. In most cases, mutation methods will take parameters to indicate what sort of change to make and/or to specify which entities to update or delete. Let's take a look at how we might use a mutation method to create a Portfolio object, as follows:

```
@GraphQLApi
public class PortfolioGraphQLApi {
    //...

    @Mutation
    public Portfolio createNewPortfolio(@Name("portfolio")
      Portfolio portfolio)
        throws DuplicatePortfolioOwnerException,
            UnknownPortfolioException {

        portfolioDB.addPortfolio(portfolio);
        return portfolio(portfolio.getOwner());
    }
```

There are a few things to notice here. First, the createNewPortfolio method returns the Portfolio object it just created—it actually calls the portfolio method we wrote in the last section to ensure that the new Portfolio object was created successfully in the database. Mutations, as with queries, must always return something. Void mutation or query methods are not allowed.

> **Suggestion**
>
> If you really don't want to return anything, consider returning a `boolean`
> value to indicate whether the mutation was completed successfully, or consider
> returning an `int` value, indicating how many entities were created/updated/
> deleted.

The second thing to notice about this code is that it accepts a complex object as a
parameter. This will cause some new entries to be generated in the schema. Let's take
a look, as follows:

```
input PortfolioInput {
  accountID: ID
  loyalty: Loyalty
  owner: String
  stocks: [StockInput]
  total: Float!
}

input StockInput {
  commission: Float!
  shares: Int!
  symbol: String
}
```

These input types look very similar to the types we saw when we generated the schema
for our query method. The difference is that these types are appended with `input`.
GraphQL differentiates between types used for input and types used for output. One
advantage of this is that it means it might be possible for clients to view things that they
cannot modify or vice versa. So, what might the mutation look like in **GraphiQL**? Let's
take a look, as follows:

Figure 11.3 – Mutation creating a new portfolio

Figure 11.3 shows how to specify a complex parameter, `portfolio`. The syntax is very similar to JSON, but not exactly—notice that the field names are not in quotes. Notice also that the mutation specifies a return value, `owner`—a valid query or mutation must contain at least one return value.

> **A note about parameters and pagination**
>
> Parameters in a query or mutation do not need to be related to the underlying business entity. You could also use parameters for **pagination**, allowing a client to control the number and range of the entries it wants to receive. For example, suppose a client wants to iterate over all the stock portfolios in the database, but it has a limited capacity for processing. In this case, it might be advantageous to add parameters for `pageNumber` and `entriesPerPage` so that the client can process the portfolios at its own pace.

Now we've covered queries and mutations, let's take a closer look at entities and how we can shape them into what we want in the GraphQL world!

Writing entities

Entities are all complex types (not **scalars**) used for input or output. The MP GraphQL runtime will compute all entities that are referenced by root-level queries and mutations, and it will automatically add them to the schema. It will differentiate between entities that are used as parameters (input) and entities used as return values (output). And, as we discovered in the last section, the framework will also add entities referenced by other entities that may not necessarily be directly referenced by root-level queries and mutations. This includes classes, enums, and **interfaces**.

Using GraphQL interfaces

We've already covered basic classes and enums as entities, so let's now take a look at interfaces. Just as with interfaces in Java, GraphQL interfaces can be implemented by concrete GraphQL types. One difference is that input types cannot implement interfaces, which can make things tricky. Let's take a look at an example to get a better understanding. Suppose we want to have a portfolio owner *profile* that contains the contact information of the account owner. Since some portfolio accounts might be managed by somebody other than the owner, we might want two different types of profiles—one for single-person owners and one for accounts with a designated manager. To meet this requirement, we might code up something like this:

```
@Interface
public interface OwnerProfile {
    String getOwnerId();
    String getEmailAddress();
    void setEmailAddress(String emailAddress);
}


public class OwnerProfileImpl implements OwnerProfile {

    private String ownerId;
    private String emailAddress;
    // ... public getters / setters
}


public class ManagedOwnerProfileImpl extends
    OwnerProfileImpl implements OwnerProfile {

    private String managerName;
```

```
    private String managerEmailAddress;
    // ... public getters / setters
}
```

In the preceding code snippet, we see the @Interface annotation applied to the OwnerProfile interface. This tells the MP GraphQL framework to treat this interface as a GraphQL interface in the schema. The framework will then search for implementations of this interface and add them to the schema as well.

Next, let's take a look at what the API class might look like, as follows:

```
@GraphQLApi
public class ProfileGraphQLApi {
    @Inject
    OwnerProfileDatabase db;

    @Query
    public OwnerProfile profile(String ownerId) {
        return db.getProfile(ownerId);
    }

    @Mutation
    public boolean addProfile(OwnerProfileImpl profile)
            throws DuplicatePortfolioOwnerException {
        db.addProfile(profile);
        return true;
    }

    @Mutation
    public boolean addManagedProfile
       (ManagedOwnerProfileImpl profile)
            throws DuplicatePortfolioOwnerException {
        db.addProfile(profile);
        return true;
    }
}
```

Notice that the API class has separate mutation methods for creating each type of profile. This is an unfortunate side effect of GraphQL not allowing input types to implement interfaces—even though the Java code implements the interface, the GraphQL code does not. This means that the parameters must not be interfaces. On the other hand, output types don't have this limitation, so we can use a single-query method that will handle both profile types. The combination of this API class and the entity interface and classes will generate a schema that looks like this (abbreviated):

```
interface OwnerProfile {
  emailAddress: String
  ownerId: String
}


type ManagedOwnerProfileImpl implements OwnerProfile {
  emailAddress: String
  managerEmailAddress: String
  managerName: String
  ownerId: String
}


type OwnerProfileImpl implements OwnerProfile {
  emailAddress: String
  ownerId: String
}


input ManagedOwnerProfileImplInput {
  emailAddress: String
  managerEmailAddress: String
  managerName: String
  ownerId: String
}


input OwnerProfileImplInput {
  emailAddress: String
  ownerId: String
}
```

As we'd expect, the `ManagedOwnerProfileImpl` type implements the `OwnerProfile` interface. It has the same fields as the interface, and it also has a couple of extra fields. So, how do we access these extra fields in a query? The magic happens on *lines 6* and *14* of the query, as shown in the following screenshot:

```
1
2 ▾ query profiles {
3 ▾   emily: profile(ownerId: "Emily J") {
4       ownerId,
5       emailAddress
6       ... on ManagedOwnerProfileImpl {
7         managerName,
8         managerEmailAddress
9       }
10    }
11 ▾   andy: profile(ownerId: "Andy M") {
12      ownerId,
13      emailAddress
14      ... on ManagedOwnerProfileImpl {
15        managerName,
16        managerEmailAddress
17      }
18    }
19  }
20
```

```
▾ {
    "data": {
      "emily": {
        "ownerId": "Emily J",
        "emailAddress": "emilyj@notmyrealaddress.com"
      },
      "andy": {
        "ownerId": "Andy M",
        "emailAddress": "andym@notmyrealaddress.com",
        "managerName": "John A",
        "managerEmailAddress": "johna@notmyrealaddress.com"
      }
    }
  }
```

Figure 11.4 – Query using interfaces

As seen in *Figure 11.4*, the `... on ManagedOwnerProfileImpl` code is similar to casting the interface to the implementation class and then invoking getter methods that only exist on the implementation class in Java. Notice in the output that the profile type returned for `Emily J` is not a `ManagedOwnerProfileImpl` type, so it does not contain the additional fields.

Just as with Java, interfaces can be quite useful for organizing and reusing entities. Now, let's look at how we can further refine entities.

Using entity annotations

It's not uncommon to have an entity class that you want to expose as part of the GraphQL schema, but maybe rename a field (or exclude one) or make a field read-only, or make some other modification. This is possible using annotations on entity fields and/or getter/setter methods. Since MP GraphQL integrates with **JSON Binding (JSON-B)**, many of the MP GraphQL-specific annotations can be replaced by JSON-B annotations to avoid annotation overload.

We've already seen the @Name annotation used on parameters in query/mutation methods, but we can also use this annotation on entity fields and getters/setters to *rename* the field in the generated GraphQL schema. As with all of the annotations described in this section, if you put the annotation on the getter method it will only apply to the output type. If you put the annotation on the setter method, it will only apply to the input type. If you put it on the field, it will apply to both.

The following table lists the annotations that can be quite useful when adding entities to your GraphQL applications:

GraphQL annotation	JSON-B annotation (if applicable)	Description
@Name	@JsonbProperty	These annotations rename the Java property when generating the schema and **input/output (I/O)** types.
@Description	-	This annotation provides additional details about entities and fields in the schema.
@NotNull	-	This annotation ensures that null values are not allowed. If a null value is passed as a parameter or is returned as part of the return value, the MP GraphQL framework will return an error. By default, all Java primitives are automatically configured as @NotNull.
@DateFormat	@JsonbDateFormat	For date-related fields, this annotation controls the I/O conversion of the type. By default, **International Organization for Standardization (ISO)** date formats are used.
@NumberFormat	@JsonbNumberFormat	For numeric fields, this annotation controls the conversion of the type.
@Ignore	@JsonbTransient	This annotation prevents the field from appearing in the schema.

Table 11.1 – MP GraphQL entity annotations and their JSON-B equivalents

Applying these annotations to your entity types allows you to better control the external view of your model classes and better reuse existing classes.

Outsourcing

Suppose you have an entity with a field that is expensive to compute—maybe it requires intensive mathematical computation, or perhaps it requires querying a remote database, and so on. It seems wasteful to compute that field when the client isn't interested in it. Fortunately, it's possible to avoid expensive computation by **outsourcing** the field from the entity class and using the @Source annotation.

For example, let's suppose that the profile service wants to be able to check the loyalty level of a given portfolio owner, but that information is in the portfolio database, not the profile database. So, in this example, a client wanting to see profile data would end up asking the server to connect to two different databases to get the results. We can optimize this situation by only checking the portfolio database if the client requests the loyalty field. We do this by putting a getLoyalty(@Source OwnerProfileImpl profile) method in the ProfileGraphQLApi class, like so:

```
@GraphQLApi
public class ProfileGraphQLApi {

    @Inject
    PortfolioDatabase portfolioDB;

    public Loyalty getLoyalty(@Source OwnerProfileImpl
        profile) throws UnknownPortfolioException {
        String ownerId = profile.getOwnerId();
        Portfolio p = portfolioDB.getPortfolio(ownerId);
        return p.getLoyalty();
    }
    // ...
}
```

What this does is *adds* a new field, loyalty, to the OwnerProfileImpl entity in the schema. From the client's view, this new field is just like any other field, but the getLoyalty method is only invoked if the client specifically requests that field. This is a useful way to avoid paying for expensive operations when the client has no use for the resulting data.

> **Best practice**
>
> Use the @Source annotation for expensive data fetching in order to optimize server-side performance. This also enables you to reduce memory consumption on the server for large queries.

If the @Source method throws an exception, the MP GraphQL framework will return a null result for that field and will send error data but will continue to send the data from other fields as partial results.

Sending partial results using GraphQLException

We've now seen two ways that we can send **partial results** with error data—firstly when the client sends multiple queries in the same request and one or more goes bad, and secondly, when using the @Source annotation to outsource a field's data fetcher.

A third way to send partial results is by using a GraphQLException exception. This exception allows you to include partial results before throwing the exception back to the MP GraphQL framework. The framework will then attempt to send the partial results with the error data back to the client. Here is an example of this:

```
@Mutation
public Collection<Portfolio> createNewPortfolios(
        @Name("portfolios") List<Portfolio> newPortfolios)
        throws GraphQLException, UnknownPortfolioException {
    Tuple<Collection<Portfolio>, Collection<String>>
        tuple = portfolioDB.addPortfolios(newPortfolios);
    if (!tuple.second.isEmpty()) {
        // some of the portfolios to be added already exist;
        // throw an exception with partial results
        throw new GraphQLException(
            "The following portfolios already exist and "
            + "cannot be re-added: " + tuple.second,
            tuple.first); // here are the partial results
    }
    return tuple.first;
}
```

This mutation allows clients to create multiple new portfolios in one request. If the client attempts to create a portfolio for an owner that already exists, this will cause an exception, but all of the other portfolios will still be created and their results will be sent back to the client, along with a list of portfolios that could not be created in the error data.

In this section, we've learned how to construct a server-side GraphQL application in Java using MP GraphQL. While not specifically covered in this section, it should be noted that MP GraphQL integrates nicely with other MicroProfile features, such as Fault Tolerance and Metrics. The MP GraphQL 1.0 specification is officially released and supported in open source Java servers such as Open Liberty, Quarkus, and WildFly. Future versions of the specification will add new features such as support for subscriptions, the ability to define custom scalars, union types, built-in pagination support, and client APIs.

In this section, we learned how to write simple and advanced GraphQL services using MicroProfile APIs. So far, we've only invoked these services using the **GraphiQL** tool. In the next section, we'll learn how we can invoke these services using Java APIs.

Consuming GraphQL services with client APIs

The client APIs are not officially part of the MP GraphQL specification yet. At the time of writing, these APIs are still under development in the **SmallRye GraphQL** project, with the intention of formalizing them into the specification.

> **Disclaimer**
>
> Since these APIs are not official yet, they are subject to change. The information in this section pertains to the SmallRye GraphQL version 1.2.3 client APIs. These APIs may change when added to the official MP GraphQL specification, so please check with the official documentation at `https://github.com/eclipse/microprofile-graphql` for any changes.

The MP GraphQL project intends to support two flavors of client APIs. Similar to the JAX-RS client and the MicroProfile REST client (see *Chapter 4, Developing Cloud-Native Applications*), there is a **dynamic client** API and a **type-safe client** API. As with the JAX-RS client, the dynamic client allows users to specify the nitty-gritty details of the request, while the type-safe client allows users to construct an interface to model the remote service and simply invokes it when it wants to make a new request.

Both of these client APIs are demonstrated as integration tests in the GitHub repository at `https://github.com/PacktPublishing/Practical-Cloud-Native-Java-Development-with-MicroProfile/tree/main/Chapter11/src/test/java/com/packt/microprofile/ch11/client`. They test an `allProfiles` query that returns all of the profiles known to the server. In our example, we've created two profiles for testing purposes. Let's take a look at the dynamic client first.

Dynamic client

The dynamic client works by building a `DynamicGraphQLClient` instance and then passing it as either a `Request` or a `Document` object. The `Request` object usually contains a plain text string with the query or mutation you wish to execute, while a `Document` object must be constructed programmatically. Let's take a look at the `Request` approach first, as follows:

```
@Test
public void testAllProfilesWithStringDocument()
   throws Exception {
     verify(() -> executeSync(
         new RequestImpl("query allProfiles {"
                      +"   allProfiles {"
                      +"       ownerId, emailAddress"
                      +"   }"
                      +"}")));
}


private Response executeSync(Request req) {
    try (DynamicGraphQLClient client = newClient()) {
        return client.executeSync(req);
    } catch (Exception ex) {
        throw new IllegalStateException(ex);
    }
}


private DynamicGraphQLClient newClient() {
    return DynamicGraphQLClientBuilder.newBuilder()
        .url(URL)
        .build();
```

```
}
```

```
private void verify(Supplier<Response> responseSupplier)
        throws Exception {
    Response resp = responseSupplier.get();
    JsonObject data = resp.getData();
    assertNotNull(data);
    JsonArray allProfiles =
        data.getJsonArray("allProfiles");
    assertNotNull(allProfiles);
    JsonObject emily = allProfiles.getJsonObject(0);
    assertNotNull(emily);
    assertEquals("Emily J", emily.getString("ownerId"));
    assertEquals("emilyj@notmyrealaddress.com",
        emily.getString("emailAddress"));
    JsonObject andy = allProfiles.getJsonObject(1);
    assertNotNull(andy);
    assertEquals("Andy M", andy.getString("ownerId"));
    assertEquals("andym@notmyrealaddress.com",
        andy.getString("emailAddress"));
}
```

In this code snippet, we create a new `DynamicGraphQLClient` instance using the builder pattern and specifying the **Uniform Resource Locator (URL)**—for our example, the URL is `http://localhost:9080/ch11/graphql`. We then call the `executeSync` method on that client instance, passing it as `RequestImpl` with our query in a plain text string. This returns a `Response` object that we can extract a JSON-P `JsonObject` instance from that contains the data from the GraphQL result.

Another way that we could write this is more like a builder pattern, where we build each part of the query into a `Document` object using Java code. Here is an example of this:

```
@Test
public void testAllProfilesWithConstructedDocument() throws
    Exception {
    Field query = field("allProfiles");
    query.setFields(Arrays.asList(field("ownerId"),
        field("emailAddress")));
    verify(() -> executeSync(document(operation
```

```
          (OperationType.QUERY, "allProfiles",query)))) ;
}
```

In this code, we create an `allProfiles` field for the query itself, and then create the sub-fields we are interested in: `ownerId` and `emailAddress`. We then construct an `Operation` from the query field and a `Document` object from the `Operation`. We then pass the `Document` object to the `executeSync` method in order to invoke the query, and our `Response` object is the same as in the previous code snippet. This may seem more complicated than simply writing up the query in plain text, but the advantage is that you could use this approach to build more complicated queries depending on the situation—for example, you could programmatically request additional fields in your query for certain situations.

The dynamic client is a nice way to write GraphQL queries and mutations that might require changes, depending on when they are invoked. For situations where you expect the query to be somewhat static, the type-safe client is more appropriate. Let's see what that looks like next.

Type-safe client

The type-safe client borrows a lot of its design from the MicroProfile REST client. It uses annotations and interfaces to represent the remote service and then either a builder pattern or CDI injection to create a client instance. Let's take a look at how we might code this up in an integration test case. First, we'll need to represent the actual response object, the `OwnerProfile` object, as follows:

```
class OwnerProfile {
    String ownerId;
    String emailAddress;
    // public getters/setters
}
```

This is very similar to the same class on the server side. Let's now see what the client interface looks like, as follows:

```
@GraphQLClientApi
interface ProfileApi {
    List<OwnerProfile> allProfiles();
}
```

This interface is annotated with `@GraphQLClientApi` to indicate that it represents the remote service. Because we are only interested in the `allProfiles` query, we only have one method: `allProfiles`. We could add other methods to match other queries or mutations. Since this is a single-query method, we don't need to annotate it with `@Query`, but if we wanted to include mutations, then we would need to specify which methods are which, with the `@Query` and `@Mutation` annotations.

Let's now tie this all together with the builder code and the execution, as follows:

```
@Test
public void testAllProfiles() throws Exception {

    ProfileApi api = TypesafeGraphQLClientBuilder
        .newBuilder()
        .endpoint(URL)
        .build(ProfileApi.class);
    List<OwnerProfile> allProfiles = api.allProfiles();
    assertNotNull(allProfiles);
    assertEquals(2, allProfiles.size());
    assertEquals("Emily J",
        allProfiles.get(0).getOwnerId());
    assertEquals("emilyj@notmyrealaddress.com",
        allProfiles.get(0).getEmailAddress());
    assertEquals("Andy M",allProfiles.get(1).getOwnerId());
    assertEquals("andym@notmyrealaddress.com",
        allProfiles.get(1).getEmailAddress());
}
```

We build an instance of the `ProfileApi` client interface using `TypesafeGraphQLClientBuilder`. Then, once we invoke a method on this interface, the query is sent to the server and returns with a list of owner profiles identical to the data returned using the dynamic client in the previous section.

Both of these client options provide a lot of power and flexibility for invoking remote GraphQL services, even those not built with MicroProfile—or even Java.

Summary

In this chapter, we've learned about GraphQL and how it addresses some of the gaps in REST. We've also learned how to create and consume GraphQL services using MP GraphQL, without the overhead of maintaining a schema in addition to Java code. We've learned that we can build queries and mutations by applying annotations to our API classes and that we can enrich them by adding descriptions, parameters, formatting, and more. By outsourcing, we've learned that we can avoid executing expensive operations when they are not necessary. We've also learned how to send partial results when exceptions occur. We've learned that there are some useful tools such as **GraphiQL** that can simplify testing. And while the client APIs aren't fully supported from the specification, we've been able to view two different clients, and we've seen how we could use them for integration testing or to consume GraphQL services.

With what we've learned in this chapter, combined with the tools available at our disposal, we are now able to develop and test cloud-native GraphQL applications or apply a GraphQL frontend to our existing applications. Our microservices can now avoid over-fetching and under-fetching, reducing network traffic and giving clients exactly what they want.

In the next chapter, we will take a look at the future of MicroProfile and see what changes we can expect to see in the years to come.

12
MicroProfile LRA and the Future of MicroProfile

You have reached the final chapter of this book. Congratulations on making it this far! In this final chapter, we will briefly discuss the newly released MicroProfile **Long-Running Action** (**LRA**) and then look at the future of MicroProfile.

While writing this book, MicroProfile LRA 1.0 was released to address the need for microservice transactions. A traditional **transaction**, as we all must know, is a movement of money, such as an online payment or a withdrawal of money from a bank. In a traditional application, you normally use technologies such as the **two-phase commit** or **eXtended Architecture** (**XA**) protocol to manage transactions. However, these technologies do not suit cloud-native application transactions. In this chapter, we will explore how MicroProfile addresses the need to manage cloud-native transactions. We also will have a look at the transaction architecture for cloud-native applications. After that, we will take you through the latest MicroProfile platform release. Finally, we will learn about the future roadmap of MicroProfile as well as its alignment with the Jakarta EE community.

We will cover the following topics:

- Cloud-native application transactions
- Using the latest MicroProfile platform release
- MicroProfile's technical roadmap
- MicroProfile and Jakarta EE alignment

By the end of this chapter, you should be able to use MicroProfile LRA for cloud-native application transactions and describe the roadmap for MicroProfile, which will help you to architect applications for the future.

Cloud-native application transactions

Cloud-native application transactions try to ensure data consistency and integrity, similar to a traditional transaction. Traditional transactions normally use the two-phase commit or XA protocol. The two-phase commit protocol ensures that transactional updates are committed in all databases or are fully rolled back in the case of a failure. It is widely supported by many databases. As its name implies, this protocol consists of two phases: the **voting phase** and the **commit phase**. In the voting phase, the transaction manager gets approval or rejection from the participating XA resources. In the commit phase, the transaction manager informs the participants about the result. If the result is positive, the entire transaction will be committed. Otherwise, it will be rolled back. This protocol is very reliable and guarantees data consistency. The drawback is that it locks resources and might lead to indefinite blocking. Therefore, it is not suitable for cloud-native applications, because they do not scale well and the latency of held locks is problematic. Consequently, the **saga pattern** was established for cloud-native application transactions to achieve eventual data consistency. The saga pattern commits local transactions and then either completes or compensates the transactions. MicroProfile LRA is a realization of the saga pattern. In the upcoming subsections, we will discuss more on LRA.

Using MicroProfile LRA for cloud-native application transactions

MicroProfile LRA (https://download.eclipse.org/microprofile/ microprofile-lra-1.0) provides a solution for cloud-native application transactions. It introduces two main concepts:

- **LRA participants**: LRA participants are transaction participants, which are cloud-native applications.

- **LRA coordinator**: The LRA coordinator is a transaction coordinator that manages the LRA processing and LRA participants. The LRA coordinator manages all LRAs and invokes LRA methods based on the LRA status.

The following illustrates the relationships between LRA participants and the LRA coordinator:

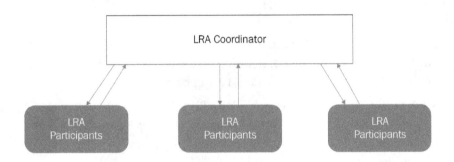

Figure 12.1 – LRA coordinator and participants

As shown in *Figure 12.1*, the LRA participants enlist with the LRA coordinator, which will then call back with the relevant JAX-RS methods based on the transaction status. We will now discuss LRA participants in more detail.

LRA participants

LRA participants are JAX-RS methods that are involved in a transaction and are annotated with the following LRA annotations in the `org.eclipse.microprofile.lra.annotation` package:

- `@LRA`: A method with this annotation will be associated with an LRA. The `@LRA` annotation registers the method with the LRA coordinator. When using this annotation, the following **LRA types** can be specified. `LRA.Type` is like the `TransactionAttributeType` enum in **Enterprise JavaBeans** (**EJB**), indicating whether an LRA is a new one or an existing one. The commonly used `LRA.Type` variants are as follows:

  a) `REQUIRED`: With this type, the method invocation will run with a new LRA context if called outside an LRA context. Otherwise, it will run with the same context.

  b) `REQUIRES_NEW`: With this type, the method invocation will always run with a new LRA context.

c) MANDATORY: With this type, the method invocation will run inside an LRA context. If it is called outside an LRA context, an error will be returned.

d) SUPPORTS: With this type, if the method is called outside an LRA context, it will be executed outside an LRA context. If it is called inside an LRA context, it will be executed inside an LRA context.

e) NOT_SUPPORTED: With this type, the method is always executed outside an LRA context.

f) NEVER: With this type, if the method is called outside an LRA context, it will be executed outside an LRA context. If it is called inside an LRA context, the method execution will fail and the return code 412 will be returned.

g) NESTED: With this type, when the method is called, a new LRA will be created, which can be either top-level or nested based on whether it is called inside an LRA context or not. If invoked outside a context, the new LRA will be top-level. Otherwise, the new LRA will be nested.

You might be wondering how to determine whether a method is called inside an LRA context. If the LRA_HTTP_CONTEXT_HEADER header is present, it means the method is called inside an LRA context.

- @Complete: A method with this annotation will be called when the LRA closes.

- @Compensate: A method with this annotation will be invoked if the LRA is canceled.

- @Forget: A method with this annotation will be invoked if either the @Complete or @Compensate method invocation fails.

- @Leave: A method with this annotation causes the LRA participant to be removed from the LRA participation.

- @Status: A method with this annotation reports the status of the associated LRA.

- @AfterLRA: A method with this annotation will be called when an LRA ends.

The @Compensate, @Complete, and @AfterLRA annotations are for the PUT operation, while the @Status annotation is for the GET operation and @Forget for the DELETE operation. Let's go through this code snippet to explain these annotations further:

```
@LRA(value = LRA.Type.REQUIRED, end=false)
@POST
@Path("/book")
public Response  bookHotel(@HeaderParam
```

```
        (LRA_HTTP_CONTEXT_HEADER) String lraId)    {
        // code
    }
    @Complete
    @Path("/complete")
    @PUT
    public Response completeBooking(@HeaderParam
        (LRA_HTTP_CONTEXT_HEADER) String lraId,
            String userData) {
        //code
    }
    @Compensate
    @Path("/compensate")
    @PUT
    public Response cancelBooking(@HeaderParam
        (LRA_HTTP_CONTEXT_HEADER) String lraId,
            String userData) {
        //code
    }
```

In the code snippet, when the bookHotel() method is called inside an LRA, this method will run with the same LRA context. If it is called outside an LRA context, the method will run with a new context. This method might call in to another service. If this method succeeds, the completeBooking() method will be invoked. Otherwise, the cancelBooking() method will be invoked. You might be wondering which service calls the completeBooking() and cancelBooking() methods. It's the job of the LRA coordinator, which will ensure the corresponding method is invoked. In the next section, we will discuss how to make the APIs from LRA available to your Maven and Gradle projects.

Making MicroProfile LRA available

To use the MicroProfile LRA APIs, you need to make these APIs available to your application. If you create a Maven project, you can directly add the following to your pom.xml:

```
<dependency>
    <groupId>org.eclipse.microprofile.lra</groupId>
    <artifactId>microprofile-lra-api</artifactId>
```

```
    <version>1.0</version>
</dependency>
```

Alternatively, if you create a Gradle project, you need to add the following dependency:

```
dependencies {
  providedCompile org.eclipse.microprofile.lra
    :microprofile-lra-api:1.0
}
```

With this, you have learned how to perform transactions in your cloud-native application. Congratulations! You have now learned about all the MicroProfile specifications. In the next section, let's discuss how best to use the latest MicroProfile platform release.

Using the latest MicroProfile platform release

In *Chapter 2, How Does MicroProfile Fit Into Cloud-Native Application Development?*, we mentioned the MicroProfile platform release and its content. So far, the latest MicroProfile platform release is MicroProfile 4.1, which can be found at `https://download. eclipse.org/microprofile/microprofile-4.1/`.

MicroProfile 4.1 was built on top of MicroProfile 4.0, with MicroProfile Health updating from 3.0 to 3.1. MicroProfile 4.1 aligns with the following Jakarta EE 8 specifications:

- Jakarta Contexts and Dependency Injection 2.0
- Jakarta Annotations 1.3, Jakarta RESTful Web Services 2.1
- Jakarta JSON-B 1.0
- Jakarta JSON-P 1.1
- Jakarta Annotations 1.3

It also includes the following MicroProfile specifications:

- Config 2.0
- Fault Tolerance 3.0
- Health 3.1
- JWT Propagation 1.2

- Metrics 3.0
- OpenAPI 2.0
- OpenTracing 2.0
- Rest Client 2.0

If you want to use a few of the MicroProfile specifications from MicroProfile 4.1 for your cloud-native applications, you need to follow these steps:

1. Make the APIs from MicroProfile 4.1 available for compiling your cloud-native applications.

2. If you build a Maven project, add the following dependency in your `pom.xml` to make the APIs available to your cloud-native applications:

```
<dependency>
    <groupId>org.eclipse.microprofile</groupId>
    <artifactId>microprofile</artifactId>
    <version>4.1</version>
    <type>pom</type>
    <scope>provided</scope>
</dependency>
```

Alternatively, specify the following dependency for your Gradle projects:

```
dependencies {
providedCompile org.eclipse.microprofile
    :microprofile:4.1
}
```

3. Choose a MicroProfile 4.1 implementation to run your cloud-native applications.

   Open Liberty was used as the compatible implementation to release MicroProfile 4.1. Open Liberty, as mentioned in *Chapter 7, The MicroProfile Ecosystem with Open Liberty, Docker, and Kubernetes,* is a very lightweight and performant runtime for supporting MicroProfile specifications. It is also a composable runtime. Specifying the following MicroProfile 4.1 feature in your `server.xml` causes the implementation of MicroProfile 4.1 to be loaded:

```
<feature>microProfile-4.1</feature>
```

4. To use the standalone specifications, such as MicroProfile GraphQL, MicroProfile Context Propagation, MicroProfile Reactive Messaging, and MicroProfile LRA, you will need to specify the relevant API Maven dependencies as mentioned in the previous chapters and then include the corresponding feature elements in your `server.xml`, as shown next. The following line pulls in the implementation of MicroProfile GraphQL 1.0:

```
<feature>mpGraphQL-1.0</feature>
```

This line enables the support of MicroProfile Context Propagation 1.2:

```
<feature>mpContextPropagation-1.2</feature>
```

This line pulls in the implementation of MicroProfile Reactive Messaging 1.0:

```
<feature>mpReactiveMessaging-1.0</feature>
```

This line enables MicroProfile LRA participants of MicroPorfile LRA 1.0:

```
<feature>mpLRA-1.0</feature>
```

This line enables the MicroProfile LRA coordinator of MicroProfile LRA 1.0:

```
<feature>mpLRACoordinator-1.0</feature>
```

The support for MicroProfile LRA 1.0 is available in the Open Liberty beta driver from 20.0.0.12-beta onward.

With this, you have gained up-to-date information about MicroProfile. In the next section, we will discuss the future roadmap for MicroProfile.

MicroProfile's technical roadmap

MicroProfile is used to define a programming model for developing cloud-native applications. It helps to establish a great ecosystem using different cloud infrastructure technologies. These cloud infrastructure technologies include some cloud-native frameworks such as Kubernetes, Jaeger, Prometheus, Grafana, and OpenTelemetry. Kubernetes, Jaeger, Prometheus, and Grafana are mature technologies, and you probably know about them already. You might not know a great deal about OpenTelemetry. OpenTelemetry is a new sandbox project from the **Cloud Native Computing Foundation (CNCF)**, and we will spend some time explaining it a bit.

Adopting OpenTelemetry in MicroProfile

OpenTelemetry (`https://opentelemetry.io/`) is a new CNCF observability framework developed by merging of **OpenTracing** (`https://opentracing.io/`) and **OpenCensus** (`https://opencensus.io/`). Since MicroProfile OpenTracing, covered in *Chapter 6, Observing and Monitoring Cloud-Native Applications*, was based on OpenTracing, OpenTelemetry was bound to be adopted by MicroProfile eventually.

A lot of effort has been gone to in the MicroProfile community to investigate how to utilize OpenTelemetry in MicroProfile. One suggestion is to continue supporting the OpenTracing API, but its implementation adopts OpenTelemetry by using the following code snippet to transform an OpenTelemetry tracer to an OpenTracing tracer:

```
io.opentracing.Tracer tracer =
   TracerShim.createTracerShim(openTelemetryTracer);
```

With the tracer transformation, the current MicroProfile OpenTracing should be able to continue working. However, the OpenTracing Tracer API won't be maintained anymore because the community has moved to working on OpenTelemetry APIs. The ultimate goal is to expose the Tracer API (`io.opentelemetry.api.trace.Tracer`) from OpenTelemetry. The MicroProfile community is trying to find the best way of adopting OpenTelemetry.

You might be aware that OpenTelemetry also provides metrics support. Do we need to pull OpenTelemetry metrics to MicroProfile? This is an open question. Let's discuss the future roadmap of MicroProfile Metrics in the next section.

What is the future of MicroProfile Metrics?

MicroProfile Metrics, explained in *Chapter 6, Observing and Monitoring Cloud-Native Applications*, was based on **Dropwizard** (`https://www.dropwizard.io/en/latest/`), a Java framework for developing ops-friendly, high-performance, RESTful web services. Dropwizard has been very popular in the past few years. However, recently, **Micrometer** (`https://micrometer.io/`) has gained more momentum and become a prominent metrics framework. The MicroProfile Metrics specification team is investigating how to adopt Micrometer while keeping the current APIs working with either Micrometer or Dropwizard.

As mentioned previously, OpenTelemetry also contains metrics support. The other suggestion is for MicroProfile Metrics to align with OpenTelemetry Metrics. If OpenTelemetry Metrics is the new metrics standard in the future, MicroProfile should adopt OpenTelemetry Metrics instead. So, MicroProfile offers two metrics candidates to choose from. Now, the question arises: *Which one should you choose*? It depends on which one will become the mainstream. The ideal situation is that Micrometer integrates with OpenTelemetry. if Micrometer integrates well with OpenTelemetry Metrics, adopting Micrometer would naturally align with OpenTelemetry Metrics. Maybe MicroProfile Metrics should wait for OpenTelemetry Metrics to settle and then work out which framework to adopt.

Apart from the existing MicroProfile specifications, the MicroProfile community is also interested in new initiatives, such as gRPC.

Adopting gPRC

Apart from the evolution of the current MicroProfile specifications, the community is interested in adopting new technologies to provide better support in cloud-native applications. One potential new specification is gRPC.

gRPC (`https://grpc.io/`) is a modern high-performance **Remote Procedure Call (RPC)** framework that can run in any environment. To make gRPC easier to use in cloud-native applications, it would be great if it can be integrated with CDI, JAX-RS, and so on. If MicroProfile adopts gRPC to create a new specification MicroProfile gRPC, this specification will be able to work closely and seamlessly with other MicroProfile specifications.

Now that we have discussed the specification updates, we will discuss MicroProfile alignment with Jakarta EE releases.

MicroProfile and Jakarta EE alignment

MicroProfile adopts a few Jakarta EE technologies, such as CDI, JAX-RS, JSON-B, JSON-P, and Common Annotations. MicroProfile 4.0 and 4.1 align with the Jakarta EE 8 release. This book is based on the MicroProfile 4.1 release. MicroProfile has been working very closely with Jakarta EE. Most major players in MicroProfile are also involved in Jakarta EE. MicroProfile and Jakarta EE form a great ecosystem for developing cloud-native applications. It is very important that they always keep in sync and are compatible with each other. Jakarta EE 9.1 (`https://jakarta.ee/release/9.1/`) was released in 2021, which adds a requirement for MicroProfile to work with this release so that end users can use APIs from both frameworks. Due to this requirement, we will discuss MicroProfile 5.0 in the next section, which is planned to align with Jakarta EE 9.1.

Aligning MicroProfile 5.0 with Jakarta EE 9.1

The focus of MicroProfile 5.0 is to align with Jakarta EE 9.1. The eight component specifications, including Config, Fault Tolerance, Rest Client, Health, Metrics, OpenTracing, OpenAPI, and JWT Propagation, need to be updated so that they are aligned with Jakarta EE 9.1. Some of these specifications do not directly depend on the Jakarta specifications in their APIs, but their **Technology Compatibility Kits (TCKs)** pull in Jakarta specifications. For these specifications, only a minor release is needed. To make all the MicroProfile specifications work with Jakarta 9.1, the specifications under the standalone releases such as Reactive Streams Operators, Reactive Messaging, LRA, GraphQL, and Context Propagation all need to be updated to align with Jakarta EE 9.1.

Apart from the alignment with Jakarta EE, some of the MicroProfile specifications extend the current Jakarta specifications. Since these MicroProfile specifications were created while Java EE was stagnant, it might be the right time for these MicroProfile specifications to become Jakarta specifications so that other Jakarta specifications can benefit from them. Let's look at those specifications.

Moving some MicroProfile specifications to Jakarta EE

Some Jakarta EE specifications, such as **Jakarta NoSQL** (GitHub repository: `https://github.com/eclipse-ee4j/nosql`), would benefit from MicroProfile Config for configuration. If Jakarta EE depended on MicroProfile, this would create a circular dependency as MicroProfile aligns with Jakarta EE specifications. The other problem is that Jakarta EE specifications have traditionally maintained backward compatibility more carefully, while MicroProfile specifications can introduce backward-incompatibility changes from time to time. Therefore, it might be problematic for Jakarta EE specifications to directly depend on MicroProfile specifications. To solve this problem, a new proposal, **Jakarta Config**, was put forward to collaborate with MicroProfile Config. Jakarta Config (GitHub repository: `https://github.com/eclipse-ee4j/config`) could become the centerpiece of Jakarta EE. Jakarta Config aims to be included in Jakarta Core Profile so that other profiles and MicroProfile can depend on this specification.

Apart from alignment with Jakarta EE, MicroProfile is also trying to adopt **Long-Term Support (LTS)** Java releases such as Java 11 and Java 17.

You might still remember the two releases in MicroProfile: platform and standalone. The MicroProfile community needs to look at the specifications included in the standalone release to see whether it is time to move some specifications back to the platform release bucket. The other area the MicroProfile community needs to improve is the end-user experience. The MicroProfile community will continue improving its entry page (`https://microprofile.io/`).

We can't believe that we have reached the end of this book. There are so many topics to cover. For further information on MicroProfile, please go to `https://microprofile.io/`. If you would like to learn about anything related to MicroProfile, please visit the Open Liberty guides (`https://openliberty.io/guides/`).

Summary

With that, we come to the end of this book. Let's revisit what you have learned. Throughout this book, we learned how to create cloud-native applications using Jakarta REST, JSON-P, JSON-B, CDI, and the MicroProfile Rest Client; then enhance cloud-native applications using MicroProfile Config, Fault Tolerance, Open API, and JWT Propagation; and finally monitor cloud-native applications using MicroProfile Health, Metrics, and Open Tracing. We then learned about the MicroProfile ecosystem with Open Liberty, Docker, Kubernetes, and Istio. After we covered all the technologies, we then looked at an end-to-end project that utilized different MicroProfile technologies. Afterward, we discussed deployment and day 2 operations. We then looked at the standalone specifications: MicroProfile GraphQL, MicroProfile Context Propagation, and MicroProfile Reactive Messaging.

In this final chapter, we discussed the latest release of MicroProfile LRA 1.0. We then discussed the future roadmap in MicroProfile, followed by the plan with Jakarta EE alignment. The takeaway from this chapter is that MicroProfile and Jakarta EE are complementary to each other, and they form a great ecosystem that supports cloud-native applications.

We hope you have enjoyed reading this book and learned how to use the amazing features of MicroProfile to help you with your cloud-native application development, deployment, and management. If you would like to contribute to MicroProfile, please click on the **Join The Discussion** link on the microprofile.io website (`https://microprofile.io/`) to express your interest in being on the mailing list.

Packt.com

Subscribe to our online digital library for full access to over 7,000 books and videos, as well as industry leading tools to help you plan your personal development and advance your career. For more information, please visit our website.

Why subscribe?

- Spend less time learning and more time coding with practical eBooks and Videos from over 4,000 industry professionals

- Improve your learning with Skill Plans built especially for you

- Get a free eBook or video every month

- Fully searchable for easy access to vital information

- Copy and paste, print, and bookmark content

Did you know that Packt offers eBook versions of every book published, with PDF and ePub files available? You can upgrade to the eBook version at packt.com and as a print book customer, you are entitled to a discount on the eBook copy. Get in touch with us at customercare@packtpub.com for more details.

At www.packt.com, you can also read a collection of free technical articles, sign up for a range of free newsletters, and receive exclusive discounts and offers on Packt books and eBooks.

Other Books You May Enjoy

If you enjoyed this book, you may be interested in these other books by Packt:

Jakarta EE Cookbook Second Edition

Elder Moraes

ISBN: 978-1-83864-288-4

- Work with Jakarta EE's most commonly used APIs and features for server-side development
- Enable fast and secure communication in web applications with the help of HTTP2
- Build enterprise applications with reusable components
- Break down monoliths into microservices using Jakarta EE and Eclipse MicroProfile
- Improve your enterprise applications with multithreading and concurrency
- Run applications in the cloud with the help of containers

- Get to grips with continuous delivery and deployment for shipping your applications effectively

Supercharge Your Applications with GraalVM

A B Vijay Kumar

ISBN: 978-1-80056-490-9

- Gain a solid understanding of GraalVM and how it works under the hood
- Work with GraalVM's high performance optimizing compiler and see how it can be used in both JIT (just-in-time) and AOT (ahead-of-time) modes
- Get to grips with the various optimizations that GraalVM performs at runtime
- Use advanced tools to analyze and diagnose performance issues in the code
- Compile, embed, run, and interoperate between languages using Truffle on GraalVM
- Build optimum microservices using popular frameworks such as Micronaut and Quarkus to create cloud-native applications

Packt is searching for authors like you

If you're interested in becoming an author for Packt, please visit `authors.packtpub.com` and apply today. We have worked with thousands of developers and tech professionals, just like you, to help them share their insight with the global tech community. You can make a general application, apply for a specific hot topic that we are recruiting an author for, or submit your own idea.

Share Your Thoughts

Now you've finished *Practical Cloud-Native Java Development with MicroProfile*, we'd love to hear your thoughts! Scan the QR code below to go straight to the Amazon review page for this book and share your feedback or leave a review on the site that you purchased it from.

`https://packt.link/r/1-801-07880-7`

Your review is important to us and the tech community and will help us make sure we're delivering excellent quality content.

Index

CPSIA information can be obtained
at www.ICGtesting.com
Printed in the USA
LVHW020753050422
715110LV00001B/1

9 781801 078801